Christmas 1934

To my very dear
friend Ann

Bud

*WHILE
ROME
BURNS*

ALEXANDER
WOOLLCOTT
☼

# WHILE
# ROME
# BURNS

☼


☼


☼

THE VIKING PRESS
NEW YORK · MCMXXXIV

PUBLISHED MARCH 1934
SECOND PRINTING MARCH 1934
THIRD PRINTING MARCH 1934
FOURTH PRINTING MARCH 1934
FIFTH PRINTING MARCH 1934
SIXTH PRINTING APRIL 1934
SEVENTH PRINTING JUNE 1934
EIGHTH PRINTING JUNE 1934
NINTH PRINTING JULY 1934
TENTH PRINTING AUGUST 1934
ELEVENTH PRINTING AUGUST 1934
TWELFTH PRINTING OCTOBER 1934

*To Beatrice Kaufman*

# CONTENTS

*WHILE*
*ROME*
*BURNS*

*THE chapter which Brand Whitlock should have written (but might not write) about the great and gallant Marquis of Villalobar, sometime Ambassador from Spain to Belgium.*

# IN THAT STATE OF LIFE

A STRAY on a spring evening in the old library of William and Mary at Williamsburg in Virginia and admonished to silence by the grim female in charge, who kept warning me at the top of her lungs that all about me the young were at their studies, I took down from a shelf the fat volumes of Brand Whitlock's *Belgium* and renewed an old acquaintance with the stirring story he had to tell. From this reunion, I came away with fresh enthusiasm for one character in that story, a great gentleman from Spain whose odd, stiff little figure moved jerkily across the stage of the World War and seems to me now, through the dust and smoke still hanging in the air, as near to a hero as walked the earth in that time.

He was the Marquis of Villalobar. As Spanish Ambassador to Belgium when the rest of the world took up arms, he shared with Whitlock the extra burdens which the war deposited on the doorsteps of the two great neutral embassies in the cockpit of Europe. Fastidious, sensitive, chivalrous, proud, witty, sardonic, the little Marquis, in his huge English car with his chauffeur brave in a livery of red and green, moves like a thread of relieving color through the somber fabric of Whitlock's story. But not once in the two volumes is there so much as a hint of the dreadful and magnificent truth about Villalobar which must have filled Whitlock with wonder and pity and awe every time he saw him, every time he thought of him.

When, still at his post in Brussels, Villalobar died in the summer of 1926 and the news was cabled to America, the obituary in the *New York Times* next day told all the routine facts about him—his ministry to Washington, his services in the great war—but left untold that single salient fact which still shapes the lingering legend about the man and puts up on the wall of every chancellery in the world a portrait done in whispers. Now surely the full story can be told. Now, while in Tokyo and Constantinople and Berlin, in Washington and Brussels and Madrid, there still be men who might bear witness; above all, while I, myself, am still here to read that story, I hope it *will* be told.

For the little Marquis had been born, they say, with a greater blight laid upon him than was the portion even of Sir Richard Calmady. An aging few must still recall Lucas Malet's extraordinary novel of that unhappy baronet who, in obedience to a curse laid upon his line in olden days, was born into the world with the head and torso of a young god, but with feet that came above where his knees should have been —a grotesquely truncated figure that stumbled and scrambled across the world while the heartless laughed and the pitiful turned away. Well, according to the legend I still hope to see filled out and documented, that very curse had been laid also upon the Villalobar line, and this heir to the great house, who was born in 1866, came into the world misshapen in the self-same fashion. They say there were even heavier odds against him. For his head was hairless and he had only one hand he could let anyone see. The other he carried, whenever possible, thrust into the bosom of his coat. It was, they say, a kind of cloven claw.

I do not know by what heavy and intricate contrivance Villalobar raised himself to the stature of other men and managed a kind of locomotion. It was serviceable enough, however, to carry him to the ends of the earth, and his will lent him seven-league boots. Furthermore, it was so deceptive to one who did not see him move that when first he appeared at court in Madrid, a fledgling diplomat already booked for some minor post in Washington, a great lady—some say the Queen Mother, but I do not believe that part of the legend—turned quickly when she heard his name and told him how as a girl she had visited in his part of Spain and how she had always wondered whatever became of the Villalobar monster. It seems she had heard curious countryside tales of a monster born to the Villalobar line, just such a one as shadowed Glamis Castle in those days and shadows it today. Such a fascinating story, my dear Marquis. Quite gave one the creeps. One heard it everywhere. Had the creature died? Or been killed? Or what?

"Madame," said young Villalobar, with a malicious smile twisting the rich curve of his lips, "I am that monster," and, bowing low, he shuffled away, leaving her to wish she had never been born.

Whitlock has a hundred anecdotes of the Marquis in his prime—tales of his exquisite tact, of his generous rages, of his devotion to the exiled Eugénie, who had been kind to him when he was a little boy, of his vain, scornful, passionate, night-long fight to save Edith Cavell from a German firing squad. Whitlock tells about a time when a roaring Prussian martinet bellowed at Villalobar only to have the little Marquis, who, of course, spoke German fluently, turn on him and say with glacial calm:

"*Pardon, Monsieur, je ne vous comprends pas. Parlez lentement, poliment—et en français.*"

And about the time when he was halted in his rounds of Brussels by another Prussian, who asked him brusquely what he was doing there. Villalobar, with the accent of history and doom, made answer:

"Sir, what are *you* doing here?" and stumped off about the business of his king.

Whitlock tells all about the spotless, delicately perfumed, and beautiful embassy in the Rue Archimède, filled with the loot of Villalobar's life, gifts from kings and queens, portraits, family silver, even his grandmother's sedan chair. The American Ambassador could not imagine his own workaday forbears associated with a vehicle so elegant. The Italian Ambassador had no such difficulty. "Mine," he said, "were here." And he stepped between the shafts.

Whitlock envied Villalobar the lovely Louis XVI table which served as a desk, with the row of silver dispatch boxes standing like sentinels on its gleaming surface. The Marquis said he had picked it up in a second-hand shop in Toledo. Whitlock sighed and murmured something about the luxury of rummaging in these old European cities. Villalobar interrupted him with a chuckle.

"Oh, it wasn't in *my* Toledo in Spain," he said; "it was in *your* Toledo in Ohio. That time I was there, you remember, for the carnival; I was going down that street—what's it's name? . . ."

Whitlock reports that on that desk and in that embassy, no paper was ever, by any chance, out of place. But he says nothing about the despotism, at once comical and terrifying, whereby that order was maintained. Nor does he tell with what bated breath the Marquis was always served. Nor how each thread of the embassy life, however trivial, had to lead to Villalobar's one available hand. Even when finally the vast concerns of America and England were added to the French and Spanish business, Villalobar would have only one telephone in the embassy. You see, he wanted to hear each mes-

sage. It might be only the market calling up about the cauli-
flower. No matter. The Marquis would take the message. It
might be a light-o'-love calling up the young third secretary.
The Marquis would take that, too. If a picture postcard came
for the cook, the Marquis saw it before the cook did.

It was an embassy ruled by a crotchety bachelor. Once
Whitlock told Villalobar that had he been born in an un-
feathered American nest, he might, with his many and varied
talents, have been anything he chose: lawyer, journalist, politician, artist, financier, and certainly as guileful a stage manager as Irving or David Belasco. If Whitlock wondered privately whether, had he so chosen, Villalobar might also have
been a husband, he could scarcely have given voice to that
inevitable speculation. Yet when he was approaching sixty,
Villalobar did marry. He married a cousin whom he had
wooed in vain when she was a young girl, and who came to
the shelter of his name and power when the long years had
played strange tricks on both of them.

But that is another story. What Whitlock saw was an embassy run by a bachelor, and one thing all its staff knew was
that the chief would tolerate no physical assistance while anyone was looking. If, as sometimes happened, he fell, the secretary who ventured to help him or even to notice the mishap
would go unthanked and soon be mysteriously recalled to
Madrid for transfer to some other capital. Not everyone knew
this. It is part of the legend that on the night of a wartime
Christmas party at the British Embassy in Madrid, in a scuffle
under the mistletoe which hung from the chandelier, the
Marquis came down with a crash. The lights were put out
lest anyone see him getting to his pins. But in Brussels, the
consciousness of him was so acute that once when he was
mounting the grand stairway at a tremendous postwar reception and slipped as he was nearing the top, a kind of catalepsy
seized the whole sumptuous assemblage as over and over, over
and over, over and over, that little figure rolled with a tre-

mendous clatter to the foot of the stairs. In the distance an oblivious orchestra was fiddling away for dear life, but among the actual onlookers no one dared breathe. And that agonized paralysis lasted while he righted himself somehow, and, tap-tap-tap, tap-tap-tap, began again—and finished—the difficult ascent.

There is a photograph of him in the lovely Spanish Embassy at Washington—taken, I suppose, at the time of his first assignment to this country. Whitlock speaks of him as handsome and here you see why. He is dressed as a Maestrante Knight of Zaragoza, and something in the white cape, the beplumed helmet, and the amused, contemptuous curve of the sensuous lips makes you think of him as having just come from some torchlit conspiratorial gathering in Zenda or Graustark. At the embassy, too, you can find in the files the list of his honors:

Grand Cross of Charles the Third. Grand Cross of Isabella the Catholic. Gold Medal of the Sieges of Zaragoza. Grand Cross of St. Gregory the Great of the Holy See. Grand Cross of St. Maurice and St. Lazarus of Italy. Grand Cross of the Rising Sun of Japan. Grand Officer of the Legion of Honor of France. Knight Commander of the Order of Christ and of Villaviciosa of Portugal. Lord of the Bedchamber of His Majesty. Maestrante Knight of Zaragoza. Burgess of Brussels. Burgess of Ghent. Burgess of Lille.

Thus interminably. A little it recalls the list of titles which Thornton Wilder, with wide-open eyes and elegiac voice, read out over the dead princeling in *The Cabala*. The list ceased to be a mere string of words and became a roll of drums.

Not in that embassy, however, nor in any other, but only in far cafés in moments of unleashed confidences will those who worked under him tell the tales that make up the living legend of Villalobar. They still talk in whispers as if a little afraid to this day that he might reach out and punish them.

I have heard in Berlin at second-hand—and only so does one even begin to know how great a man their little Marquis was —the experience of one minor secretary who remembers still, and will, I think, remember while he lives, a wartime night in Brussels when he was homing at three in the morning from some clandestine mischief. Silk-hatted and caped resplendent, he was passing through the guarded dark of the Rue Archimède when, as he passed the embassy, he remembered with a panic clutch of fear that he had gone off that afternoon and left an indiscreet paper in full sight on his desk. If only he could let himself into the chancellery wing and retrieve it, there might even yet be a chance that the chief had not seen it.

When, on this slightly burglarious enterprise, the secretary reached his desk in the office, he found the paper gone. But whether the Marquis had seen it and taken it away the young man never really knew. For next morning he was recalled to Madrid with no chance to bid his chief good-by. But that night, just as he realized his mission was fruitless, he saw there was a light in the hallway at this unaccountable hour and heard a puzzling noise there as of some animal scuttling across the floor. Alarmed, he tiptoed through the intervening rooms, reached the lighted doorway, and on the threshold stood transfixed. He swears he stopped breathing altogether. There on the rug, crouched as if for a spring, was a small, unrecognizable creature clad in some kind of white nightshift. It had a human head. Its burning eyes met his. The witness says that before he could move or force a sound through his paralyzed lips, the creature turned, scampered to the foot of the stairs, and then—a streak of white in the dusk of the stair-well—whisked up and along the gallery and out of sight.

*HOW such oddly assorted char-*
*acters as Damon Runyon and a*
*certain celebrated Nazi became*
*involved in one pursuit of a will-*
*o'-the-wisp picture.*

## THE SACRED GROVE

O NCE upon a time, a great architect sat on the floor
and spread out before me the plans for an apartment house that was to be a tower of copper and
glass. One could picture the homing householder catching
sight of it from afar, an opalescent shaft agleam and winking
in the afternoon sunlight. It was when the architect added
casually that he himself would design each interior, even unto
the uttermost ashtray, and permit each tenant to bring with
him only his own piano, that I made a mulish mental note
*not* to take a flat in that iridescent tower. For it seems to me
that the loveliest product of an unrestrained, unsubservient
decorator is, as Edna Ferber once said of Switzerland, beautiful but dumb, with just about as much character as a birthday
cake.

I would not mind a home of my own being an affront to
every other eye so long as it was full of the accidentals of my
own life. I doubt if I am any longer equal to such spasms of
quaintness as animated young J. M. Barrie when, more than
forty years ago, he was furbishing his first flat in London and
used to paste on the back of each piece of furniture a copy of

the newspaper or magazine article which had paid for it. But I do think that a man who is at least half-full of years is missing something of the salt of life if every stick and patch on which his lamplight falls does not tell him sad or funny stories of where and what he has been.

Surely it is so even with one's pictures. My own lean gallery, from which one thrilling Utrillo has gone back home, to which another has just come for a visit and an early Noel Coward for good, and which is now even aspiring to shelter some day, if only for a few memorable weeks, the inexplicable magic of a serenely powerful O'Keeffe—my own gallery, I say, has pictures which no one else would take as a gift because they could not mean to anyone else what they happen to mean to me. In that sense, I have one fading photograph which I would not swap for a Vermeer. And in that sense, I cherish with an especial affection a certain Böcklin, even though it represents a kind of ham painting I have not enjoyed for years. You are doubtless familiar with it. It is the one with the file of white-clad priests emerging from a bosky dell to kneel at a Druidical altar. It is, mind you, only a reproduction, for the original, which that sentimental Helvetian painted in Florence fifty years ago, still hangs in the gallery at Basel—and may go on hanging there for all of me. It is the reproduction I want—this reproduction.

It was in 1916 that I entered upon the long train of inquiry, chance, skullduggery, and blandishment which finally brought this Böcklin to my door and hung it on my wall, there to remain until death, bankruptcy, or the dawn of Communism do us part. One fine afternoon of a day in that year, when I happened to be solvent, I went into a picture store on Fifth Avenue and asked the clerk there if they had a print of "The Sacred Grove." A large and somewhat tumultuous-looking young man who was tending shop at the time said, "Ah, *'Der heilige Hain,'*" and brushed me aside, a trifle summarily, I thought, as if I were perversely asking the impossible. Well, if they didn't have it in stock, how long, I persisted doggedly, would it take them to get me one? This innocent query wrung from him a very roar of displeasure.

That, remember, was in the time of strain when the American people were trying to hold on to their neutrality much as a voyager in the English Channel tries to hold on to his breakfast. With my perceptions sharpened by years of journalism, I had realized at once that the young art-dealer was not precisely what would have been called pro-Ally. If, however, I not only left his shop hastily but thereafter stayed away from it, it was not so much because I felt alienated by his failure to share my own wartime prejudices, but because, after all, it did seem improbable that, by further traffic with him, I would acquire what I had come for. Indeed, being one of little faith, I saw in those dark days no prospect of my ever owning "The Sacred Grove" at all.

Yet two years later, when, after America had taken to shipping men as well as munitions, I was ordered to Paris from my lowly post in Brittany, what should I see looking out at me enigmatically from a shop window in the Rue Drouot but a print of "The Sacred Grove"? Surely this was a sign unto me. Then and there I decided to buy it, even though I would need another sign to tell me how to get the money for the purpose, and even though I had not the slightest notion what I should do with the pesky picture when I got it. For the most part, impulses to mural decoration in the A.E.F. found expression in covers of *La Vie Parisienne* pinned on barrack walls. The welfare agencies, though addicted to culture and dedicated to ameliorating the bleak life of the enlisted man, had not yet reached the point of insuring to each soldier his own personal art gallery.

The purely financial aspect of the problem was cleared up a few nights later on the floor of the Yale rooms at the University Union. Among the participants or the kibitzers of that

crap game were F.P.A., J. T. Winterich of *The Colophon,*
Lee Wilson Dodd, and John Erskine. I remember the details
of this contest not only because of its singularly pleasing outcome but because it was interrupted by an air raid which
plunged the game (and, incidentally, the rest of Paris) into
impenetrable darkness. As the lights went out, each winner
flung himself shrewdly down upon his pile of francs, but
Captain Adams, having been recently relieved by the fall of
the dice from the oppressive burden of private property, was
free to put on his helmet, drift out onto the balcony, and
cravenly murmur *"Kamerad! Kamerad!"* in the general direction of the heavens. Owing, perhaps, to the shriek of the
sirens, the spatter of anti-aircraft guns, and the occasional
boom of a bomb falling in the city, this propitiatory effort
went unnoticed by those to whom it was addressed. According to the heroic press next day, the damage done by the raid
of the night before had been negligible, but I can testify that
at least one building was completely demolished. I can so
testify because when, with pockets agreeably stuffed with
francs, I hurried next morning to the Rue Drouot, I discovered that on the night before, in the middle of the air raid,
my picture shop had gone out of business in a big way. One
German victory after another. I was minded to say with Shylock: "I never felt it until now."

Even for the sake of the story, I will not pretend that this
minor misadventure stiffened my will to victory. But I do
remember feeling a faint if unjustifiable glow of personal triumph when, on a day in early December, after the American
troops had marched to the Rhine and we were all savoring
the experience of strolling unchallenged through the streets
of Coblenz, there, looking out at me from a shop window, I
saw a print of *"Der heilige Hain"* as ever was. Five minutes
later, Damon Runyon, himself astroll in the thoroughfares of
the bridgehead, found me still standing in front of the shop,
staring pensively at a will-o'-the-wisp which seemed bent on

both pursuing and eluding me, for the price tag was in full view and I had just remembered that in my jeans was no money at all. I did not even have that which was even more acceptable as currency in the Rhineland just then—a cake of soap. Indeed, all the soap supply of our outfit was gone, and our dreamy old mess sergeant was even then languishing in the brig, awaiting trial on the charge that he had given it all to sundry matrons in Trier in return for favors unspecified in the indictment.

The kindly Runyon was so puzzled by my anachronistic absorption in the art of the late Arnold Böcklin that I was forced to tell him the story just as I have told it to you, and then work up a fairly convincing start of grateful surprise when he walked grandly into the shop and bought the picture.

*"Fröhliche Weihnachten,"* said the lavish old linguist, as he put it into my hands. *"Und,"* I replied, *"ein glückliches Neujahr."* I rather had him there.

I shall not describe the immense amount of shenanigan involved in getting that print to Paris, beyond saying that it made the journey by ambulance, hidden under a blanket which also, by the way, concealed the tremulous person of the aforesaid mess sergeant, who had escaped from his guard and was starting A.W.O.L. for parts unknown. Nor shall I tell you how, against all the laws of the A.E.F., the picture went from a French post office to a guardian appointed in New York. I need only describe how, myself back in New York the following year, I regained custody of it and, with the print still rolled in its cardboard mailer, hurried around to the nearest picture-framer. This was a little place in Fifty-seventh Street across from Carnegie Hall, and blandly in charge as I walked in was the once distraught young picture-dealer of yesteryear. This time he was all affability, and at the sight of me he delved deep into what must be a prodigious memory.

"Ah," he cried, "the man who likes Böcklin! Which one

was it? Yes, yes, *'Der heilige Hain.'* Ah, well, my friend, I can get it for you now."

I suppose I derived some slight malicious pleasure from unrolling my picture and sticking it under his nose. He was properly astonished.

"Well, well," he said, "where did you get it?"

When I answered "In Coblenz," he suppressed a visible and creditable impulse to tear it up and throw it in my face, but the rest of the transaction was carried out in moody silence. Anyway, he did frame it for me.

All of which I remembered when in the spring of 1933 I came upon his photograph in the rotogravures. He was seated at an elegant desk, signing things furiously. Beside him stood some minor functionary in such an obsequious posture as must have given him pleasure to watch. From the caption I learned that he was a Harvard man named Hanfstaengl and that he had just become confidential secretary to some German politician whose name, as I recall, was Hitler.

*THE true story of crackpot Marigold to whom, when it befell that all men turned from her, a consoling and eventful lover came out of the blue.*

# A PLOT FOR MR. DREISER

THIS is an account of my neighbor, Marigold Jones. It is an unfinished story. When first I came to New York, she was a most lovely sight to see, not unlike Miss Justine Johnstone in her fair beauty, we all thought, but taller and graver and more serene. She had that sweet composure of the spirit which made it an effortless thing for her to sit hour after hour on the model-stand till the afternoon light faded from the studio. Then, in the twilight, she would make us some tea before she had to leave to meet her sweetheart on the corner. In those, her untroubled years, all artists clamored for Marigold. If anyone needed a goddess for coin or poster, Marigold would oblige. Or she would sit with an ermine wrap flung back from her white shoulders, her long, gloved arm resting on the rail of an improvised opera-box, while on the easel there took form a picture of Our Lady of the Diamond Horseshoe, which, if cunningly used as an advertisement for some frippery, would incite to the point of purchasing it a myriad girls even humbler and poorer than Marigold herself.

16

Well, all that was long ago. Today, in her early forties, she is a scarred and haggard creature with frightened eyes. She gets a chance to pose at all only when some artist remembers her with a pang, and lets her sit for old times' sake while he draws a sleeve, a shoulder, the back of a head. They cannot draw her face any more. They cannot even look at it. Wherefore, I have been thinking that this story could end only with some such fond cry as was wrung from Sylvia Warner in her moment of parting forever with the manuscript of her beloved *Mr. Fortune's Maggot.* My poor Marigold, good-by. I do not know what will become of you! But she herself does not share my apprehensions.

It was during the war that the peace first went out of Marigold's eyes. She lost her lover then and was herself as dreadfully wounded as any casualty that was carried on a stretcher from a battlefield in France. This lover of hers was an Irish boy who drove a freebooting taxi, and when he was drafted, she took all her savings and bought him a wrist-watch, with two hearts engraved on it, and their initials intertwined. The week before his outfit sailed, she went down to Spartanburg to say good-by to him. It would be some hours before he could come in from camp to meet her. While she waited on a bench in the park, she fell to talking, as sister to sister, with a tart who was doing a thriving trade in the national emergency. Some of those soldier boys, it seems, were real crazy about her. For instance, there was one dizzy guy from New York who, only the night before, had given her his wrist-watch. See! Pretty, ain't it? It was Marigold's watch.

Then some years after the war came that automobile collision which flung a taxi onto the sidewalk where our Marigold was mooning along. The surgeons had to do a good deal of guessing as they worked on the jigsaw puzzle of her face. The damage awarded scarcely paid the hospital bills. I suppose the jury was unimpressed with the long line of famous painters who took the stand to tell how fair a sight this pale, trembling ruin once had been. What of it? She could still scrub floors, couldn't she?

I have said her eyes were frightened. But not always. At times now, quite suddenly, they grow large and dark and fill up with wonder. Once this strange and visible change took place while I was present. For a moment she sat like one who hears distant music. Then she jumped from the model-stand and ran to the window. "He's come! He's come!" she cried, looking up into the sky. "Don't you hear him?" And with a pretty flurry of apology, she caught up her hat and coat and rushed out of the studio.

It seems that, for some months past, Marigold has been happy in the devotion of an aviator. It is no violation of confidence to tell you so, for she herself unpacks her singing heart in the sight of everyone—the news-dealer at the corner, the boy who runs the elevator, the girl at the switchboard. Marigold gets the sweetest notes from him. He writes them in the sky and she reads them as she walks in Central Park. At first she affected to be displeased by this correspondence writ large that the whole world could read it. She vowed he was a nuisance. It was downright embarrassing to have him fly over the park like that, writing in characters of smoke "I love you, Marigold." Just that, penciled in black on the limitless blue. "I love you, Marigold. I love you, Marigold."

When she remembers, she is in terror lest he come too close and see the ravage of her face. In this mood one night she locked herself in her room and lay till dawn with her shamed cheeks hidden in her pillow, the while the wings of his plane brushed the glass of her window in nightlong quest of her. But mostly she is happy with him. One day in July she begged the oldest of her artists to give her some of the ragged finery he uses for his models. Ah, there, Marigold, going to the ball? But she only laughed and went off in triumph with a sleazy chiffon scarf, a fan of weatherbeaten ostrich plumes that had been dyed an emerald green, and a lace gown that had seen better days—but not recently. If they were damaged goods, you would not have known it had you seen her on the roof of her tenement at midnight, dancing in the moonlight for her lover.

The good people with whom she finds lodging are worried about her—especially when that flier of hers writes a message in the sky, bidding her meet him at such and such a street corner. Once she waited in the rain from dusk to dawn, and when the agony of that disappointment had been eased by a little time, they tried to reason with her, arguing that she ought not pin her hopes on one so faithless. She smiled at them pityingly. Why, he had explained that one defection. You see, he had had to go to the moon that day and it took him longer than he expected.

Well, that is the story of Marigold. I have no title for it because the one that fits has already been used by Theodore Dreiser. He used it for the heading of a clinical case he reported in the *Mercury* some years ago. It was the case of an ugly and unsought virgin who bewildered her family by taking, late in life, to paint and gaudy raiment, suspecting every man she passed—every visitor to the house, even the bishop—of dishonorable intentions, and generally living in a festive delusion that she was a *femme fatale* of devastating allure. It made a pathetic story. Dreiser called it "The Mercy of God."

*HOW Anne Parrish, in the divine scheme of things, crossed the sea to keep, beside the River Seine, an unconscious tryst with a companion of her childhood.*

## REUNION IN PARIS

THIS is a story—a true story—of an adventure which befell Anne Parrish one June day in Paris. I mean *the* Anne Parrish, the one who wrote *The Perennial Bachelor,* the maliciously surgical *All Kneeling,* and that uncomfortably penetrating and richly entertaining novel called *Loads of Love.* Although she comes of Philadelphia and Delaware people and has used their backgrounds and folkways for her books, she herself grew up out in Colorado Springs and it was not until one summer about ten years ago that she first experienced the enchantment of Paris. It was all new to her—the placid sidewalk cafés, the beckoning bookstalls along the river wall, the breath-taking panorama of the city from the steps of Sacré-Cœur, the twisting alleys of the Marais, murmurous with the footfalls of two thousand years.

No day was long enough for her. But to her husband Paris was an old story and one Sunday, after they had been to Notre-Dame for Mass, then to the bird-market, all a-twitter in the June sunlight, and finally (with detours to a dozen bookstalls) to the Deux-Magots for lunch, he swore he had seen all of Paris he could bear to see that day. Not one more bookstall, even if there was another only just across the way, all stocked, no doubt, with First Folios of Shakespeare, unrecognized by the witless bookseller, who would part with them at two francs each. Even so, he would sit him down at this table on the *quai* and take no further needless steps that day. From where he sat, obdurately sipping his *fine,* he could see her a-prowl on the riverbank, watch her as she hovered over the rows of books. At last he saw her pounce on one, wave it in triumph, haggle with the vendor, and come back with her purchase under her arm.

Just see what she had found for a franc! It was a flat, pallid, dingy English book for children, called *Jack Frost and Other Stories.* He inspected it without enthusiasm, implying by his manner that, personally, he would rather have had the franc. But she explained that, valueless as this admittedly insipid volume might seem to him, she was delighted to have it because it was a book she had been brought up on in her nursery days and she had not seen a copy since. For her it would provide material for just such a debauch of memory as I myself might enjoy if ever I could come upon a certain dilapidated volume of *Chatterbox,* from which I was wrenched by harsh circumstance nearly forty years ago. But he was skeptical. Could she, for instance, recall a single story in the lot? Yes, she could. After a spasm of concentration, she fished up out of her memory the fact that one of the stories concerned a little girl named Dorothy—she could even remember the pen-and-ink illustration—a little girl named Dorothy who did not like her own nose.

This bit of testimony confounded him, for indeed there was such an item in the inane collection. There, you see! While she was basking in this triumph, he turned the dog's-eared pages in quest of further data. There was a moment of silence while her glance drifted along the river to the close-packed green of its islands and the towers beyond. This silence was broken abruptly by his admitting, in a strained voice, that after all he was inclined to think she *had* known the book in her younger days. He handed it to her, open at the fly-leaf. On the fly-leaf was penciled in an ungainly, childish scrawl: "Anne Parrish, 209 N. Weber Street, Colorado Springs."

Well, that is the story. How and when the book had first passed out of her possession, she could not recall, if indeed she ever knew. She did not remember having seen or thought of it in twenty years. She could only surmise by what seemingly capricious circumstances and against what dismaying, incalculable odds it had made its journey across five thousand miles of land and sea to take up its place on the bank of the Seine and wait there for the right day and hour and moment in June when she would come drifting by and reach out her hand for it.

Surely the finding of it gave her more deeply nourishing pleasure than any collectors' item—any mere First Folio, for instance—could possibly have afforded her. Pleasure for her and pleasure, too, I think, for all of us. In fact, what interests me most about this story is a result of my own experience in hearing it and, from time to time, telling it. There is something so curiously tickling, so warming to the foolish heart in the phenomenon we call coincidence that the most indifferent stranger is somehow delighted by Anne Parrish's adventure, delighted and cheered by a strong and probably valid sense of good fortune.

I know that when I myself first heard it, I walked down the street in quite a glow, for all the world as if I had just found a tidy sum on the pavement. I had to keep reminding myself that my affairs were, when examined separately and coldly, in just about as parlous a state as they had been before. If the tidings of so uncommon a coincidence thus have all the tingle of good news, if they come to us with the force of a boon and a benison, it is, I suppose, because they carry with them the reassuring intimation that this is, after all, an or-

dered universe, that there is, after all, a design to our existence. When we thus catch life in the very act of rhyming, our
inordinate pleasure is a measure, perhaps, of how frightened
we really are by the mystery of its uncharted seas. At least, I
know that when I first heard the tale, I carried it about with
me as a talisman, more than half disposed to believe that
when the oblivious Anne Parrish crossed the street to that
bookstall, somewhere in fathomless space a star chuckled—
chuckled and skipped in its course.

*WHEREIN it is related how
an aging scribe, having escorted
his unnerving goddaughter to the
play, is rewarded by an introduction to several members of the
youngest set.*

## HANSOM IS

ON a Saturday in January, in pursuance of a promise
recklessly made long ago to my firm, young goddaughter, I engaged a hansom and in it escorted
her, cloppety-clop, to the theater where *Alice in Wonderland*
was playing. This innocent excursion was attended by rather
more publicity than had been foreseen, and was viewed from
the sidewalks with just such a jaundiced eye as I myself
would have turned upon it had I been on the outside looking
in. Here, I would have said, is someone pretty grim in his
resolution to be quaint. Here, perhaps, is even someone seeking public attention in the manner of Mae Murray when, in
the presence of photographers, that whimsical creature went
down to the Grand Central and kissed the Twentieth Century—kissed it, as a great poet said at the time, with a hey
nonny nonny and a mae murray murray.

Well, it was this way. It seems that, like every chronic winner of second prizes, I have three godchildren. Three times a
godfather and never a father. To be sure, one of the three
was christened while I was in the trenches (old soldier's slang
for war service in Paris) and another, thanks to the heathen-

ish habits of her parents, has not yet been officially called to God's attention. But one of these wards I actually sponsored. When, at a certain point in the service, these old arms opened to receive her minute person, she dissented with such a shriek of frank distaste that, as one who can take a hint, I avoided her thereafter for several years. It was when she was very six that my latent interest in her was renewed. Two overheard remarks of hers provoked this grudging attention. One was on a sunlit day when her mother was hell-bent on teaching her to dive. Finally, she took the child by the neck and ankles and swished her through the water to give her a foretaste of what a header might be like. "There, dear," said this aquatic Madonna with that dreadful false gusto which nurses employ in a doomed effort to convince their charges how simply delicious spinach is, "there, dear, wasn't that *fun!*" To which my goddaughter, shaking the water out of her eyes, replied coldly, "Not for me." Then we heard she was going to school and could actually spell. It seemed improbable, but one day, in the presence of skeptical guests, her over-confident mother put an arm around the small shoulders and asked seductively, "Joan, dear, what is c-a-t?" After some thought, Joan replied, "Thirty-four." I have revered her from that moment.

Then one July, when I realized she was going on eight, I proposed taking her to a matinée some day in the winter and escorting her there in a hansom cab. It is so easy to promise anything six months ahead, especially in an age when all one's really intellectual neighbors give daily assurance that the clock of the world will have run down by three weeks from the following Tuesday. As for the vehicular detail with which the promise was complicated, perhaps I should confess an old weakness for all archaic means of transportation. They are not much on speed, but, after all, I am in no hurry. My favorite is a rickshaw, and next to that the victoria combines the greatest comfort with the best view. Unfortunately, the view works both ways and the lolling occupant of a victoria does sometimes have a sense of being uncomfortably conspicuous. I remember one occasion when, in jogging up Fifth Avenue through the midsummer twilight, we were caught and embedded, as a raisin in a cake, in the herd of angry pedestrians swarming from curb to curb. The nightmare unreality of that moment was heightened when my companion—could it have been Dorothy Parker?—rose and blew kisses to the crowd, calling out, "And I promise to come back and sing *Carmen* again for you some time."

Hansoms have the advantage of semi-privacy, and what their drivers lack in chic they make up in saltiness. I recall an evening when it was my privilege to escort the most fascinating American actress to the stage door of her theater. As there was time to spare, we hailed a hansom in front of the Plaza and were soon ensconced, with the whip cracking and the horse dashing off in great style. It took some time for me to attract the driver's attention by beating on the ceiling with my stick. Once he had drawn rein and opened up his peep hole, I inquired bitingly, "Wouldn't you like to know where we want to go?" "Oh, no," he replied cheerfully, and, closing his trap, dashed off into the Park. Yes, I do think hansom rides are likely to be rewarding experiences. Besides, there is something in my goddaughter which makes a vintage vehicle seem an appropriate conveyance for her. She has an undeniable 1840 air. In her character I detect an alarming admixture of some such rough ferriferous substance as Molly Pitcher, but the substratum is straight from Haworth Parsonage. Emily Brontë at eight must have been very like her.

Anyway, it was a hansom that had been promised, and at the last moment I was discovering with dismay that none was parked somnolently in front of the Plaza in January. After some negotiation, I persuaded an aged charioteer named Ben Solomon to take his out of winter quarters. It was not precisely new, he admitted, but it did have red wheels. Meanwhile, rumbles from afar assured me that my guest was getting ready, and with such effective protests about having nothing to wear that, by the appointed hour, she had wangled a new pair of shoes and a new red dress, and had acquired for the occasion, from a gentleman-friend named Connelly, a pair of opera glasses. A promise had been lightly made in a dead-and-gone July, and here we were bowling down Eighth Avenue.

I was not long in discovering that some anxiety was weighing on my guest. She confessed at last a fear that the horse would not know where to go. As this was obviously preying on her mind, I pointed to the vanishing reins and explained that somewhere out of sight the driver had hold of them and thus controlled the situation. It was clear from her polite smile that she regarded this as just some more of the dreary nonsense with which grown-ups insult and fatigue the intelligence of the young. "But," she persisted, "does the horse know what play we want to see?" I realized with a shudder that city-bred children of the machine age are no more familiar with the technique of the bit and rein than I am with the mechanics of a trireme. I was just about to assure her that our steed was one of the original guarantors of the Civic Repertory who had since had to go to work, when fortunately there arose at that moment the question of the horse's name. I had thoughtlessly neglected to ask, and after some meditation (about six blocks) she decided to name it Fluff. Then at last, miraculously, we were drawing up at the right curb— good old Fluff had known the way after all—and pretty soon the curtain was up and we were both, I think, enthralled. With an infallible and gracious gesture, Miss Le Gallienne had summoned from immortal pages a lovely cavalcade and, with this achievement, surely all lingering doubts about her must vanish. I might say—and have said—many things about her. One thing I must say. She is—if there be one in our time —a great woman.

In all her enchanting pageant, my goddaughter and I detected only one flaw. In telling about the children who lived at the bottom of the treacle well, the dormouse did speak of them as Elsie, Lucy, and Tillie, when of course it should be Lacie, not Lucy. Lucy, indeed! Good God! We pounced on this error with punditical pleasure, and scowled and tossed our arms about in What-is-the-world-coming-to gestures and were pretty indignant. Afterwards, there was a delightful visit to the turbulent regions backstage, a meeting with Miss Le Gallienne and with Alice herself and with the incredibly small pickaninny who plays the littlest rabbit. There was even a moment when we were allowed to try on the White Queen's crown. Then began the ride home through the gath- ering dusk. My guest seemed lost in thought as one entranced. What dreams! What sweet saunterings through a looking-glass world of her own! Ah, to be young enough again to share so perfect an illusion! Made gross by the debauching years, I feared, by so much as a word, to crash through the gossamer of her fancies. Finally, she herself broke the silence. "I don't think," she said, "that that lady keeps her theater very clean."

This hansom took me further than I had anticipated. Through strange byways, it led me into the alarming company of my goddaughter's contemporaries. It introduced me to one formidable Miss Osland-Hill.

After brooding for many weeks upon Nora Waln's *The House of Exile,* I gave voice to some accumulated misgivings. Under the caption "A Doll's House for Nora," I tried to make the point that this young Quaker woman, by picturing Chinese life with all the dirt, smell, neglect, and dissolution left out, had achieved an effect so pretty as to leave one wondering whether her book quite deserved the high honor of being enrolled in the best-seller lists as *non*-fiction. This mutinous mutter of dissent elicited from a stern young reader a reprimand which—perhaps because of its eventually mitigated severity—I am willing to quote in full. Here it is:

DEAR MR. WOOLLCOTT,

I am Nora Waln's daughter. Mummy is not just a pacifist by inheritence. She is one by conviction also. No matter what any one does to her, she will not take any action. I am not a birthright Quaker. Both parents have to be one or the child is not. My father is a member of the Church of England but does not go to Church. I will probably not be a pacifist. Anyhow I am not one yet. I think that you ought to be written to and I am doing it.

I have read your article. I was born in China and lived nearly all my life there. I have read Mummy's book carefully and I do not find any untruth in it. Certainly she does not put everything down. Mummy never mentions nasty things in her conversation. I do not think she concentrates on them in her mind. She may see them but I do not think she could write them. Filth makes her vomit. When she has to pass anything horrid she goes quickly and does not look. If anyone mentions anything not nice, such as blood on the meat platter as my cousin Brenda did at lunch, Mummy is sick right then. Uncle Jim says she has always been like that. I feel that it is naughty of you to write that she shouldn't notice only beauty. Why shouldn't she? If you want something else written then can't you write it yourself?

But if you write anything bad about China I shall not like it. China is the best country in the world. I am young but I have been twice around the world. I have not seen any other place to compare with my birthland. Mai-da's life is told correctly.

Besides having read your article about Mummy, I have read your article about taking a little girl to the theater in February, and I have seen your picture in the *Cosmopolitan*. My conclusion is that you are not a bad man but a too hasty one.

Yours sincerely,

MARIE OSLAND-HILL.

The foregoing missive, which my executor will eventually find among my papers, is hereby gratefully acknowledged. It is my guess that the writer is the Small Girl referred to in this letter which Shunko wrote to Nora Waln from the

House of Exile on the last day of the Kindly Moon in 1923:

Uncle Keng-lin has trained a bird-of-one-thousand-bells to sing for thy Small Girl. En route to Shanghai Camel-back will bring the bird to thee with instructions how to feed and exercise it. The one-thousand-bells has a lovely plumage and a wonderful repertoire of trills. His red cage is pagoda-shaped. It was made to Uncle's own design in the birdcage shop on the Street-of-the-Sound-of-Thunder-on-the-Ground.

Later we see Small Girl borne supine on a sedan-chair cushion through the streets of Canton, watch her rescue from the murderous rage of Chang, the house steward, and accompany her through sundry later alarums and excursions of China in revolution.

Little I thought I would one day get a letter from Small Girl. I could wish she were not so far away that it is impractical at present for me to call a hansom and pay my respects in person. I should do so in the hope and belief that we would get along famously. To be sure, the prospect of such harmony would be brighter if there could be tactful provision made for my getting off in a corner from time to time for a good, rough, gory talk with Cousin Brenda, who is, I suspect, more my style. But to Marie Osland-Hill I must ever be grateful for the best epitaph I seem likely to get. Indeed, arrangements are now being made at Woodlawn for a simple headstone engraved with the legend "Too Hasty, But Not a Bad Man."

Once in my hebdomadal musings I raised the question whether nowadays there *were* any children who, after a *petit déjeuner* of Bekus Puddy or Lishus, really liked to run off and romp in the Tot Lot. My own spasmodic encounters with the members of the youngest generation had tended to suggest they were made of sterner stuff. My own goddaughter, I said, more closely resembled Lady Macbeth (or the glorious Florence Atwater) than she did the vacuous Dora Copperfield. To this chance and passing remark I owe the incalculable boon of an introduction to a young woman whom I shall call Sally because that is her name.

Sally lives in a New England town and her years on this earth have been seven. Sally has an aunt who (fortunately for you and me) is good at shorthand; a four-year-old brother Wallie, who, like myself, regards her with awe; and, living just down the street, a little girl, slightly older and taller than herself, whom she looks upon as her mortal enemy and in whose shoes I most decidedly would not care to be.

The other day the mortal enemy could be descried through the window, mincing offensively past Sally's house, with, I suspect, such a flirt of her skirts as served only to fan the ever-smoldering embers of Sally's animosity. Anyway, beyond earshot of this noxious neighbor, Sally began to croon a war song.

"There she comes! Isn't she *dirty!* Shoot her, Wallie."

Wallie responded with a dutiful "Bang! Bang!"

"There!" cried Sally. "You shot her right through the little hole in her stomach and she is dead. Oh"—this is a spurious tone of concern—"somebody stepped on her! See the foot mark? Her brains will run out. And her insides. The chickens will eat them and we will give her bones to the cat to chew on. We will skin her in the old-fashioned way and I will make a little, sleeveless dress—a tan dress—out of her skin. To match my tan shoes."

Wallie was getting into the spirit of the thing. "To wear on Sunday?" he suggested, respectfully.

"Yes," said Sally, "and we will take out her brains and all the blood will run into a bowl. We will cut the freckles out of her skin so that it will be a *plain* tan dress. We will put her on the ground and let snakes crawl on her. Now she is dying, and when she has gone to Heaven," Sally said, with what I have no doubt was a clairvoyant glimpse of the spectacle best calculated to perturb the spirit of her enemy, "and when she has gone to Heaven, her little sister *will wear all her dresses.*"

The war song was over. It had been a solace and a luxury, but Sally is one who can see the moon in her daydreams and still not overlook the sixpence at her feet. There were more limited objectives that could interest her, *faute de mieux.*

"When I see her tomorrow," she concluded, lapsing moodily into the practical, "I will poke her with a stick and trip her up when she is skating."

Well, there you have Sally, in a nutshell. I am at work now on a suitable bedtime story for her. To her mind, I am afraid, the aforesaid Lady Macbeth would seem indistinguishable from Elsie Dinsmore. She might be mildly interested in Brunehaut and Fredegonde, those rival queens of Frankish Gaul who, in their squabbles, killed off most of each other's children and grandchildren. Fredegonde was the better of the two and, full of years, died peacefully in bed. Somewhat like the late Miss Borden of Fall River, she was buried by the side of her husband, whose violent death she had personally negotiated. But I think Sally would relish more the death of Brunehaut. They caught the old girl at last, accused her of the death of ten kings, and for three days set her on a camel for the army to mock at. Then they tied her to the tail of a horse and lashed the creature to fury. "Soon," says the chronicle, "all that remained of the proud queen was a shapeless mass of carrion." Of course they were simple fellows, and never thought of making her into a little sleeveless dress.

*THE night of the strange, swift inspection, held under a fitful light at all of the camps which American troops had pitched in the mud of Brittany.*

# HANDS ACROSS THE SEA

IN the World War, when chance made me a spellbound witness of some great occasions, some part of me—the incorrigible journalist, I suppose—kept saying: "This will be something to remember. This will be something to remember." Well, it seems I was wrong about that. I find I do not often think of the war at all, and when I do, it is the small, unimportant days that come drifting back, the ones that have no part in history at all. For example, of late my thoughts have taken unaccountably to jogging back along the road to Savenay, an ancient Breton village of steep, cobbled streets, and windmills that still, I suppose, turn sleepily against the sunset sky. And here I am, bent to the task of telling you about the evening of the strange inspection there.

It was at Savenay, in August of '17, that the base hospital recruited at the Post-Graduate in New York was established, with an enlisted personnel consisting, to an impressive extent, of bouncing undergraduates from Princeton and Rutgers who had enlisted early in May in order to escape the June exams. This frustrated group was part of a shipment of two thousand soldiers who sailed stealthily from Hoboken on a hot morn-

33

ing in July aboard the *Saratoga,* which aged transport got as
far as Staten Island before being rammed and sunk. A week
later, the same outfit tried again with another boat and got as
far as Savenay. Then followed an interminable and corrupt-
ing wait through that bleak autumn of '17 when the war
seemed to stretch ahead of us as a sterile condition of life of
which we, at least, would never see the end. A time when
only the real stalwarts were strong enough to keep from becoming silly or servile or both. A time of inaction and sus-
pense and only the most sporadic and belated news from
home. A time when no rumor could be too monstrous to be
believed.

I emphasize this matter of rumors riding on every wind
which came up the valley of the Loire only so that you may
remember what tinder we all were for wild surmise, and
what an outbreak of fantastic speculation there must have
been one frosty December afternoon when, just after sundown, the bugles began blowing a summons which none of
us, as we came tumbling out of quarters, could account for.
"Line up, everybody! Line up! Line up!" This from the ser-
geants, all conscientiously gruff and authoritative, exhorting
us and pushing us in any order into hastily formed queues
which at once began shuffling docilely along in the quick-
gathering darkness. Within sight, there were several such
lines, each apparently working its way up to an appointed
table, where there seemed to be muster-rolls spread out. We
caught the gleam from officers' caps, bent in candle-lit conference. At the table, the line would pause for a moment, then
move on and be swallowed up in the darkness. During this
pause a light would flash on and off, on and off, like a winking beacon. What was up? It seemed to be some new kind of
inspection. A curious hour for any kind. It was like a nightmare payday. But we had just *been* paid the week before.
Perhaps the fool quartermaster wanted his francs back. Too
late. Too late. There was smothered laughter, and a few foul

but constructive suggestions as to what the quartermaster could do if he felt so inclined. A distant line had started up a song, and in a moment you could hear nothing else in the courtyard. It was that fine old pessimistic refrain to the tune of "Glory Hallelujah":

> Every day we sign the pay-roll,
> Every day we sign the pay-roll,
> Every day we sign the pay-roll,
>   But we never get a
>   God-damned cent.

By this time my place in line was so far advanced that I could see something of what was going on. As each soldier reached the table, his name would be checked on the roll. Then he would be told to spread his hands on the table, palms down. An electric flash would spotlight them. The officers all bent low to examine them. Then palms up. Again the light. Again the close inspection. And that was all. No more than that. Well, for Christ's sake, was it leprosy they thought we had *this* time? The soldier would move on, bewildered. The next man would take his place. A moment later my own hands were spread out. By now the entire outfit was humming with surmise. It was a kind of off-stage hubbub with only the recurrent word "hands" distinguishable. Hands. Hands. Hands. Why did they want to see our hands? From the gossipy orderly in the adjutant's office we learned there had been a telephone call from the base and within half an hour, every hand in that outfit was being checked. Patients', orderlies', doctors', cooks', mechanics', everybody's. Except the nurses'.

We drifted out through the gate onto the road to Nantes. It lay hard as flint in the frost, white as snow in the light of the new-risen moon. Across the fields was a camp of the Seventeenth Engineers. There, too, the same puzzled line was forming, writhing. The same candle-lit table, the same winking flashlight. They were looking at all the American hands in Savenay. We later learned that, at that same moment, in Nantes, some thirty kilometers away, and in all the camps pitched in the frozen mud outside St. Nazaire, the same swift inspection was going on. Also, still later, we learned why. In a barn near the port that afternoon, a fourteen-year-old girl in a torn black smock had been found unconscious. She had been raped. They could learn from her only that she had been dragged there by a soldier in a brown uniform, and that, while she was struggling with him, she had caught his hand and bitten it. Bitten it until she tasted blood.

Well, that is the story. Not, as you see, an important one. It was unrelated to the major forces launched to make the world safe for democracy. But, every now and again, some sight of a line shuffling in the torch-lit darkness—a not altogether unfamiliar sight in *this* rescued democracy—some Proustian invocation of a bygone moment brings it all back to me.

And the end of the story? You want to know, perhaps, whether they found a man with a bitten hand. Yes, they did.

*BEING the brief history of an illiterate but golden-hearted clown, much admired by all who enjoy the inestimable boon of his acquaintance.*

## MY FRIEND HARPO

ONCE in a moment of special disaffection caused by some troubling paragraph I had contributed to the public prints, John Barrymore predicted that an autopsy would reveal these old veins as flowing, not with blood at all, but with printer's ink. Some years later, my erstwhile colleague, Charles Brackett, expressed a cognate thought when he said that I never really liked anyone whose life story would not make a good magazine article. I would have to admit that, on several occasions, I have caught myself in the very act of thinking, even as I was gossiping across the fence with some neighbor whom I profoundly admired, that it would be a pleasure to write his obituary. On such occasions the happily unconscious subject would be somewhat disconcerted were he able to read my faintly vulturine thoughts. But he would be even more disconcerted if he could ever read the piece I might write about him when once I got warmed up. *Nil nisi bonum?* Why, only of the dead can one say one's hearty say unchecked by fear of causing embarrassment, uninhibited by the dreary diffidences of human relations.

If, therefore, I consider myself free to set down here some

37

small part of the affection and enthusiastic regard I feel for my friend Harpo, if I put it in black and white that there is no creature on earth whose company I find more entertaining and none in the warmth of whose generous heart I place more implicit trust, I do so only because I know that the printed word never bothers him. For among his many accomplishments—born of generations of show-folks, he is, for instance, not only a skillful pantomimist and an infallible comedian, but he is good at games too, and if you could see him in aquatic sports you would know he simply was not human— among his many accomplishments, I started to say, it so happens that the much over-rated art of reading is not included.

That circumstance, which has the effect of turning this into a confidential communication, lets me mention that my enthusiasm for Harpo is, I know, reciprocated. Indeed, when I go to the ends of the earth and come back again, there is no welcome which I can count on quite so surely as I can on his, for then his loving-kindness invents a score of ways to warm the foolish cockles of my heart. Furthermore, he carries his approval of me to the mad length of thinking I have a kind of beauty. Many a time and oft have I read as much in the melting glance of his topaz eyes when he has been sitting with his head on my knee, the while I stroked his tousled foretop and tweaked his roguish ears. There is even some evidence that he thinks I smell delightful.

I owe my friendship with him to Booth Tarkington. I owe it to my first encounter in the matchless book called *Gentle Julia* with his chronicle of Gamin, the French poodle which stormed the citadel of that aged and peculiar man, the father of Julia Atwater; the poodle which, seemingly turned out by some frenzied topiarian, had a bang like a black chrysanthemum, eyes like winking garnets, and a clown's heart so golden that he sometimes reminded Mr. Tarkington of the Jongleur of Notre-Dame. When I first read the story of Gamin, I made a secret resolve some day, somewhere, somehow, to get me a French poodle of my own. Wherefore, when a great lady of my acquaintance who has bred these dogs for some time past announced that there was a born clown in the new litter at her kennels, I spoke up for him. He was not black like Gamin but brown—or plum-colored, rather— and because of the ruddy tinge to his curly head, she had named him Harpo. The celebrated Harpo Marx, though he has "walked with kings" and rolled on the floor, they say, with princesses, was never more honored than when this enchanting dog was named after him.

I could write here endlessly of the younger Harpo's engaging ways. I could tell you of his ingenuity in the matter of opening windows, bolted doors, and ice-boxes. Quite annoying, sometimes, that last accomplishment. I could tell you of the splendor of the leap with which he clears a six-foot fence. The trajectory is motion become lyric and sets one to remembering Nijinski. Or I could enlarge upon his morbid passion for landscape gardening, which involves a good deal of trench-work and some little moving of stones and even bowlders. I could describe his manners, which are of a fastidious perfection in spite of the fact—or perhaps because of the fact—that he was born in a manger. Then I wish I had words to report the tacit rebuke his patient dignity conveys when, as sometimes happens, his piquant appearance provokes people into behaving in an excessively whimsical manner toward him. He is so deeply embarrassed—for them, of course. It upsets his idealism to see *homo sapiens* being silly.

But I mean to speak only of the puzzling enthusiasm for our species which these French poodles have manifested since time out of mind. When Harpo and I shared a cottage at Locust Valley one winter, he was neighborly enough with all the dogs living in the big house up the hill. He was gracious, for instance, toward Erich Maria Remarque, a dachshund who fitted under him like a nesting table. He was perhaps a thought too intimate with a Scotty light-o'-love named Margaret Ogilvy, although on one occasion the widely voiced suspicion that he would have to make an honest woman of her was proved baseless when subsequent developments all too clearly implicated a nitwit Cocker spaniel living down the road.

But Harpo would leave all the wondering dogs flat for the chance of watching a good croquet game, and at such desertion I think they looked upon him with vague irritation as a kind of handshaking teacher's pet. Certainly they behaved like resentful hoodlums when he would come back from his coiffeur's, fancily clipped and mighty elegant. On these occasions they would offend him by hooting and jeering in their oafish ignorance of the fact that such poodles have worn their hair that way since Augustus ruled in Rome. But I meant to suggest only that Gamin and Harpo clearly regarded themselves as having a special relation to the human species—a bond traceable, I suppose, to the fact that for a thousand years their forbears traveled with the French circuses, and in all that time had no fixed point in their lives except a person, no home at all save the foot of the boss's bed wherever it might be.

Strictly speaking, I belonged to Harpo for only a year. Then my pitiably urban habits, complicated by an incurable vagrancy, made it seem best—to him, too, I hope—that he should adopt someone else. He therefore matriculated at Hamilton College, where he has much lovely woodland to investigate, acres of greensward to race over, and a houseful of children to look after and check in at night. His present master—I use the term conventionally, for everyone concerned realizes that the delicate balance of ownership inclines, if anything, the other way—is a member of the faculty and all through Freshman year, Harpo's emotional dependence led him to sit on the campus and moan a good deal during the lectures from which he was excluded. Now he goes right into the classroom where his deportment is beyond criticism, unless you count the windy yawn he emits when he feels the lecture is running just a little too long. When, as sometimes happens, I visit his part of the country, he first conveys to the professor, with the nicest tact imaginable, that here is just an old friendship which need not worry *him* at all. Then, in my honor, he has the churchbells rung and orders dancing in the streets. Immensely flattered, I go on my way, deciding anew that New York, with the opera and the theaters and such, is all very well, but that there is only one word to describe a community in which there is no place for the likes of my friend Harpo. The word is "uninhabitable."

*A FOND report on the reap-
pearance of Maude Adams, returning to the stage after a thirteen year absence as Portia in
"The Merchant of Venice."*

# REUNION IN NEWARK

DECEMBER 1931.

I T is a commonplace that nothing can so poignantly evoke
the flavor of the receding past as some remembered tune,
some melody that has caught up and woven into its own
unconscious fabric the very color and fragrance of a day gone
by. I am sure, for example, that this Juventino Rosas (I have
just copied his unfamiliar name from a phonograph record)
who once wrote a pleasant and rather hoppy waltz called
"Over the Waves," would be astounded if he could know
what overtones I hear when that old tune of his comes to me
across a lake at sundown, or floats up through the darkness
from a distant orchestra. I myself could not detect all its associations but first among them is certainly the heart-breaking
gayety in the third act of *The Cherry Orchard*. Then there
are the peanut-strewn paths at Willow Grove with Sousa's
band playing of a Sunday afternoon long ago. And of course
every prom of my salad days, with the girls in organdy and
the stag-line miserable in white gloves and stiff shirts, and
chaperones, with frozen smiles, ever on the prowl. Then I
think a few jugglers' acts are mixed in somewhere.

42

I know that the blend was too much for a certain aging and mellow traveler one day in the May just past when, along with some scores of others, he was bidden to a cocktail party at the British Legation in Peking. The drinks, of which he took perhaps too many, were served in the largest of a succession of scarlet pavilions set in the greensward. Beyond the furthest one, the sentries could be seen ceaselessly pacing. In the shelter of another, the band of the Queen's Own, which had come up from Tientsin for the polo game, was staying over to play for the party. And just as the aforesaid traveler was taking his departure and stepping into his apprehensive rickshaw, the band struck up the familiar opening bars of "Over the Waves" and its melody followed him through the streets of the Legation Quarter. Whereupon the traveler began to weep in a quiet way. Perhaps it was just as well that the already sufficiently puzzled rickshaw-boy understood no word of English, for it would have been difficult to explain to him (or to anyone else, for that matter) what the old fool was crying about.

To anyone "sufficiently decayed," such an evocation of a bygone day is tinged with a sadness inexplicable to the young fry. One might warn them, however, that they will live to learn that all music is full of such mischief. But, as it happens, I never realized until one Wednesday afternoon early in the present month when, to my considerable surprise, I found myself in Newark, that there are other sounds which can come across the years as sweetly freighted with associations numberless and indefinable. For, sitting as one unresisting spectator in the largest audience I have seen in any theater in many a season, I found myself yielding to the spell of a music familiar, dear, and ineffably touching. It was the music of a speaking voice I had not heard in years nor ever thought to hear once more. It was the voice—unchanged and changeless—of Maude Adams. And the sound of it filled me with an almost intolerable nostalgia for a day that is not now and

never can be again. I was under the distinct impression that
the play was *The Merchant of Venice* and that the admirable
Shylock was Otis Skinner—the same Shylock (and wearing,
by the way, the selfsame cloak) that I had seen with Ada
Rehan eight-and-twenty years before from a hard-earned seat
in the gallery of the Garrick in Philadelphia. Then I knew,
too, that Miss Adams was supposed to be Portia, but I kept
hearing the glee of Babbie laughing through the rowan ber-
ries at the little minister and once—I think through some
lovely intonation in the "Quality of Mercy" speech—I suddenly saw not Portia at all, but Peter standing white, wraithlike, and consecrate, on guard outside the house they built
for Wendy.

I have no quarrel with the young reviewers who went all
the way out to Cleveland to discover that Maude Adams was
not a young and lustrous Portia, and am only a little amused
at their implication that she ever would have been. For even
when she was a youngster, she was a timeless gnome, and
there never was a day when she could have played Portia
to a good press. After all she was never considered a great
actress in the sense that Ada Rehan and Mrs. Fiske were
great. Another adjective described her more happily and still
does—described her unmistakably and more nearly than
any other player of my time. That adjective was "dear." Also
am I a little amused at the recurrent observation that the selection of this particular play for her return was "ill-advised."
If there is one thing I am sure of, it is that it was not *advised*
at all. For she was ever a person apart, and long ago she
learned to shut herself, such as she was, away from the distracting sounds of the managers, the critics, and the public.
I am glad of that for only such a one could, in 1905, have
saved the newborn *Peter Pan* from being the dire failure
which the managers, the critics, and the public at first so confidently regarded it.

The audience in Newark was made up of gaffers and

school-children. For instance, I was not unaware of several comely minxes but recently arrived in their teens who were sitting just behind me. When we came to the moon-drenched loveliness of the final scene and heard from Lorenzo how the floor of heaven was thick inlaid with patines of bright gold, the young females behind me giggled. I realized that, to them, bred at the movies, this scene was just a coupla young people in funny clothes necking in a garden. And right they were, I suppose. But beyond them stretched an acre or so of gray heads, and at some familiar gesture of this Portia, or at some fondly remembered caress of the funny, throaty little voice, which ever defeated the mimics of its day, a ripple ran across that audience as a gust of wind traverses a field of grain —a ripple that was part sigh and part contented chuckle and, to my notion, most pleasant to hear.

Probably she hears it every night, and as she steps on to the stage at Ford's in Baltimore next Friday, she must know how many of us all over the land are wishing her, with all our hearts, a Merry Christmas.

*THE funeral of a great priest as reported by one who had come to know him during his genial missions "in partibus infidelium."*

# FATHER DUFFY

AFTER her last tour in *The Rivals,* that celebrated Mrs. Malaprop who was the grandmother of these latter-day Barrymores used to sit rocking on her veranda at Larchmont. Joseph Jefferson, himself getting on towards seventy, would rock beside her. "What mystifies me, Joe," she said one day, "is why you should traipse all the way across New England just to visit an old woman like me." He told her why. You see, she was the only person left in the world who called him Joe. You who are young now cannot hope to postpone until so ripe an age the first sense of your own world coming to an end. By the time you have reached the middle years, it may well be that people dearer to you than anyone can ever be again will already be ashes scattered to the winds. Thereafter, one by one, the friends slip away. Death seems to come oftener into your street than he used to do, now knocking at the house next door, now touching on the shoulder the neighbor you were talking to only yesterday at sundown. You grow quite accustomed to the sound of his step under your window.

It is a life thus successively and irremediably impoverished

46

which you yourself give up at last—the less reluctantly, I daresay. At least that is the feeling I have when I try looking squarely at the fact that I shall never again read a new page by Lytton Strachey, never again hear the wonder of Mrs. Fiske's voice in the theater, never again experience on Christmas Eve, as in so many jolly years gone by, the heart-warming benediction of Father Duffy's smile. I seem to remember it more often than not as a mutinous smile, the eyes dancing, the lips puckering as if his conscientious sobriety as a priest were once more engaged in its long, losing fight with his inner amusement at the world—his deeply contented amusement at the world. I thought that smile one of the pleasantest sights in America, and I find unbearable the thought that I shall not see it again.

They buried Father Duffy from St. Patrick's at the end of June in 1932. The huge cathedral might as well have been a tiny chapel for all it could hope to hold those of us who wanted to say good-by to him. As I waited in the cool, candle-lit dusk of the church for the procession to make its way up the sunny avenue, all around me lips were moving in prayer and gnarled fingers were telling their rosaries. But even the heathen could at least count over their hours with him. There were many of us there, outsiders who, without belonging to his outfit, had nevertheless been attached to him for rations—of the spirit. One had only to stop for a moment and speak to him on the street to go on one's way immensely set up, reassured by what he was that there might be a good deal, after all, to this institution called the human race.

While we waited, my own wry thoughts jumped back to that desperate October in 1918 when his regiment, the old 69th of New York, was cut to ribbons in the Argonne. Especially I recalled the black day when Colonel Donovan was carried out of the battle on a blanket—Wild Bill, who was the very apple of the Padre's eye. Father Duffy had always scolded him for his gaudy recklessness, and there he was at last with his underpinnings shot from under him. As they carried him into the dressing-station he had just strength enough left to shake a defiant fist. "Ah there, Father," he said, "you thought you'd have the pleasure of burying me!" Father Duffy shook a fist in reply. "And I will yet," he said. But it was not to be that way. For here, fourteen years later, was Wild Bill and a thousand others of the old regiment coming up the avenue to bury Father Duffy.

One by one there came back to me all the times our paths had crossed in France and on the Rhine. He would always have tall tales to tell of his Irish fighters, who, with death all around them, heard only the grace of God purring in their hearts. It delighted him that they spoke of the Ourcq as the O'Rourke, and he enjoyed their wonderment at the French presumption in dignifying so measly a creek by calling it a river. He loved the story of one wounded soldier who waved aside a proffered canteen. "Give it to the Ourcq. It needs it more than I do." And he loved all stories wherein the uppity were discomfited. On the Rhine he relished the spectacle of Pershing vainly trying to unbend a bit and play the little father to his troops. The Commander-in-Chief paused before one Irish doughboy who had three wound stripes on his arm. "Well, my lad," asked the great man in benevolent tones, "and where did you get those?" "From the supply sergeant, Sir," the hero answered, and Father Duffy grinned from ear to ear.

Most often he would talk not of France and the war at all, but of New York. He liked nothing better than to sit in a shell-hole with Clancey and Callahan and Kerrigan and talk about New York. I have stood beside him ankle-deep in the Argonne mud and, above the noise of the rain pattering on our helmets, heard him speculate about the gleam of Fifth Avenue in the October sunshine and say how he would like to see once more that grand actress who called herself Laurette Taylor, but who, mind you, was born a Cooney. And

for him the most electric moment in all the war came on a
night of June moonlight in Lorraine when the troops of the
old 69th discovered that the shiny new outfit which was relieving them was also from New York. The war had picked
them both up by the scruff of the neck, carried them across
the world, and dropped them in the French mud, and here
they were passing each other on the road. At that time the
Rainbow had been in the line only a few weeks, and the
Baccarat Sector was a tranquil one. The real slaughter of July
and October lay ahead of them but at least they could feel
battle-scarred and scornful when compared with these green
boys of the 77th, fresh from the transports. Being themselves
volunteers, they jeered at the newcomers as conscripts, who
retorted, to their surprise, by calling them draft dodgers.
There was some excitement as old neighbors would identify
each other in the moonlight, and one unforgettable moment
when Father Duffy saw two brothers meet. In their emotion
they could only take pokes at each other and swear enormously. Then, lest all these ructions draw the attention of the
enemy artillery to this relief, order was somehow restored
and the march went on, mingling prohibited, speech of any
kind forbidden. So these passing regiments just hummed to
each other very softly in the darkness. "Give my regards to
Broadway." The rhythm staccato, the words unnecessary.
"Remember me to Herald Square." The tune said the words
for all of them. "Tell all the boys in Forty-second Street that
I will soon be there." In the distance the sound grew fainter
and fainter. Father Duffy had a lump in his throat.

For he was the great New Yorker. Born in Canada, Irish
as Irish, schooled in Maynooth, he was surely the first citizen
of our town. This city is too large for most of us. But not for
Father Duffy. Not too large, I mean, for him to invest it with
the homeliness of a neighborhood. When he walked down
the street—any street—he was like a *curé* striding through his
own village. Everyone knew him. I have walked beside him

and thought I had never before seen so many *pleased* faces. The beaming cop would stop all traffic to make a path from curb to curb for Father Duffy. Both the proud-stomached banker who stopped to speak with him on the corner and the checkroom boy who took his hat at the restaurant would grin transcendently at the sight of him. He would call them both by their first names, and you could see how proud they were on that account. Father Duffy was of such dimensions that he made New York into a small town.

No wonder all the sidewalk space as far as one could see was needed for the overflow at his funeral. To my notion, the mute multitude in the June sunlight made the more impressive congregation. To alien ears the Latin passages of the Mass seem as automatic and as passionless as the multiplication table, and at least those who could not get in missed the harangue delivered from the pulpit with the vocal technique of a train announcer. One woman I know saw an unused bit of pavement and asked a huge policeman if she might not stand there. He told her the space was reserved. "But," she explained, as if offering credentials, "I was a personal friend of Father Duffy's." The policeman's answer was an epitaph. "That is true, Ma'am," he said, "of everyone here today."

*A SHORT history of the magician's daughter who was the managing mother of the Four Marx Brothers.*

# OBITUARY

L AST week the Marx Brothers buried their mother. On the preceding Friday night, more from gregariousness than from appetite, she had eaten two dinners instead of the conventional one, and, after finishing off with a brief, hilarious game of ping-pong, was homeward bound across the Queensboro Bridge when paralysis seized her. Within an hour she was dead in her Harpo's arms. Of the people I have met, I would name her as among the few of whom it could be said that they had greatness.

Minnie Marx was in this world sixty-five years and *lived* all sixty-five of them. None knew better than her sons that she had not only borne them, brought them up, and (with a bit of coaxing here and a *schlag* there) turned them into successful play-actors. She had done much more than that. She had *invented* them. They were just comics she imagined for her own amusement. They amused no one more, and their reward was her ravishing smile.

It was her idea that they should go into the theater at all. She herself was doing sweat-shop lace-work when she mar-

ried a tailor named Sam Marx. But for fifty years her father
was a roving magician in Hanover, and as a child she had
known the excitement of their barn-storming cart-rides from
one German town to another. Now here she was, sidetracked
in a Third Avenue tenement, with a swarm of children on
her hands. But hadn't her brother deserted his career as a
pants-presser to go into vaudeville? You remember the song
about Mr. Gallagher and Mr. Shean? Well, that was her
brother—Mr. Shean. His first success only strengthened her
conviction that she came of showfolks, and she was determined that her sons should enter into that inheritance. She
had six, in all. One died as a baby. After the war, she lost
another to the silk-dress business. This defection from her
now notable quartet did not baffle her long. Reaching for
Zeppo, her youngest, she yanked him out of high school and
flung him into the breach.

At first she had an undisputed monopoly of the idea that
her boys would do well in the theater. Even they did not
share it with her. To be sure, Chico, her eldest, was a piano
player. Fortunately for her peace of mind, she didn't know
where. But she knew he was a piano player, for she herself
had amassed the weekly quarter which paid for his lessons.
Then her Julius—that's Groucho—had a promising soprano
voice. After cleaning up the breakfast things, she used to
tether the youngest to the kitchen table and sit all day in
agents' offices, until finally she got her Julius a job. Then,
when she had incredibly launched her vaudeville act—it consisted of a son or so, pieced out with a pretty girl and a tenor
—she couldn't bear the thought of setting forth on tour while
her Harpo stayed behind, a bellhop at the Seville, with no
one to see that he ate properly. It was a woman of magnificent decision who therefore called a cab, drove to the Seville,
snatched Harpo from his employment and, en route to Hen-
derson's at Coney Island, transformed him with a white duck
suit, so that, just as the curtain was rising, she could catapult

him into the act. Really, one cannot say that the Marxes ever *went* on the stage. They were pushed on.

The uphill stretch was a long one, humble, worrisome, yet somehow rollicking. The Third Avenue flat, with the rent money never once on time in ten years, gave way to a Chicago house, with an equally oppressive mortgage. And when in their trouping through that territory they would grow so harumscarum that there was real danger of a fine by the management, she would have to subdue them by a magic word whispered piercingly from the wings. The word was "Greenbaum." You see, Mr. Greenbaum held the mortgage aforesaid.

It was eighteen years after her first homespun efforts as an impresario that her great night came. That was when, for the first time, the words "Marx Brothers" were written in lamps over the door of a Broadway theater. For the première of *I'll Say She Is,* she felt entitled to a new gown, with which she proposed to sweep to her seat in the proscenium box. But while she was standing on a chair to have it fitted, the incompetent chair gave way, and she broke her ankle. So she couldn't exactly sweep to her seat on the first night. They had to carry her. But she got there.

Her trouble was that her boys had got there too. They had arrived. Thereafter, I think she took less interest in their professional lives. When someone paid them a king's ransom to make their first talkie, she only yawned. What she sighed for was the zest of beginnings. Why, I hear that last year she was caught hauling her embarrassed chauffeur off to a dancing-school, with the idea of putting *him* on the stage. In her boredom she took to poker, her game being marked by so incurable a weakness for inside straights that, as often as not, her rings were missing and her bureau drawer littered with sheepish pawntickets. On the night *Animal Crackers* opened she was so absorbed that she almost forgot to go at all. But at the last moment she sent her husband for her best wig, dispatched her chauffeur to fetch her new teeth, and, assembling herself on the way downtown, reached the theater in time to greet the audience. Pretty as a picture she was, as she met us in the aisle. "We have a big success," she said.

Minnie Marx was a wise, tolerant, generous, gallant matriarch. In the passing of such a one, a woman full of years, with her work done, and children and grandchildren to hug her memory all their days, you have no more of a sense of death than you have when the Hudson—sunlit, steady, all-conquering—leaves you behind on the shore on its way to the fathomless sea.

She died during rehearsals, in the one week of the year when all her boys would be around her—back from their summer roamings, that is, but not yet gone forth on tour. Had she foreseen this—I'm not sure she didn't—she would have chuckled, and, combining a sly wink with her beautiful smile, she would have said, "How's that for perfect timing?"

*THE teasing mystery of an anon-
ymous benefaction and how it
was solved at last.*

# THE EDITOR'S EASY CHAIR

THE question as to who killed the late Arnold Roth-
stein remains as yet unanswered, and there seems no
present likelihood of the world ever knowing just
what became of that most vanishing lady of them all—Miss
Dorothy Arnold. But now one mystery that for many weeks
had plagued and vexed your frantic correspondent has at last
been solved. The events leading up to the tragedy could be
recounted in a brochure entitled *The Mystery of the Easy
Chair*.

It was on a tranquil, lulling day last May that the chair
arrived at Wits' End. As though it were yesterday, I remember my first glimpse of its noble profile, when I came in and
found it glistening amid the shabbier furnishings. I had been
up the street on some errand or other—had probably trudged
off, let us say, to take an ailing neighbor a glass of guava jelly
nesting in a basket under a snowy napkin. At all events, the
chair arrived during my absence. That notorious dawdler,
my man Saturday, explained that two melodramatic delivery-
men had borne it triumphantly into the living room, cut the
strings, whipped off and taken away the encasing paper, and
gone their way, saying no words as to whence it had come,

and leaving not a tittle of evidence behind to help me guess. It was a new chair, copied, I suspect, from some classic model of an ampler age, and built to sustain without misgivings a person of considerable bulk—should any such chance to pay me a visit.

Being a burnt child, my first suspicion led me to telephone one of those harpies called interior decorators. I know their tricks and their manners, and I just wanted to warn this one that I *would* not have my flat fixed by duress, that if she thought to tempt me with the sight of this masterpiece on the premises, and thereafter mail me a staggering bill for it, she might better send a dray around for it at once. The harpy in question repelled this "horrid implication" with some little asperity.

I was then driven, blushing, to the conclusion that the chair was a gift from some unknown admirer. But from whom? Of course in the days when I was a dramatic critic I was showered with presents. Anyway, at Christmastime there would always be a few tasty bottles of this or that from Jones & Green; a box from Dixie Hines containing three pencils with my name lettered in gold on each, and almost correctly spelled, too; and several cartons of Camels from old Santa Lee Shubert. But, with my retirement from the turmoil of journalism, the neighborly affection of these gentlemen withered as if from some sudden frost. An unsuspected gift, therefore, had become a rarity. I could not begin to guess who had sent the chair.

The chair, though superb in architecture, was upholstered in one of those flagrant chintzes, designed, apparently, by the art editor of a seed catalogue. I itched to have it reupholstered in some stout denim, but dared not thus affront the veiled unknown. Therefore I decided, like Bunker Bean, to play the waiting game, keeping up the while an artfully careless watch on every visitor for some telltale gesture—perhaps a blush of pride at the reminder of so costly a gift, perhaps an irrepressible spasm of regret at having parted with it. Inevitably, several wags, hearing of my researches, wrote me, handsomely confessing that in a moment of impulse *they* had ordered the chair sent to me. But these shy admissions lacked the ring of authenticity. Finally I came to the conclusion that the giver must be one of two persons, and I set myself to the task of discovering which.

To be safe, I showered each of the suspects with orchids, bonbons, and theater tickets, in the manner of a nineteenth-century gallant, writing them little notes which besought them to drop in to tea and sit in a great, new wonderful chair which I had acquired for their comfort. As each sank into its beckoning depths, I watched for some blush of complicity, but came at last to the conclusion that I was on the wrong scent. After a pointblank question, indeed, each suspect disavowed all previous knowledge of the chair, but not before I had spent enough on their entertainment—orchids, bonbons, theater tickets, orange pekoe, crumpets, and the like—to have paid for the chair, and a couple of ottomans thrown in.

Then, the other day, just as the mystery was receding into a pigeonhole alongside the Charlie Ross *dossier,* a quite hysterical furniture dealer broke through the cordon of sentries while I was nibbling my breakfast rusk. He rushed at me in saucer-eyed excitement, holding out a dingy business card and muttering, "A terrible predicament, yo, a terrible predicament." He was in the middle of a stuttering explanation that a chair had been ordered by an apparently fussy family named Talcott—he had got that far in the story of his terrible predicament when he spied his lost chair, as good as new, save for a few nicks in the woodwork and a few caviar-stains and splotches of fountain-pen ink, barely perceptible in the rank *flora* of the upholstery. With a loud, glad cry he signaled his henchmen, who were, I discovered, even then crouched in the hallway.

The last thing I saw of the mystery it was on its way down the freight elevator. The Editor's Easy Chair, forsooth! *Too* easy, it seems. Altogether too easy.

*AN enemy alien spies upon the
centennial revelries held by the
brotherhood of the Star and Crescent.*

# FOR ALPHA DELTA PHI

IN these random notes on contemporary American life,
the conviction has been not infrequently expressed that
banquets are bores, that he who arranges one (especially
in warm weather) is at least a semi-public-nuisance, and that
those who attend them are defectives. Yet on Labor Day in
1932 your apostate correspondent drove a hundred and fifty
miles across the mountains through the holiday traffic and
wedged himself panting into a dinner coat, merely to be
present at such a function, whereat many speeches were
made, including one by himself. The banquet, with Bruce
Barton in the chair, was the wind-up of the Alpha Delta
Phi Centenary convention, for it was just one hundred years
since this most distinguished of the Greek Letter societies
had been founded on the lovely hilltop of my own college.
Before you are lost in wonder at the heroic lengths to which
a sentimental old grad will go in behalf of his beloved
fraternity, perhaps I should explain that Alpha Delta Phi
is not my fraternity at all, beloved or otherwise. I was there
as spokesman for the other Greek Letter societies. I was
immensely set up by the assignment until it occurred to me,

too late, that, after all, it was not they but the Alpha Delts
who had appointed me, with the notion, perhaps, that, as a
specimen of the kind of man whom the other crowds took in,
I would add a relish to their dinner.

It is an eerie experience on an evening of song and fond
recollection to be the only Bœotian present. I knew then how
George S. Kaufman's famous ancestor, Sir Roderick Kaufman, must have felt. He was the one, you may remember,
who went on the crusades—as a spy. I had an uneasy feeling
that some aged and myopic alumnus would give me the grip.
The Alpha Delt salute is, I believe, no such complicated and
embarrassing stranglehold as that with which the brethren
of Sigma Phi assault each other on meeting. Still, I thought it
best to run up my colors at once. Wherefore I explained to
the famous banker on my left that I was a Theta Delt.
"Thank God," he exclaimed, in the manner of one already
fed up, "I don't have to call you brother." I was not quite sure
how I should take this, but he went on in a kindly way to
suggest that I might have a reunion of my own with the
waiters. "From your Tuskegee chapter," he explained. Later,
when some speaker recalled how an early and valorous Alpha
Delt had once climbed to one of the high peaks of the world
to carve the star and crescent in the everlasting rock, I took
pleasure in reminiscing to my neighbor, the banker, about the
night in college when some of us had been at great pains to
etch that same insignia in the snowbank outside the Alpha
Delt hall.

Some of my best friends are Alpha Delts. To two members
of that society from the Hamilton College chapter I owe
much. It was Samuel Hopkins Adams of the Class of 1891
who, when I came out of college, persuaded the *New York
Times,* against its better judgment, to take me on as a reporter. But already Walter Scott Kimball of the Class of '51
had come to my aid at a time of even greater need. Dr. Kimball was a general practitioner in Little Silver, New Jersey.

On a bleak day in 1887, he drove seven miles to our house through the snow, and on his way home was able to spread the news throughout the countryside that it was another boy at the Woollcotts'. Dr. Kimball's daughter drove the cutter on that momentous occasion, and often spoke afterward of how bitter cold it was and what an unconscionable time I spent on the mere business of being born. Even so, it seems to have put ideas into her head. For (of course, after the proper legal and biological formalities) she went my mother one better and gave birth to Edmund Wilson.

Kimball, '51, and Adams, '91—I felt no little satisfaction in acknowledging my debt to these men. But I think I most savored the dinner as a reminder of, and a sequel to, the September afternoon in my college days when I was thrown off the veranda of the Alpha Delt hall. The word "thrown" is an insufficient description. I was picked up and carried off as to an incinerator. It happened during the rushing season in my senior year—that feverish period when the different fraternities must seduce incoming freshmen with an air of conferring a favor upon them, must pursue yet seem pursued. It is no work for men. The comedy of such a time has been immortalized by George Fitch (*olav hasholem!*) in his memoirs of dear old Siwash. The anguish, as far as I know, is yet to be written. It was a season in the college year when I felt myself peculiarly inadequate. Then, if ever, I knew I was not the type. My own brothers in Theta Delta Chi were clearly of the same opinion. Not by words so much as by manner, they suggested that, whereas, once a freshman had been pledged, he would begin to discover I had a heart of gold and would come in time (years, perhaps) to be proud of knowing me, I might, at first glance, be frightening to a callow observer. I was, they intimated, an acquired taste. They were struggling to express an idea which the late Mrs. Janis was later to put into words when I overheard her explain to someone that I was like a fine old olive. More bluntly, they said that if I *would* persist in wearing those old corduroys, that paint-daubed turtle-neck sweater, and that red fez, it might be best for the future of Theta Delta Chi if the freshman class were not to see me at all. Well, I could take a hint. It was clear that I must vanish for a time from the temple of friendship. Where to go? That was the only question. After some thought, I hit on a rather good answer. I cut all my classes for the day, drew *Anna Karenina* from the college library, stole some apples, went up to the Alpha Delt hall, and sat on the veranda, prepared to spend the day. As speculative knots of freshmen drifted by, I would look up from my book, lean over the rail, leer at them seductively, and cry out: "Don't you want to join our frat?" Some Alpha Delt seniors, returning from classes late in the day, caught me in the act. The aforesaid ejection took place in due course. But it was too late. They had a hard time getting a delegation that year. It was almost the end of the chapter.

Dear me, that had been four-and-twenty years before, and here was I, forgiven at last and breaking bread with them in convention assembled. Through the smoke-haze of the dining-room, I could see one of the plug-uglies who performed that memorable act of dispossession—he and a couple of other fellows. Today it would take the whole fraternity.

*IN reading this chapter from an as yet unwritten autobiography, you may be in some doubt as to which is the central figure—the Lady or the Tiger.*

# AUNT MARY'S DOCTOR

I SAW by the newspapers one morning in the first weeks of 1929 that the doctor who attended my Aunt Mary in her last illness was engaged in writing a book. I did not anticipate an Adlerian treatise entitled *The Case of Aunt Mary,* or even *The Doctor Looks at Aunt Mary*. Indeed, I imagined that he had forgotten all about her, for his was a crowded, tempest-tossed life, and she has been dust in the graveyard these many years.

Even into my time the faint, fragrant memory of her still lingered around the house where she and I were born. This is a shabby, rambling old caravansary in Jersey, bleak as a skull in winter. I am afraid it has not been painted since the Civil War. But in the spring, the vines that encase it and hold it up against the winds break into myriad blossoms. In May it is fantastically festooned with wistaria, and when their lavender petals flutter down to the eaves of the veranda roof, the crimson rambler takes up the task of making the old house seem gay and important.

The place is thronged with ghosts. Ghosts, for instance, of the Van Mater slaves, who, back in the early part of the

eighteenth century, forged the nails and hewed the beams
of the barn that went up in flames in 1919, and whose burial
ground still stands between two fields, the wooden crosses
long since moldered away, but the soil itself somehow spared
each spring by diffident plowmen.

Or ghosts of Washington's troops, buried, my elders always told me, there on the lawn across the noisy brook that
winds through the hazel thicket and cuts across our place
on its bustling, undiscouraged way to the sea. Certainly the
Redcoat retreat to the waiting ships at the Highlands ran
across our fields, and now and again the spring plowing will
bring up a bit of salvage. Once the potato diggers came upon
a British officer's sword, emblazoned with a forgotten and
almost indecipherable importance.

Then there is the ghost of Mr. Greeley, who used to take
his nap in a chair on the veranda, the red bandanna, which
would be thrown across his face, bellying rhythmically with
his snores, and all the young fry compelled to go about on
tiptoe because the great editor was disposed to doze.

And of course the ghosts of mine own people—above all,
the ghost of little Aunt Mary. She was a tiny, fragile, merry
child, born into a husky and surprised tribe. It was the way of
her time to say that she faded like a wild rose from the roadside. She had become a dim legend in my time, but I knew
the daguerreotype, with a locket clasping the fichu on her
breast, and the black hair parted in the middle above a forehead ivory white. On frosty, moonlit nights I used to think
I saw her, with her crinolines and her hood and her mittens,
standing half lost in the shadows under the big walnut tree
that was an old-timer even in her day.

She was in her early twenties when she died. They spoke
of the malady that carried her off as "a decline," and I suppose that some species of anemia afflicted her. The medical
talent available then in Monmouth County was unequal to
cope with the sickness that seized her, and the young French

painter who was in love with her came up to New York to seek advice and help in the French colony here.

It was 1866—a time when New York looked to Paris for everything, from the *corps de ballet* for *The Black Crook* to the styles in bonnets and shawls affected by the lovely Eugénie. And just as anyone with an endocrine perplexity would have turned, a few years ago, to Walter Timme, new come from Vienna with all the latest wisdom about the glands, so in the sixties Aunt Mary's anxious suitor hunted up a young French doctor, bursting with all the latest theories from the University of Paris. He had come to America to make his fortune and see the world, I suppose, but more particularly to escape from a France ruled by a rouged Napoleon sitting on the nervous edge of a recent throne. Paris just then was unhealthy for radicals and the fiery young doctor, in the days of his internship, had already tasted the experience of spending two months in the lockup for writing pieces distasteful to the party in power.

Now, in New York, he responded to the call for help from down home. The trip was more of an undertaking in those days. There were no trains running to Red Bank. The young doctor must needs take a boat to South Amboy, and from there travel across country on horseback.

All his new-garnered wisdom was not enough for his task, but in the days when he stood by he proved himself sympathetic and winning and must have made friends with all the family. For afterward, when he was teaching French to a school of young misses up in Stratford, Connecticut, and desired, or at any rate agreed, to marry one of his pupils, it was to my grandfather that he came to borrow the cost of his wedding trip and the price of a fine new suit of clothes.

I never heard whether he settled that score, but I think he must have, for it was a tradition in the family to speak fondly of him. Another baffling detail I cannot supply would explain how, contrary to all the old family customs, my grandfather happened to have the money to lend him.

Aunt Mary's doctor paid another visit to America in 1922 to make a speaking tour. In the newspaper comment heralding that tour, one viewpoint puzzled my uncles and aunts, as they rocked on the veranda and let their memories run back to the days when the dapper young doctor had come galloping up from Amboy more than half a century before. Being his seniors, they could not understand why anyone should think he was too old to make this tour. Why, he was only eighty-one, going on eighty-two. Perhaps, they decided, he had let the life of Paris sap him, and was, in consequence, poorly.

And now, seven years later, he had outlived them all and, or at least so the cables from Paris reported, was spry enough to be engaged in writing a book. His name, of course, was Clemenceau.

*AN attempt to winnow out some*
*of the chaff in the legend of a*
*woman from Rockland, Maine,*
*who has entered into American*
*mythology.*

# THE TRUTH
## ABOUT JESSICA DERMOT

I KNOW an ancient mariner who sits in the sun at Honolulu and remembers the days when, as an orphaned kid, he escaped from the old Cape Cod spinsters in charge of him and ran away to sea. Most of all he likes to tell about the first time he got a berth as mate on a ship sailing round the world. Her captain was the weather-beaten Thomas Dermot of Rockland, Maine, who, in his turn, had been a Liverpool wharf-rat when the sea scooped him up and adopted him. Now Dermot's motherless little daughter Jessica was flowering just then into such loveliness that the skipper felt a deep uneasiness about leaving her behind in Rockland. So, whether he thought of her as an innocent to be guarded or as a pearl he might sell some day for a good price, he took her to sea with him. When she stood on the bridge beside him, with the salt wind whipping her dark hair, she must have been as fair a sight as ever greeted mortal eyes.

I wish I might have seen her in those days. When I did see her a dozen years later (the skipper could not keep her

at sea forever), her beauty was breath-taking enough in all
conscience, but by then there was no surprise in it, for it was
famous the world around. At the time she was on the stage,
to which great beauty has ever gravitated as to a show window. She was playing with Nat Goodwin in a sentimental
romance fabricated around the slim, proud figure of Nathan
Hale. Before he went forth to be hanged at dawn, there was
a heart-wrenching scene of farewell which drenched the
house in tears and left the younger set in the gallery quite
inconsolable. Indeed, I quit the theater so bemused that to
this day I cannot pass the bronze Nathan Hale in City Hall
Park in New York without thinking how sweet at her side
might have been the one life he had to give for his country.

Well, that was many a year ago and Jessica Dermot has
long since left the stage. Today, she has white hair and a great
fortune, and she lives in a villa she has built for herself on
the shore at Cannes, where, when she goes out to drive, she
can see the depressing and faintly repulsive statue of her old
friend Edward VII, erected by the grateful citizens of this
French resort which his favor made fashionable. It is a fearsome sight, but at that it may sometimes remind her mis-
chievously of the venturesome days when he was astroll one
afternoon in the park at Marienbad and passed this young
American woman in a dove-colored gown with puffed sleeves
who, not without design, sat seemingly engrossed in a becoming book of poetry, her ruffled parasol tilted to shade the
page. As Royalty went by, she chanced to look up from beneath the wide brim of her hat, and, for the space that a
breath is held, their eyes met. Then she looked down at her
book again and went on reading until, in ten minutes or so,
an equerry came bowing and scraping with an invitation to
dine that evening. But in her villa now her windows look out
on the sea she used to sail when she was a kid from Rockland,
long ago. That villa, by the way, was swept by flames in the

spring of 1933. If its fate had rested with the local fire department, her home would now be ashes, but the damage was restricted, thanks to the valiant help volunteered by the English battleships at anchor in the harbor. It was so like her to employ the British Navy as her personal fire-extinguisher.

When she herself indulges in such retrospects, hers are, I suppose, the mixed emotions which must be the portion of any woman who knows that already, in her own lifetime, she is a myth. Irrevocably the skipper's daughter, under her assumed name of Maxine Elliott, has entered into American legend. It is the substance of that legend that her great catch was none of the men she married but the late Pierpont Morgan. The legend has it that, fascinated and ensnared by her loveliness, he showered on her the gifts which leave her still, after the hurricane of the depression, a fabulously rich woman, and that, as a magnate's kiss for Cinderella, he built and gave her the marble-front theater in Times Square which has borne her name now for more than five-and-twenty years. That the first financier and the first beauty of an era should be thus linked in people's minds has almost the force of a folk wish. That Mr. Morgan built the Maxine Elliott Theater as a slight token of his regard has been an article in the simple creed of New York ever since I can remember. If I repeat it here, it is for the purpose and the satisfaction of saying something new about it.

What I wish to contribute to the legend is the fact that it is not true. I do not mean merely that it is not quite true. It is not true in any degree. Dollar by dollar, Miss Elliott paid for her share of that theater out of her own shrewdly multiplied savings, and, mind you, it was not merely that she did not know Mr. Morgan well enough to expect or accept such gifts from him. She did not know him at all. It was not merely that they did not exchange favors. They did not even exchange words. The force of gossip is such that it has woven a probably indestructible fabric of faintly scandalous romance about two people who, as it happens, were not even acquaintances.

I confess myself fascinated by this evidence that a legend can spring up and flourish untended without a particle of truth to sustain it. If you have any doubt about the sturdiness of this one, you have only to ask any man in the street, or glance through the pages of Master Winkler's *Morgan the Magnificent,* or attend the play called *Dinner at Eight.* As Mr. Winkler was obliged to write his biography without access to the Morgan archives and without co-operation from the Morgan family, he had to fall back on clippings and gossip and guesswork to such a degree that inevitably so cherished and firmly rooted a myth as the one about Maxine Elliott found a place in his pages. Morgan, according to Mr. Winkler, permitted her to "tame" him. "Maxine Elliott," he says, "had a peculiar influence over Morgan." Very peculiar, indeed!

Then there is no mistaking her identity behind the florid, if somewhat neglected, figure of Carlotta Vance in *Dinner at Eight.* Into that comedy strolls this erstwhile beauty of the stage, brought back from her villa at Antibes by the depression. She must look into her once fruitful investments, and, in particular, get rid if she can of the theater named after her. It had fallen on evil days. Listen to Carlotta herself:

"May I take you for a stroll down Forty-second Street and a little look at the Carlotta Vance Theater? It's between the Flea Circus and a Hamburger-and-onion Eatery. It's had six weeks of booking in the past two years. And what were they! Special matinées of a Greek actress named Maria Koreopolous playing Sophocles' *How Are You?* in the original Greek. *That* filled a long-felt want. Then there was a movie week. A big educational film called *The Story of Evolution; or, From Ooze to Hoover* in ten reels. It then swung back to the legitimate with a little gem entitled *Papa Love Mama.* Three days. For the past six months they haven't taken the lock off the door. It's now known as the spiders' rendezvous, but you can't collect rent from *them!* . . . So my little problem is to find somebody I can sell it to. Though I don't know what they'd do with it, unless they flood it and use it for a swimming pool. I wonder if I couldn't sell it back to the Stanfield estate. There's an idea. You know, when he gave me that theater I thought it was pretty magnificent of the old boy. I wish now I'd taken a sandwich."

At which revelation on the first night in New York, there was a great rustle in the audience, the sibilant sound of a thousand complacent wiseacres all whispering "Maxine Elliott" in unison. Of course it is quite possible that should you ask George Kaufman and Edna Ferber about it, they would blandly insist they were just two great dreamers who had invented that character without a thought of Maxine Elliott so much as crossing their minds. If they should say that, you have my permission to tell them they are lying in their teeth.

What is peculiarly maddening about the Maxine Elliott legend is that the truth itself is so much more interesting. After all, a pretty lady of the stage who thriftily hoards the gifts of rich men as a provision for her old age is a fairly stereotyped character. But here is one who was herself a genius in finance. She helped many men in her time, and needed the help of none. If, baffled by the loss of such a cherished old toy as the Morgan myth, you at least try to suggest that Miss Elliott owed a great deal to the market tips given her by great men of affairs, those who worked with her in the old days will smile a rueful smile, knowing that, as it happened, great men of affairs were more likely to get their tips from her. She had an infallible instinct in investments. I know of one instance when her lawyer had bought ten thousand shares of a copper-mine stock he thought well of when it was selling at 15. She decided to follow him to the extent of a thousand shares. When he sold out at 44—and glad to get it—he was good enough to warn her that he had done so. But she replied, by wire, that *she* was selling at 115 or nothing. The stock went to 117. The instance would hardly be worth telling if it were not so characteristic. Multiply that by a hundred and you have her story. "If she had been a man," the lawyer says in dreamy reverence, "Morgan would have been her secretary, and Jacob Schiff her office boy."

Of course her going into partnership with Lee Shubert in the building of her theater represented an irritated impulse to get her strong and competent hands into the cheerful muddle of the great American box office. But there was a time when she had a better idea even than that. She dreamed a theater with no Shuberts in it at all. It was her notion that the ten most successful stars of the day might form a circuit, and, by thus dispensing with the middleman, themselves take all the profit. She worked out this scheme in such actuarial detail as would have warmed a banker's heart. Armed with her prospectus, she went to the first star on her list, John Drew, knowing that he at least had a good-enough head to grasp her argument, and that with him in her pocket the rest would follow. He studied the scheme with care. "Yes, it would work," he said, "but what will become of Charley Frohman?" And he handed it back to her. She tore it up and went her way, cursing the fate that had thrown her into a profession where everyone else but herself was a muddle-headed softy. If she was to make her fortune she would have to do it alone.

Seemingly she cared little about accumulation for its own sake. Secretly she decided upon a specific sum as her objective. She was on tour in the Middle West when the word came from her bankers that the sum had been reached. That night the notice went up on the bulletin board. She paid her company to the end of the season, dismissed them, and walked out of the stage door an independent woman. If some years later she came back to it for a season or two, it was because the war and a houseful of nieces brought needs for more money, which she had not foreseen.

The truth about Jessica Dermot, if I may make a clause out of my own title, is less something I myself might presume to tell than something I would like to read. It is a biography I hope someone better qualified will write while I am still around to read it. I suppose it will have to deal, to some extent, with Maxine Elliott as an actress. She never was one, really. It was the habit of her friends to say that her beauty handicapped her, but that was nonsense. Indeed, her beauty was all that let her into the theater at all. Certain quite homely little women among her contemporaries had, as a compensation, the capacity to make Maxine Elliott on the stage seem a woman of no importance. She was not so much a bad actress as a non-actress. She had everything that beauty, wit, great intelligence, ambition, industry, and a will of iron could contribute to the making of an actress. It was not enough. The strange, incommunicable gift was not hers.

Then the book will have to deal with her marital adventures. She attempted two husbands before deciding that marriage was no career for which she was equipped. The first, whom, to judge from her paragraph in *Who's Who in the Theater,* she seems to have forgotten, was a man named Mc-Dermott. According to Rockland tradition, he was a man much older than herself whom she married because her family needed his money. Later—as who did not in those days—she married Nat Goodwin. Afterwards in his memoirs he classified his brides. The first was an angel, the second a dear little thing, and the third, Maxine, a Roman senator. Roman general would, I think, have been more apt. That selfsame paragraph in *Who's Who* makes up for its first oversight by marrying her off to Tony Wilding, the British tennis player who was killed in the war and to whom, as a matter of fact, she was never married at all. Just before the war the cables hummed with prophecies that she *would* marry him. Her old friend, Melville E. Stone, as head of the Associated Press, sent her a wire of confidential inquiry in the matter. She wired back: "I have honorable intentions towards no man." But, for that matter, there was a time when half the hearts of England were left hopefully on her doorstep, including one noble coronet that she would have none of. It was her difficulty that she would be the appanage of no man, and yet could not like a man who would be an appanage of hers. I happen to have known the husbands of some women of great achievement. Most of them were the lowest form of animal life. Whether great women have a taste for such, like a predilection for Roquefort, or inevitably make poor things of the men they marry, I do not know. I merely appreciate the validity of Miss Elliott's predicament.

I hope that the chapter on Hartsbourne Manor will be written by someone who savored its brilliant hospitality. It was her English country home during and before the war. Edward and his ministers and all the glittering people of that time were guests under its roof. In the first startled autumn of 1914 the youngsters interspersed the bridge games with target practice. When she sold the place at last, she paid a farewell visit to its haunted gardens, and stayed looking long at the beech tree pockmarked with bullets fired by those young friends of hers who never came back from France. There is a legend at Hartsbourne that once the King was minded to visit her unattended for the week-end. She wrote him she knew that no one who had been so good a friend would thus destroy her. Majesty replied crossly that not even his own subjects were suffered to advise him in such matters. She began packing her trunks, and some of them, marked for America, were already in the van when a breathless equerry arrived with a list of guests the reconsiderate King would bring with him.

Two stories which I myself can vouch for will belong in that biography. The first concerns an English actress who, stricken with a once-fatal malady, was sent abroad to die. At some hospital in Switzerland they guessed she had three months to live. Just then a car arrived with a great lady who wanted to know if there were any hope. Well, there was talk of a new specific recently discovered in America. It was as yet a little-tried remedy and this patient, the doctors said, was so worried about her dependents back in England that any experiment seemed hopeless. The visitor took out a check book. The new treatment was ordered forthwith, the hospital expenses for the next six months were paid in advance and all the worries in England were shouldered on the spot. This gesture saved the day. That actress is still playing triumphantly, owing, as many of her sisters do, much to Maxine Elliott.

Then I would have you know that when her career as a hostess at Hartsbourne was at its zenith, she used to say a good-by to her guests on Sunday night, whether or not they were lingering till Monday. Then she herself would withdraw into a plain little two-room wing which was inviolably hers. There for five days of the week she satisfied her Rockland soul by practicing the art of dressmaking. Her nieces and friends, firmly she adorned them every one. It was a bit of the Maine coast transplanted to the heart of Hertfordshire. It was Jessica Dermot having her way behind the lovely mask called Maxine Elliott.

*WHEREIN a young cadet from
the Saint-Cyr of yesteryear has a
bit of luck and learns how great-
hearted a French cocotte can be.*

LEGENDS: I

# ENTRANCE FEE

THIS, then, is the story of Cosette and the Saint-Cyrien,
much as they tell it (and these many years have been
telling it) in the smoky *popotes* of the French army.
In the nineties, when one heard less ugly babel of alien
tongues in the sidewalk cafés, the talk at the *apéritif* hour
was sure to turn sooner or later on Cosette—Mlle. Cosette of
the *Variétés,* who was regarded by common consent as the
most desirable woman in France. She was no hedged-in
royal courtesan, as her possessive fellow-citizens would point
out with satisfaction, but a distributed du Barry, the *chère
amie* of a republic.

Her origins were misty. Some said she had been born of
fisher folk at Plonbazlanec on the Brittany coast. Others
preferred the tale that she was the love-child of a famous
actress by a very well-known king. In any case, she was now
a national legend, and in her pre-eminence the still-bruised
French people found in some curious way a balm for their

wounded self-esteem. Her photographs, which usually showed her sitting piquantly on a café table, were cut from *L'Illustration* and pinned up in every barracks. Every French lad dreamed of her, and every right-minded French girl quite understood that her sweetheart was saying in effect, "Since I cannot hope to have Cosette, will you come to the river's edge at sundown?" Quite understood, and did not blame him.

Everyone had seen the pictures of Cosette's tiny, vine-hung villa at Saint-Cloud, with its high garden wall and its twittering aviary. And even those for whom that wall was hopelessly high took morbid pride in a persistent detail of the legend which said that no man was ever a guest there for the night who could not bring five thousand francs with him. This was in the nineties, mind you, when francs were francs, and men—by a coincidence then more dependable—were men.

The peasant blend of charm and thrift in Cosette filled the cadets at Saint-Cyr with a gentle melancholy. In their twilight hours of relaxation they talked it over, and all thought it a sorrowful thing that, so wretched is the soldier's pittance, not one of those who must some day direct the great *Revanche* would ever carry into battle a memory of the fairest woman in France. For what cadet could hope to raise five thousand francs? It was very sad. But, cried one of their number, his voice shaking, his eyes alight, there were a thousand students at Saint-Cyr, and not one among them so lacking in resource that he could not, if given time, manage to raise at least five francs.

That was how the Cosette Sweepstakes were started. There followed then all the anxious distraction of ways and means, with such Spartan exploits in self-denial, such Damon-and-Pythias borrowings, such flagrant letters of perjured appeal to unsuspecting aunts and godmothers, as Saint-Cyr had never known. But by the appointed time the last man had his, or somebody's, five francs.

The drawing of numbers was well under way when a perplexed instructor stumbled on the proceedings and reported his discovery to the Commandant. When the old General heard the story he was so profoundly moved that it was some time before he spoke.

"The lad who wins the lottery," he said at last, "will be the envy of his generation. But the lad who conceived the idea—ah, he, my friend, will some day be a Marshal of France!"

Then he fell to laughing at the thought of the starry-eyed youngster arriving at the stage door of the *Variétés* with nothing but his youth and his entrance fee. The innocent budget had made no provision for the trip to Paris, none for a carriage, a bouquet, perhaps a supper party. The Commandant said that he would wish to meet this margin of contingency from his own fatherly pocket.

"There will be extras," he said. "Let the young rascal who wins be sent to me before he leaves for Paris."

It was a cadet from the Vendée who reported to the Commandant next afternoon—very trim in his red breeches and blue tunic, his white gloves spotless, his white cockade jaunty, his heart in his mouth. The Commandant said no word to him, but put a little purse of gold *louis* in his hand, kissed him on both cheeks in benediction, and stood at his window, moist-eyed and chuckling, to watch until the white cockade disappeared down the avenue of trees.

The sunlight, latticed by the *jalousies,* was making a gay pattern on Cosette's carpet the next morning when she sat up and meditated on the day which stretched ahead of her. Her little cadet was cradled in a sweet, dreamless sleep, and it touched her rather to see how preposterously young he was. Indeed, it quite set her thinking of her early days, and how she had come up in the world. Then she began speculating on *his* early days, realized with a pang that he was still in the midst of them, and suddenly grew puzzled. Being a woman of action, she prodded him.

"Listen, my old one," she said, "how did a cadet at Saint-Cyr ever get hold of five thousand francs?"

Thus abruptly questioned, he lost his head and blurted out the tale of the sweepstakes. Perhaps he felt it could do no harm now, and anyway she listened so avidly, with such flattering little gasps of surprise and such sunny ripples of laughter, that he quite warmed to his story. When he came to the part about the Commandant, she rose and strode up and down, the lace of her peignoir fluttering behind her, tears in her violet eyes.

"Saint-Cyr has paid me the prettiest compliment I have ever known," she said, "and I am the proudest woman in France this day. But surely I must do my part. You shall go back and tell them all that Cosette is a woman of sentiment. When you are an old, old man in the Vendée you shall tell your grandchildren that once in your youth you knew the dearest favors in France, and they cost you not a sou. Not a sou."

At that she hauled open the little drawer where he had seen her lock up the lottery receipts the night before.

"Here," she said, with a lovely gesture. "I give you back your money."

And she handed him his five francs.

*THE adventure of a young med-
ico, who spent a night under an
ancient roof in Kent and with
his own eyes beheld some spectral
fancywork.*

LEGENDS: II

# MOONLIGHT SONATA

IF this report were to be published in its own England, I
would have to cross my fingers in a little foreword explaining that all the characters were fictitious—which
stern requirement of the British libel law would embarrass
me slightly because none of the characters is fictitious, and
the story—told to Katharine Cornell by Clemence Dane and
by Katharine Cornell told to me—chronicles what, to the best
of my knowledge and belief, actually befell a young English
physician whom I shall call Alvan Barach, because that does
not happen to be his name. It is an account of a hitherto un-
reported adventure he had two years ago when he went down
into Kent to visit an old friend—let us call *him* Ellery Cazalet—who spent most of his days on the links and most of his
nights wondering how he would ever pay the death duties
on the collapsing family manor-house to which he had in-
dignantly fallen heir.

This house was a shabby little cousin to Compton Wyn-
yates, with roof-tiles of Tudor red making it cozy in the

noon-day sun, and a hoarse bell which, from the clock tower, had been contemptuously scattering the hours like coins ever since Henry VIII was a rosy stripling. Within, Cazalet could afford only a doddering couple to fend for him, and the once sumptuous gardens did much as they pleased under the care of a single gardener. I think I must risk giving the gardener's real name, for none I could invent would have so appropriate a flavor. It was John Scripture, and he was assisted, from time to time, by an aged and lunatic father who, in his lucid intervals, would be let out from his captivity under the eaves of the lodge to putter amid the lewd topiarian extravagance of the hedges.

The doctor was to come down when he could, with a promise of some good golf, long nights of exquisite silence, and a ghost or two thrown in if his fancy ran that way. It was characteristic of his rather ponderous humor that, in writing to fix a day, he addressed Cazalet at "The Creeps, Sevenoaks, Kent." When he arrived, it was to find his host away from home and not due back until all hours. Barach was to dine alone with a reproachful setter for a companion, and not wait up. His bedroom on the ground floor was beautifully paneled from footboard to ceiling, but some misguided housekeeper under the fourth George had fallen upon the lovely woodwork with a can of black varnish. The dowry brought by a Cazalet bride of the mauve decade had been invested in a few vintage bathrooms, and one of these had replaced a prayer closet that once opened into this bedroom. There was only a candle to read by, but the light of a full moon came waveringly through the wind-stirred vines that half curtained the mullioned windows.

In this museum, Barach dropped off to sleep. He did not know how long he had slept when he found himself awake again, and conscious that something was astir in the room. It took him a moment to place the movement, but at last, in a patch of moonlight, he made out a hunched figure that seemed to be sitting with bent, engrossed head in the chair by the door. It was the hand, or rather the whole arm, that was moving, tracing a recurrent if irregular course in the air. At first the gesture was teasingly half-familiar, and then Barach recognized it as the one a woman makes when embroidering. There would be a hesitation as if the needle were being thrust through some taut, resistant material, and then, each time, the long, swift, sure pull of the thread.

To the startled guest, this seemed the least menacing activity he had ever heard ascribed to a ghost, but just the same he had only one idea, and that was to get out of that room with all possible dispatch. His mind made a hasty reconnaissance. The door into the hall was out of the question, for madness lay that way. At least he would have to pass right by that weaving arm. Nor did he relish a blind plunge into the thorny shrubbery beneath his window, and a barefoot scamper across the frosty turf. Of course, there was the bathroom, but that was small comfort if he could not get out of it by another door. In a spasm of concentration, he remembered that he *had* seen another door. Just at the moment of this realization, he heard the comfortingly actual sound of a car coming up the drive, and guessed that it was his host returning. In one magnificent movement, he leaped to the floor, bounded into the bathroom, and bolted its door behind him. The floor of the room beyond was quilted with moonlight. Wading through that, he arrived breathless, but unmolested, in the corridor. Further along he could see the lamp left burning in the entrance hall and hear the clatter of his host closing the front door.

As Barach came hurrying out of the darkness to greet him, Cazalet boomed his delight at such affability, and famished by his long, cold ride, proposed an immediate raid on the larder. The doctor, already sheepish at his recent panic, said nothing about it, and was all for food at once. With lighted candles held high, the foraging party descended on the offices, and mine host was descanting on the merits of cold roast beef, Cheddar cheese, and milk as a light midnight snack, when he stumbled over a bundle on the floor. With a cheerful curse at the old goody of the kitchen who was always leaving something about, he bent to see what it was this time, and let out a whistle of surprise. Then, by two candles held low, he and the doctor saw something they will not forget while they live. It was the body of the cook. Just the body. The head was gone. On the floor alongside lay a bloody cleaver.

"Old Scripture, by God!" Cazalet cried out, and, in a flash, Barach guessed. Still clutching a candle in one hand, he dragged his companion back through the interminable house to the room from which he had fled, motioning him to be silent, tiptoeing the final steps. That precaution was wasted, for a regiment could not have disturbed the rapt contentment of the ceremony still in progress within. The old lunatic had not left his seat by the door. Between his knees he still held the head of the woman he had killed. Scrupulously, happily, crooning at his work, he was plucking out the gray hairs one by one.

*HOW two wayfarers, finding shelter from the cold in a long-deserted house, encounter there, strangely but indisputably, a visitor from the sea.*

LEGENDS: III

# FULL FATHOM FIVE

THIS is the story just as I heard it the other evening—a ghost story told me as true. It seems that one chilly October night in the first decade of the present century, two sisters were motoring along a Cape Cod road, when their car broke down just before midnight and would go no further. This was in an era when such mishaps were both commoner and more hopeless than they are today. For these two, there was no chance of help until another car might chance to come by in the morning and give them a tow. Of a lodging for the night there was no hope, except a gaunt, unlighted, frame house which, with a clump of pine trees beside it, stood black in the moonlight, across a neglected stretch of frost-hardened lawn.

They yanked at its ancient bell-pull, but only a faint tinkle within made answer. They banged despairingly on the door panel, only to awaken what at first they thought was an echo, and then identified as a shutter responding antiphonally with the help of a nipping wind. This shutter was around the corner, and the ground-floor window behind it was broken and unfastened. There was enough moonlight to show that the room within was a deserted library, with a few books left on the sagging shelves and a few pieces of dilapidated furniture still standing where some departing family had left them, long before. At least the sweep of the electric flash which one of the women had brought with her showed them that on the uncarpeted floor the dust lay thick and trackless, as if no one had trod there in many a day.

They decided to bring their blankets in from the car and stretch out there on the floor until daylight, none too comfortable, perhaps, but at least sheltered from that salt and cutting wind. It was while they were lying there, trying to get to sleep, while, indeed, they had drifted halfway across the borderland, that they saw—each confirming the other's fear by a convulsive grip of the hand—saw standing at the empty fireplace, as if trying to dry himself by a fire that was not there, the wraithlike figure of a sailor, come dripping from the sea.

After an endless moment, in which neither woman breathed, one of them somehow found the strength to call out, "Who's there?" The challenge shattered the intolerable silence, and at the sound, muttering a little—they said afterwards that it was something between a groan and a whimper —the misty figure seemed to dissolve. They strained their eyes, but could see nothing between themselves and the battered mantelpiece.

Then, telling themselves (and, as one does, half believing it) that they had been dreaming, they tried again to sleep, and, indeed, did sleep until a patch of shuttered sunlight striped the morning floor. As they sat up and blinked at the gritty realism of the forsaken room, they would, I think, have laughed at their shared illusion of the night before, had it not been for something at which one of the sisters pointed with a kind of gasp. There, in the still undisturbed dust, on the spot in front of the fireplace where the apparition had seemed to stand, was a patch of water, a little, circular pool that had issued from no crack in the floor nor, as far as they could see, fallen from any point in the innocent ceiling. Near it in the surrounding dust was no footprint—their own or any other's—and in it was a piece of green that looked like seaweed. One of the women bent down and put her finger to the water, then lifted it to her tongue. The water was salty.

After that the sisters scuttled out and sat in their car, until a passerby gave them a tow to the nearest village. In its tavern at breakfast they gossiped with the proprietress about the empty house among the pine trees down the road. Oh, yes, it had been just that way for a score of years or more. Folks did say the place was spooky, haunted by a son of the family who, driven out by his father, had shipped before the mast and been drowned at sea. Some said the family had moved away because they could not stand the things they heard and saw at night.

A year later, one of the sisters told the story at a dinner party in New York. In the pause that followed a man across the table leaned forward.

"My dear lady," he said, with a smile, "I happen to be the curator of a museum where they are doing a good deal of work on submarine vegetation. In your place, I never would have left that house without taking the bit of seaweed with me."

"Of course you wouldn't," she answered tartly, "and neither did I."

It seems she had lifted it out of the water and dried it a little by pressing it against a window pane. Then she had carried it off in her pocketbook, as a souvenir. As far as she knew, it was still in an envelope in a little drawer of her desk at home. If she could find it, would he like to see it? He would. Next morning she sent it around by messenger, and a few days later it came back with a note.

"You were right," the note said, "this is seaweed. Furthermore, it may interest you to learn that it is of a rare variety which, as far as we know, grows only on dead bodies."

And that, my dears, is the story as I heard it the other evening, heard it from Alice Duer Miller who, in turn, had heard it five-and-twenty years before from Mrs. George Haven Putnam, sometime dean of Barnard College and author of that admirable work, *The Lady*. To her I must go if—as I certainly did—I wanted more precise details. So to Mrs. Putnam I went, hat in hand and, as an inveterate reporter, showered her with questions. I wanted the names of the seaweed, of the curator, of the museum, of the two sisters, of the dead sailor, and of the nearby village on Cape Cod. I wanted a roadmap marked with a cross to show the house in the grove of pines. I wanted—but the examination came to a dead stop at the sight of her obvious embarrassment. She was most graciously apologetic, but, really, what with this and what with that, she had forgotten the whole story. She could not even remember—and thus it is ever with my life in science—who it was that had told it to her.

FOOTNOTE: More recently, the Curator of the Botanical Museum in St. Louis has assured me that this tale, whispered from neighbor to neighbor across the country, has become distorted in a manner offensive to students of submarine vegetation. According to him, the visitor from the sea was seen in a house in Woods Hole, Mass. He was a son of the house who had been drowned during his honeymoon off the coast of Australia. The seaweed picked up off the dusty floor of that New England mansion was of a variety which grows only off the Australian coast. The Curator even presented me with the actual seaweed. I regard it with mingled affection and skepticism, and keep it pressed between the pages of Bullfinch's *Mythology*.

*THE adventure in Paris of a frightened girl whose traveling companion, together with the baseless fabric of her habitation, dissolves into thin air and leaves not a rock behind.*

LEGENDS: IV

# THE VANISHING LADY

THEN there was the story—told me some years ago as a true copy of a leaf from the dread secret archives of the Paris police—of the woman who disappeared during the World Exposition as suddenly, as completely, and as inexplicably as did Dorothy Arnold ten years later from the sidewalks of New York.

As I first heard the story, it began with the arrival from Marseilles of an Englishwoman and her young, inexperienced daughter, a girl of seventeen or thereabouts. The mother was the frail, pretty widow of an English officer who had been stationed in India, and the two had just come from Bombay, bound for home. In the knowledge that, after reaching there, she would soon have to cross to Paris to sign some papers affecting her husband's estate, she decided at the last minute to shift her passage to a Marseilles steamer, and, by going direct to Paris, look up the lawyers there and finish her business before crossing the Channel to settle forever and a day in the Warwickshire village where she was born.

Paris was so tumultuously crowded for the Exposition that they counted themselves fortunate when the *cocher* deposited them at the Crillon, and they learned that their precautionary telegram from Marseilles had miraculously caught a room on the wing—a double room with a fine, spacious sitting-room looking out on the Place de la Concorde. I could wish that they had wired one of those less magnificent caravansaries, if only that I might revel again in such a name as the Hotel of Jacob and of England, or, better still, the Hotel of the Universe and of Portugal. But, as the story reached me, it was to the Crillon that they went.

The long windows of their sitting-room gave on a narrow, stone-railed balcony and were half-shrouded in heavy curtains of plum-colored velvet. As again and again the girl later on had occasion to describe the look of that room when first she saw it, the walls were papered in old rose. A high-backed sofa, an oval satinwood table, a mantel with an ormolu clock that had run down—these also she recalled.

The girl was the more relieved that there would be no need of a house-to-house search for rooms, for the mother had seemed unendurably exhausted from the long train ride, and was now of such a color that the girl's first idea was to call the house physician, hoping fervently that he spoke English, for neither she nor her mother spoke any French at all.

The doctor, when he came—a dusty, smelly little man with a wrinkled face lost in a thicket of whiskers, and a reassuring Legion of Honor ribbon in the buttonhole of his lapel—did speak a little English. After a long, grave look and a few questions put to the tired woman on the bed in the shaded room, he called the girl into the sitting-room and told her frankly that her mother's condition was serious; that it was out of the question for them to think of going on to England next day; that on the morrow she might better be moved to a hospital, etc., etc.

All these things he would attend to. In the meantime he

wanted the girl to go at once to his home and fetch him a medicine that his wife would give her. It could not be as quickly prepared in any chemist's. Unfortunately, he lived on the other side of Paris and had no telephone, and with all Paris *en fête* it would be perilous to rely on any messenger. Indeed, it would be a saving of time and worry if she could go, armed with a note to his wife he was even then scribbling in French at a desk in the sitting-room. In the lobby below, the manager of the hotel, after an excited colloquy with the doctor, took charge of her most sympathetically, himself putting her into a *sapin* and, as far as she could judge, volubly directing the driver how to reach a certain house in the Rue Val du Grâce, near the Observatoire.

It was then that the girl's agony began, for the ramshackle victoria crawled through the festive streets and, as she afterwards realized, more often than not crawled in the wrong direction. The house in the Rue Val du Grâce seemed to stand at the other end of the world, when the carriage came at last to a halt in front of it. The girl grew old in the time which passed before any answer came to her ring at the bell. The doctor's wife, when finally she appeared, read his note again and again, then with much muttering and rattling of keys stationed the girl in an airless waiting room and left her there so long that she was weeping for very desperation, before the medicine was found, wrapped, and turned over to her.

A hundred times during that wait she rose and started for the door, determined to stay no longer but to run back empty-handed through the streets to her mother's bedside. A thousand times in the wretched weeks that followed she loathed herself for not having obeyed that impulse. But always there was the feeling that having come so far and having waited so long, she must not leave without the medicine just for lack of the strength of will to stick it out a little longer—perhaps only a few minutes longer.

Then the snail's pace trip back to the Right Bank was another nightmare, and it ended only when, at the *cocher's* mulish determination to deliver her to some hotel in the Place Vendôme, she leaped to the street and in sheer terror appealed for help to a passing young man whose alien tweeds and boots told her he was a compatriot of hers.

He was still standing guard beside her five minutes later when, at long last, she arrived at the desk of the Crillon and called for her key, only to have the very clerk who had handed her a pen to register with that morning look at her without recognition and blandly ask, "Whom does Mademoiselle wish to see?" At that a cold fear clutched her heart, a sudden surrender to a panic that she had fought back as preposterous when first it visited her as she sat and twisted her handkerchief in the waiting room of the doctor's office on the Left Bank; a panic born when, after the doctor had casually told her he had no telephone, she heard the fretful ringing of its bell on the other side of his walnut door.

This then was the predicament of the young English girl as she stood there at the desk of the hotel in Paris—a stranger in the city and a stranger to its bewildering tongue. She had arrived that morning from India and had left her ailing mother in charge of the house physician while she went out in quest of medicine for her—a quest in which, through a malignant conspiracy between perverse circumstances and apparently motiveless passers-by, she had lost four hours.

But now with the bottle of medicine clutched in her hand, she reached the hotel at last, only to be stared down by the clerk at the desk, only to have the very man who had shown them their rooms with such a flourish that morning now gaze at her opaquely as though she were some slightly demented creature demanding admission to someone else's apartment.

But, no, Mam'zelle must be mistaken. Was it not at some other hotel she was descended? Two more clerks came fluttering into the conference. They all eyed her without a flicker of recognition. Did Mam'zelle say her room was No. 342? Ah, but 342 was occupied by M. Quelquechose. Yes, a French client of long standing. He had been occupying it these past two weeks and more. Ah, no, it would be impossible to disturb him. All this while the lobby, full of hurrying, polyglot strangers, reeled around her.

She demanded the registration slips only to find in that day's docket no sign of the one she herself had filled out that morning on their arrival, the while her tired mother leaned against the desk and told her how. And even as the clerk now shuffled the papers before her eyes, the stupefying bloodstone which she had noticed on his ring-finger when he handed her the pen five hours before, winked at her in confirmation.

From then on she came only upon closed doors. The same house physician who had hustled her off on her tragic wild-goose chase across Paris protested now with all the shrugs and gestures of his people that he had dispatched her on no such errand, that he had never been summoned to attend her mother, that he had never seen her before in all his life. The same hotel manager who had so sympathetically helped her into the carriage when she set forth on her fruitless mission, denied her now as flatly and somehow managed to do it with the same sympathetic solicitude, suggesting that Mam'zelle must be tired, that she should let them provide another chamber where she might repose herself until such time as she could recollect at what hotel she really belonged or until some inquiries should bring in news of where her mother and her luggage were, if——

For always there was in his ever polite voice the unspoken reservation that the whole mystery might be a thing of her own disordered invention. Then, and in the destroying days that followed, she was only too keenly aware that these evasive people—the personnel of the hotel, the attachés of the embassy, the reporters of the Paris *Herald,* the officials at the

Sûreté—were each and every one behaving as if she had lost her wits. Indeed there were times when she felt that all Paris was rolling its eyes behind her back and significantly tapping its forehead.

Her only aid and comfort was the aforesaid Englishman who, because a lovely lady in distress had come up to him in the street and implored his help, elected thereafter to believe her against all the evidence which so impressed the rest of Paris. He proved a pillar of stubborn strength because he was some sort of well-born junior secretary at the British Embassy with influence enough to keep her agony from gathering dust in the official pigeon-holes.

His faith in her needed to be unreasoning because there slowly formed in his mind a suspicion that for some unimaginable reason all these people—the hotel attendants and even the police—were part of a plot to conceal the means whereby the missing woman's disappearance had been effected. This suspicion deepened when, after a day's delay, he succeeded in forcing an inspection of Room 342 and found that there was no detail of its furnishing which had not been altered from the one etched into the girl's memory.

It remained for him to prove the mechanism of that plot and to guess at its invisible motive—a motive strong enough to enlist all Paris in the silent obliteration of a woman of no importance, moreover a woman who, as far as her daughter knew, had not an enemy in the world. It was the purchased confession of one of the paper-hangers, who had worked all night in the hurried transformation of Room 342, that started the unraveling of the mystery.

By the time the story reached me, it had lost all its content of grief and become as unemotional as an anagram. Indeed, a few years ago it was a kind of circulating parlor game and one was challenged to guess what had happened to the vanished lady. Perhaps you yourself have already surmised that the doctor had recognized the woman's ailment as a case of

the black plague smuggled in from India; that his first in-
stinctive step, designed only to give time for spiriting her out
of the threatened hotel, had, when she died that afternoon,
widened into a conspiracy on the part of the police to sup-
press, at all costs to this one girl, an obituary notice which,
had it ever leaked out, would have emptied Paris overnight
and spread ruin across a city that had gambled heavily on the
great Exposition for which its gates were even then thrown
wide.

The story of this girl's ordeal long seemed to me one of the
great nightmares of real life and I was, therefore, the more
taken aback one day to have its historicity faintly impaired by
my discovering its essence in a novel called *The End of Her
Honeymoon* which the incomparable Mrs. Belloc-Lowndes
wrote as long ago as 1913. Then I find myself wondering if
she unearthed it in the archives of the Paris police or whether
she spun its mystery out of her own macabre fancy, making
from whole cloth a tale of such felicitous invention that, like
Stockton's *The Lady or the Tiger* or Anatole France's *The
Procurator of Judea,* it had moved from land to land with the
seven-league-boots of folk-music and so been told and retold
at hearths the world around by people who had never read it
anywhere.

FOOTNOTE: The story of "The Vanishing Lady" is a fair specimen
of folklore in the making. For such a story to travel round the world
by word of mouth, it is necessary that each teller of it must believe
it true, and it is a common practice for the artless teller to seek to impart that belief to his listeners by affecting kinship, or at least a life-
long intimacy, with the protagonist of the adventure related. In my
entertaining, desultory, and (with one exception) fruitless researches
into the origin of twenty such world-girdling tales, I have often challenged one of these straw-man authorities, only to have it vanish as
utterly as did the ailing lady from the Place de la Concorde. In the
case of this story, which was used not only by Mrs. Belloc-Lowndes
but by Lawrence Rising in a later novel called *She Who Was Helena
Cass,* I can report that it is a favorite, seemingly, with old ladies on
shipboard, those rootless widows who wear buttoned shoes with cloth

tops and whose families, with ill-concealed delight, persuade them to
do a good deal of traveling. The story will be whispered as gospel
truth from steamer-chair to steamer-chair, with such shakings of the
head and such Lord-have-mercy casting up of pious glances that it
seems ever new, and, with that air about it, gets submitted so regu-
larly to the fiction magazines that it has threaded many an editorial
head with untimely silver. One day I received word of its having been
published as a news story in the *London Daily Mail* as early as 1911,
the bare facts substantiated by affidavits from attachés of the British
Embassy in Paris. Here, I said with relief, is the end of my quest,
only to have Richard Henry Little point out in the *Chicago Tribune*
that the entire story had been dashed off by Karl Harriman one hot
summer night in 1889 to fill a vacant column in the next morning's
issue of the *Detroit Free Press*. Closing in on my quarry, I called upon
the blushing Harriman to tell me whether he had invented the story
or, like the rest of us, heard it somewhere in his travels. He said he
could not remember. Thereupon I felt free to consider the question
still open, for, without wishing to reflect on the fecundity of his imagination, I beg leave to doubt if any man could invent a tale like "The
Vanishing Lady" and thereafter forget that he had done so.

*HERE is a study in scarlet—*
*the ruinous red on the roulette*
*wheel, the blood-red stain upon*
*the breast of one found stretched*
*beside the sea at Monte Carlo.*

LEGENDS: V

# RIEN NE VA PLUS

WE were sitting under the midsummer stars at
Monte Carlo, eating a soufflé and talking about
suicide, when a passing newsmonger stopped at
our table all aglow with the tidings that that young American with the white forelock had just been found crumpled on
the beach, a bullet-hole in his heart. Earlier in the evening—
it was shortly before we came out of the Casino in quest of
dinner—we had all seen him wiped out by a final disastrous
turn of the wheel. And now he lay dead on the shore.

I shall have to admit that the news gave a fillip to the occasion. It came towards the end of a long, luscious dinner on
the terrace opposite the Casino. We were a casually assembled
carful, who had driven over from Antibes in the late afternoon, planning to play a little roulette as an appetizer and
then to dine interminably.

When we had arrived in the *Salles Privées* a few hours before, there was only standing room around our table at first.
In this rapt fringe, I encountered Sam Fletcher, a dawdling

95

journalist who lived on occasional assignments from the Paris offices of American newspapers. He pointed out the notables to me. There was Mary Garden, for instance, playing intently, losing and winning, losing and winning, with that economy of emotional expenditure which one usually reserves for setting-up exercises. Then there was an English dowager who looked as though she were held together by adhesive tape. She was betting parsimoniously, but Fletcher whispered to me that she lived in Monte Carlo on an ample allowance provided by her son-in-law, with the sole stipulation that she never embarrass the family by coming home. A moribund remittance woman. Next to her sat a pallid old gentleman whose hands, as they caressed his stack of counters, were conspicuously encased in braided gloves of gray silk. It seems that in his youth, he had been a wastrel, and, on her deathbed, his mother had squeezed from him a solemn promise never to touch card or chip again as long as he lived.

As for young White Lock, there was, until his final bet, nothing else noticeable about him except that he was the only man then at the table wearing a dinner coat. We heard later that at first he had lost heavily and had had to make several trips to the *caisse* to replenish his supply of plaques. By the time I came along he had settled to a more cautious play but finally, as if from boredom, he took all his plaques and counters and stacked them on the red. To this pile he added, just as the wheel began to turn, the contents of his wallet—emptying out a small cascade of thousand-franc notes, with a single hundred-franc note among them. But this one he retrieved at the last moment as if to be sure of carfare home. There was that breathless spinning moment, then the fateful *"Rien ne va plus,"* issuing in the same dead voice with which the intoning of the mass falls on infidel ears. Then the decision. *"Noir."* Around that table you could hear the word for black being *exhaled* in every language the world has known since Babel.

The young man gave a little laugh as the *croupier* called the turn. He sat quite still as his last gauge was raked into the bank. With all eyes on him, he shoved his chair back from the table, reached for his wallet, took out the aforesaid hundred-franc note and pushed it, with white, fastidious fingers, toward the center of the patterned baize. *"Pour le personnel,"* he said, with a kind of wry grandeur which hushed the usual twitter of thanks from the *croupiers.* "And that," he added, "is that." So saying, he got to his feet, yawned a little, and sauntered out of the room. I remember thinking, at the time, that he was behaving rather like any desperate young man in any Zoë Akins play. But it was a good performance. And now, it seems, he lay dead by the water's edge.

It was Fletcher himself who brought the news. It came, I say, just as we were eating soufflé and talking of suicide. This, of course, was no obliging coincidence. One always tells tall tales of self-slaughter at Monte Carlo. It is part of the legend of the principality—as strong in its force of suggestion, I suppose, as the legend of Lourdes is strong in its hint to hysterics that the time has come to cast away their crutches. Fletcher told us that the sound of the shot had brought a watchman running. The youth lay on his back, his chin tilted to the stars, one outstretched hand limply holding the revolver, a dark stain on the pleated whiteness of his breast. Before Fletcher could wire his report to Paris, he would have to await certain—well—formalities. In a conspiratorial whisper, he explained there had been so many such suicides of late that a new rule was but recently put into effect. Whenever any client of the Casino was found self-slain with empty pockets, it was customary for the Casino to rush a bankroll to the spot before notifying the police, so that the victim would seem to have ended it all from *Weltschmerz.* Even now, Fletcher said, this trick must be in progress, and in the meantime he ought to be seeking such obituary data as might be gleaned in the registry office.

We were still lingering over our coffee when he came hurrying back to us, all bristling with the end of the story. Notified in due course, the *gendarmerie* had repaired to the beach in quest of the body. But there was none. Not at the indicated spot, nor anywhere else on the shore. After further search, the minor chieftain from the Casino, who had himself tucked ten thousand francs into the pocket of the now missing suicide and was still lurking, much puzzled, in the middle-distance, returned at last to the *Salles Privées,* only to find them humming with a new chapter. It seems that that young American with the white forelock—the one somebody or other had inaccurately reported as killed—had reappeared apparently restored in spirits, and certainly restored in funds. He had bet tremendously, lingered for only three turns of the wheel, and departed with a hundred thousand francs. The attendants assumed he had merely been out to dinner. At least the careless fellow had spilled some tomato sauce on his shirt-front.

FOOTNOTE: In this same tradition is the tale of the New York matron who, oppressed by her losses in the *Salles Privées,* felt the first throb of a blinding headache. White-faced and tottery, she went to the restroom to take an aspirin, and was seen by a vigilant attendant drawing the pellet from her handbag and slipping it into her mouth. In less than another minute, strong, official hands had been laid upon her, she had been thrown, squawking, into an automobile and was being whirled at law-defying speed to Monaco's hospital, where nurses and internes were waiting with a stomach pump. The ensuing treatment was probably beneficial, at that.

One's insignificant intentions are so often misread in the heightened expectancy of that principality. I recall a night when I was apprehensively watching Miss Beatrice Lillie (Lady Peel, to you) risking her all on a game of pitch-and-toss. It was *chemin de fer,* and, as my neighbor Robert E. Sherwood once bitterly observed, none but the brave *chemin de fer.* On this Riviera occasion, Miss Lillie was suffering from the hiccups, and one spasm of them was misread by the banker as a hoarse cry of "Banquo!" A hundred thousand francs of unearned increment was being pushed towards her before she, in her pretty confusion, could explain his mistake. Afterwards, it seemed better not to embarrass him by mentioning it.

I was reminded of a day when our Miss Ferber had a rendezvous with her mother at an auction room. Arriving first, she saved a seat next hers, and, during a desultory sale of unpleasing *objets d'arts,* she kept one filial eye always on the entrance to the hall. At last she was rewarded by the sight of her mother pausing myopically on the threshold, and she made the mistake of hailing her by an uplifted hand. There was a crash of the hammer. "Sold! And, Miss F., I congratulate you!" She had acquired a grandfather's clock.

*BEING one unathletic client's grateful salute to a cheerful detachment who bestowed upon the World's Fair all of its comfort and most of its distinction.*

# THE LITTLE FOX-TERRIER

CHICAGO, JUNE 1933.

WHEN my godchild was six, a bevy of the younger set was invited in her name to occupy a box at the circus. In the week preceding this social event her mother grew haggard under the strain of the arrangements. Finally the last reassuring telephone call had been put in, the last touch given to the vitamins of the aseptic luncheon, the last exquisite guest, piloted by a skeptical nursemaid, had been delivered. The impresario of the occasion was exhausted, but her reward, she knew, would be the sweet soprano pleasure of the little ones at all the marvels in Madison Square Garden. It took these pretty innocents some time to unbend, but finally they did vouchsafe a quite gratifying, if somewhat special, delight. It was when a dejected fox-terrier, accompanying one of the lesser clowns along the sawdust trail, paused for a moment in front of them and stood sadly on his head. At this modest achievement the children were beside themselves with excitement. Oh, look at the dear little dog!

Oh, look! Oh, look! They gesticulated. They shrieked. They beat one another in their common ecstasy, and almost fell from the box in a moist heap in their effort to see the last of the pensive terrier as he trotted out of sight around the curve. And all this time the rest of the Garden was holding its breath because just then twenty-five elephants, all unnoticed by these infuriating young *flâneurs,* were standing on *their* heads.

I have an uneasy feeling that if I were honestly to assess my delights at the Fair it would be discovered that, whereas the treasure chests of the earth were ransacked for my pleasure, though caravels freighted with wonder have come even from far Cathay, though bits of Montmartre, Belgian villages, German beer gardens, Mayan temples, and glimpses of old Jehol (Re-hurr to you) have, after years of planning, been carried across the world and set down beside the waters of Lake Michigan, what really ensures my enjoyment of the Fair is the little fox-terrier who stands on his head. Or, at least, it is a detail as minor, as casual, and as clearly an afterthought. I am further embarrassed by the fact that at an exposition so unquestioningly dedicated to the latest miracles of the machine age, my greatest enthusiasm is for a device based on a mechanical principle contributed to mankind by some nameless inventor lost in the mists of unrecorded time. I refer to the unsung Edison who first conceived a wheel.

Such mulishly anachronistic behavior on my part is, I suppose, both misplaced and ungracious at a fair which is so infatuated with all the latest wrinkles in the complicated art of conveying human beings from one point to another. Airplanes, speedboats, aerial cars, the luxurious automobiles and Pullmans of tomorrow, all are here honored and displayed. Every hour a lovely pageant, which finds in Lake Michigan an adequate back-drop, rehearses the triumphal advance from the clumsy covered wagons of yesteryear to the fast planes which now race the sun from New York to Los Angeles. I am properly impressed, but even as the band plays the dismissive strains of the *Star-Spangled Banner,* I go forth on the Midway in quest of a rickshaw. It is as though each night at sundown, when the magicians pluck out of cosmic space the proud rays from Arcturus and bend them, willy-nilly, to the humble business of lighting the lamps of the Fair, I were to watch this feat with respect and then go off by myself and try to light my cigarette by rubbing two sticks together. But the fact remains that in my enjoyment of the Century of Progress I owe most to the person who thought of introducing to its bemusing paths that reactionary but most delightful of all vehicles, that gentle conveyance which combines the maximum of view with the maximum of comfort, the rickshaw. And, being one of little faith, I had thought I must cross the Pacific to enjoy another ride in one. It would almost be worth it.

The rickshaws add so much to the joy of travel in China that it is small wonder I fell to musing in Peking on how pleasant it would be if they could be introduced at Clinton, N. Y. They would make Commencement, for instance, positively enjoyable. All tourists have this notion and discard it as fantastic. For, as they reflect with a nice mixture of pride and regret, no one in the land of the free would be willing to pull the rickshaw. Indeed, it has been part of the American credo that the work of a rickshaw boy is essentially degrading, and degrades also, of course, the fellow-creature who accepts the ride. I do not know why this is so. I do not know why such sporadic outbursts of the brotherhood of man do not intervene as well in behalf of the bootblack, let us say, or of the chiropodist. Or, for that matter, in behalf of the amiable blackamoor who pushes you lazily up and down the boardwalk at Atlantic City. Just why the American mysteriously thinks it is all right for a fellow-creature to *push* him down the street but quite out of the question for a fellow-creature to *pull* him down the street, I do not know. Perhaps the distinction can be traced to some connotation of the shafts with draft animals. Anyway, so it is. Or so, at least, it was until the Century of Progress, when some thirty-odd rickshaws, tried for an unsuccessful week at an exposition in Paris and then abandoned because of labor-union protests, were imported and turned over to the muscles and good-will of some cordy, clear-eyed youngsters who volunteered from the track teams of Cornell, Pennsylvania, Wisconsin, and other universities, and who are, beyond all dispute, the pick of the land and the aristocracy of the Fair.

Each of them wears orange shorts, a white shirt, and a broad grin. They know that in the Orient the rickshaw boys run all the way, and their chief discomfort in their job derives from their fear that someone will think that *they* could not run, too, were they allowed to. Indeed, they started out to run all over the Fair, and in the process knocked so many pedestrians unconscious that the ambulances were overworked and did a lot of fretful complaining about it. In the presence of their sunny unconsciousness that there is a ticklish social question involved, the mists of embarrassment evaporate, and when you see one of them, swift, mannerly, and competent, cheerfully hauling some bulbous and stertorous merchant through the Fair, you know well enough which of the two, by any standard that makes sense, is the more dignified figure. It is a common enough experience at church to sit next a boorish bully of a financier, listen with him to a servile bootlicker in the pulpit, and then discover in the taxi-driver on the way home a fastidious and sovereign gentleman. We all need such occasional reminders that we ourselves impart to our jobs the only honor and dignity they can have. Hourly the rickshaw boys at the Century of Progress give evidence that there is no such thing as menial work. There is only the menial spirit. I think the planners of our national economy might contemplate them with profit.

The rickshaw boys fight for the privilege of trundling Katharine Cornell along the Avenue of Banners. The other night I was entranced by the sight of Constance Collier rolling majestically along, quite in the manner of Messalina on her way to the Coliseum. As a sinewy youngster from the University of Pennsylvania was affably conveying me toward the gate at midnight, I fell to thinking of a sundown at Amalfi long ago, where you seek at the top of a cliff a restaurant once patronized by Enrico Wadsworth Longfellow. It is a sheer ascent of two hundred steps, and barefoot natives fight for the chance to carry you up in chairs. I was embarrassed by their obvious conviction that they would need relays to get me to the top. They were nervously managing the last twenty steps when I was aware that popular interest in their heroic attempt had shifted to the chair behind me, in which I knew Harpo Marx had been making the ascent. There were such shrieks of local pleasure that I had to turn and look. Grinning in the seat was one of the shabbiest of the bearers. Harpo was helping carry *him* up. What just reminded me of that fraternal exchange was the sight here of our own Edna St. Vincent Millay riding gayly along in the moonlight. The carnival spirit must have gone to the head of Thornton Wilder. At least he had descended from his own rickshaw and was pulling hers through the Fair.

FOOTNOTE: The foregoing dispatch evoked an agreeable shower of letters from these somewhat different coolies, and, to the great satisfaction of your correspondent, was kept pasted all summer on the wall of their locker room. The attendant musings on pride and prejudice did, however, elicit from an injured Philadelphian an expression of sharp displeasure, which is hereby submitted.

"Fat boy, I reflected for a long time when I read your article. I thought of the four years of high-school preparation that the chiropodist must have. I thought of the years of intensive study in college. I

thought of the tedious examinations—I recalled the dreaded test before
the State Examiners. And now, along comes the wit who uses chiropodist and bootblack in the same breath. Is my face red? Not a bit, you
poor scandalmonger. Hoping you tumble from one of your beloved
rickshaws in the near future and fracture both clavicles, I am,

"Cordially yours,

"Dr. Joseph Kantor, chiropodist."

*WHEREIN one passerby, his emotions uncomplicated by any admixture of archæological erudition, records his first glimpse of the Syrian Treasure Trove called the Great Chalice of Antioch.*

THE CENTURY OF PROGRESS: II

## BELIEVE IT OR NOT

CHICAGO, JULY 1933.

THIS day, in trundling along the Avenue of Banners—how fitting a pathway it would have made for the cortège of the artist who imagined it!—I fell to recalling a day ten years ago when the late Edward Bok held me spellbound by his notions for the World's Fair then scheduled for Philadelphia in 1926. Perhaps the Sesquicentennial would have fared as well as the Century of Progress had he been suffered to have his way. Certainly his first plans for it were Napoleonic. It was his idea that each country should be sternly called upon to send to Philadelphia whatever of its national treasures seemed most likely to interest the gaping tourist. Thus, Holland, I believe, was to come across with thirty canvases by Van Dyck. France was to part, if only temporarily, with the Mona Lisa, the Winged Victory of Samothrace, and the Venus de Milo. Just those trifles. England was to let us have what Mr. Bok considered her three most cherished possessions—the crown jewels, Magna Charta, and

107

the Prince of Wales. But even in his most soaring moments, he never envisaged such an exhibit as the modest one which fills with hush the little white building—a mere shack compared with the Hall of Science—here dedicated to the world's religions. Mr. Bok could juggle with equanimity such bright balls as the Mona Lisa and the Kohinoor diamond, but even when he was dreaming most grandiosely he never conceived of bringing to Philadelphia anything to compare with the ancient and inscrutable cup called the Great Chalice of Antioch which now, to its own mild surprise, I should think, finds itself sitting on the shore of Lake Michigan, a startling anachronism in the century this exposition is celebrating, a tiny point of quiet in the noisy, colorful, complacent jubilation of the Fair.

There is no name displayed on the beautiful severe façade of this building which houses the faiths of the world, but over the door is carved a mouthful from the Proverbs—"Righteousness exalteth a nation." In the first days of the Fair, when the building had not been opened, this inscription was supplemented by a temporary sign reading "Not yet ready." Verily, an epitome of our times. In the rotunda stands the Chalice. It rests in a glass case on a pedestal, and there is a tactful railing to keep you from laying hands upon it. One of the largest diamonds in the world is soon to be exhibited in a nearby building, and there they are getting ready to protect it with collapsible floors, sprinklers of tear gas, an electric eye, and a few machine guns. But I was conscious of no such bristling guardianship around the Great Chalice. This is a silver cup of intricate workmanship which came to light in Antioch in 1910, when some Arabs, digging in the ruins of that city, found a hoard of old silver, conceivably part of the buried treasure of the cathedral which was spirited away in the hostile time of Julian the Apostate. It found its way along the familiar channels of Levantine archæology to the headquarters of Kouchakji

Frères in France, and was resting in their vaults in 1914 when quaking Paris heard the first guns of the Marne. Even as Gallieni's taxis were mobilizing, the cup went into hiding again, just as it had hid from another Apostate long ago. It turned up a little later in a Wall Street safe, and only now, after nineteen years, has it been put on view in this country.

I myself first became interested in it when in 1923 Dr. Gustavus Eisen published, at the price of $150 a copy, an antiquarian monograph on this trove. I will not pretend that I acquired one of these virtual throw-aways, but at the time I did become inflamed by the reviews. The cup is now, I believe, generally acknowledged as the earliest known example of Christian art. From a hundred and one indices in its workmanship, still visible beneath the protective wash of gold to which it was subjected in ages past, Dr. Eisen ascribes it to some nameless Greek silversmith of the third quarter of the first century. Seemingly what emerged from the dirt of many centuries was the Christian legend told, not in speech or manuscript, but in silver, and wrought at the very time when Paul had just been telling that story from one end of the known world to the other. In the dozen figures Dr. Eisen identifies certain of the disciples, and, of course, the young, aristocratic, beardless Christ—not conventional representations, any of them, but portraits all, some of them conceivably wrought from the living models. Luke and Mark and Paul —the unknown Cellini may have seen them plain. But what gives the Chalice its importance is the fact that all this loving care was expended on a mere container for another cup, a rude, egg-shaped, peasant drinking cup that can have had no value save by association. What must have made those for whom it first stood forth in Paris catch their breath was the self-evident fact that this open-work silver chalice was fashioned for the sole purpose of protecting and revealing this humbler, plainer vessel. A Christian reliquary, then, wrought to honor and preserve a cup which, within a generation after the Crucifixion, was already looked upon as holy. It is not difficult for us to imagine the excitement in the bosoms of the Kouchakji brothers when it first dawned upon them that they held in a safe in Paris just such a cup as the one about which, through at least fifteen centuries of Christian lore, there was ever a legend that it had been first treasured, then lost, and, by Galahad or Parsifal or another, would one day be found again.

The Chalice of Antioch is exhibited with almost ostentatious reticence. No placard proclaims its secret. No explanation is vouchsafed why it was never shown in America before, or by whom it is now shown. It is the only exhibit in the Fair about which there is no trumpeting. I know not what others feel about it, but for my own part I believe that after seeing Mr. Ripley's exhibit of freaks in the Midway and watching the plausible antics of a life-size, synthetic dinosaur on view in a papier-mâché, prehistoric jungle, after drinking a beer at Pabst's and escaping from the touts who advise an inspection of the nude models in the Streets of Paris, I came along at sundown in my rickshaw to this white building, and, with mine own eyes, beheld the Holy Grail.

*SOME memoranda set down in admiration for the future use of whatever hardy creature may one day attempt a biography of America's most prolific author.*

SOME NEIGHBORS: I

# A PORTRAIT OF
## KATHLEEN NORRIS

A PORTRAIT of Kathleen Norris? She had one painted when she was in France as a present to C. G. Norris, that other ink-stained wretch to whom she is married. On her way home with it, she had no sooner stepped off the gangplank in New York than he was on the wire from California, calling up to ask what she had brought him.

Her answer was truthful, though misleading. "An old map," she said, "an old map I got in Paris." A painful pause testified to his lack of marked enthusiasm. "A valuable antique?" he asked hopefully. "Well," she parried, "I'm not having to pay any duty on it, so I guess the customs men think it looks more than a hundred years old."

But a portrait of Kathleen Norris in words? Whoever is hardy enough to attempt one is bound to surprise and bewilder the vast multitude who know her only in her public appearances. Perhaps you have seen her standing, queenly

and benevolent, on the platform before some breathless con-
glomeration of women's clubs. If so, you must have noticed
how judiciously her outward aspect blends a happy approxi-
mation of Marie of Rumania, with just a dash of the late
Louisa May Alcott. Wherefore you have said that here, if ever,
was the ideal lady president of all the women's clubs in the
world. But then you did not chance to see our Mrs. Norris on
that night when she and I missed the entire first act of *The
Black Crook* because we had become involved in a singularly
bitter cribbage game with Madge Kennedy and Harold Ross
in a Hoboken saloon.

And your first impression of her would need still further
readjustment if you were to see her, as I have seen her, playing croquet against Harpo Marx, torturing her anxious partner and infuriating her painstaking opponents by making
each shot in a most lackadaisical manner, but, even so, managing never, by any chance, to miss the ball or wicket she
was aiming at. There are one or two men in America who
are as good croquet players as Kathleen Norris, but in the
real clinches of this malignant sport, no woman can come
anywhere near her.

Then those who know her only through the stories with
which she keeps the presses humming really do not know
her at all. As I am a reader who seldom attempts more than
one novel a year, and Kathleen Norris is an author who seldom writes fewer than four, she is several up on me, and
I therefore cannot pose as a final authority on her published
works. But I do think it is safe to say that, in the blend of
sentiment and romance which is her stock in trade, humor
is not the conspicuous ingredient. And yet she herself is one
of the most astonishing and delightful clowns of her day.
When the fit is on her, her mind is so dazzlingly rapid and
her thrust so strong that I would rather go back to my freshman year and be tossed in a blanket all over again than try
a joust with Kathleen Norris.

Ask Frank Sullivan. One day in a recent winter that timor-
ous little omadhaun was taking his constitutional when whom
should he spy looking speculatively into a Fifth Avenue shop
window but the slightly majestical figure of America's favorite author. It occurred to him that it might be fun to steal
up behind her and pinch her playfully. If ever in his life he
was to acquire the memory of thus roguishly accosting a
famous writer of wholesome fiction, here was his chance. He
knew her slightly, admired her profoundly, and it was all,
mind you, in the spirit of clean fun. It would, he thought, be
a good joke on her. In this he was most grievously in error.
He discovered that much as soon as he had obeyed the vagrant impulse.

Perhaps she had caught a glimpse of his reflection in the
window and so was armed with a moment's time in which
to improvise her reprisal. Anyway, he had hardly touched
her when she turned to him and in a ringing voice that could
be heard above all the hubbub of the avenue, she cried out:

"Not one penny. Not one penny more. No," she continued,
with a rush that bore down any feeble attempt at interruption which occurred to his startled mind, "you and your family have had all the money you'll ever get out of me. The
back of my hand to you, Frank Sullivan."

To the warm interest of a jostling crowd that encircled
them instanter, she went on with her denunciation. "It's useless for you to call me stingy. My check stubs are the best
answer to that. Only last week I gave you a hundred dollars
to buy medicine for your poor, sick wife. [Mr. Sullivan has
no wife, sickly or robust.] Did she get a penny of it? Not she!
No, you spent it on the drink, my lad. You guzzled it,
Frank Sullivan, and they found you in the gutter."

The crowd was now multiplying rapidly, and Sullivan
was dimly aware that its members were eying him with dis-
favor. Desperately he groped for some phrase that would let
these hostile onlookers know that it was all just a great, big

prank. But none came to him, and anyway, he could not have got a word in edgewise. For by this time she was getting her teeth into her performance. A great actress was lost to the stage when Kathleen Norris first put key to ribbon. She has a repertory of characters as varied as Ruth Draper's and, like the Margaret Anglin whom she used quite strikingly to resemble, she can turn on the tears as from a faucet. A freshet of them was now pouring down her cheeks. Her voice took on a piercing quality.

"I've given you everything I had," she cried, "and still you hound me!"

But Sullivan heard no more. Ingloriously defeated, he turned and fled, burrowing his way through the crowd which made a path for him as for a leper. By aid of the first taxi he could encounter, he asked only to put as much distance as he could between himself and that terrifying woman. Deeply content, Mrs. Norris patted her hair back into place and went on with her shopping.

A word portrait of Kathleen Norris? I had been minded, you see, to attempt one, but the difficulty of the task abashes me and what you are reading here is offered only as some rough notes to guide the bolder hand which may eventually undertake it. The material is abundant enough. There is, of course, the background of that idyllic California childhood, followed by the story of the lean and lively years when the six Thompson youngsters were left fatherless and motherless within the space of a single month. From the huddled and anxious bivouac of their San Francisco flat, Kathleen, the eldest daughter, went forth to various jobs as bookkeeper, saleswoman, companion, school-teacher, librarian. She was substituting as the society editor of a San Francisco newspaper when she first encountered Charles Norris. The acquaintance began when she telephoned him to confirm the rumor of his engagement to someone else. It was she herself who eventually scotched that rumor. It was in 1909 that they got married and came to New York, brashly setting up house-keeping on the twenty-five dollars a week which was his salary on the staff of the *American Magazine*. I think it was the quality of the manuscripts she had to help him wade through which in time aroused her old but dormant impulse to be a writer herself.

Today, she is the darling of the editors. There are beetle-browed and intense statisticians who have figured out to a penny just how much money a magazine can afford to spend on acquiring a new subscriber, and since it has been reported by lynx-eyed experts that the name of Kathleen Norris printed on a magazine cover sends up its circulation by a hundred thousand copies, you may guess for yourself why her income as a writer today is larger, year in and year out, than that of any other author in the world.

I could not—and, indeed, would not—be precise in the matter, beyond venturing a guess that Mrs. Norris must make rather more in a year than the President of the United States or I, and rather less, at present, than Greta Garbo. Therefore one need not ask why Kathleen Norris writes so many stories. What puzzles me most is *when* she writes them. But perhaps that is just because, for the most part, I have seen her only when the Norrises were taking their annual vacation in New York, sometimes seen her in an entire year only when they were giving one of their ghastly receptions at the Hotel Chatham, Charles Norris being lavish with cock-tails (made, I think, from machine oil and hair tonic) and his good wife being officially merry and gracious, but not quite successful in concealing her wild inner wonder as to why, in her husband's opinion, the trade of being an author should involve assembling, in one airless suite, so *many* people she did not want to see at all.

While being trampled underfoot at such a gathering, I usually run into one old friend of theirs who, now that I come to think of it, could do this portrait we have in mind

better than anyone else. Her path first crossed theirs back in
the days when Charles Norris was on the *American Magazine* and Kathleen, after she had put the baby to bed, cooked
the dinner, and washed the dishes, used to help him read the
manuscripts he would bring to the flat as homework. In
one batch of two hundred feeble and floundering efforts, one
story seemed alive and true. It was called "The Frog and the
Puddle," and they decided that the *American* ought to go
so far as to pay a hundred dollars for it. Easy come, easy go.
That story was the maiden effort of a young Wisconsin
newspaper woman named Edna Ferber. Now, whenever they
visit New York, you are sure to find Mrs. Norris routing Miss
Ferber out of her flossy seclusion. Once when she arrived at
the Chatham she was baffled by the discovery that the big
dreamer had moved to new quarters and retired behind the
protection of a private telephone number. But baffled only
for a day. Next morning there appeared in the personal column of the *Times,* a note running somewhat as follows:

> EDNA F.—Am at the hotel and terrible worried. Charlie is on
> the drink again. Please call me up.
>
>                                                    —KATIE.

By noon, at least fifty people had broken through the old
Ferber barricades with the news that the Norrises were at
the Chatham.

I should like to read a Ferber sketch of Kathleen Norris,
but before she attempts it, she should first visit the California
ranch where the Norrises make their summer home. It is up
in the mountains near Saratoga, and she does not know
either of them if she has not seen them in that setting. When
I think of it, I hear the click of croquet balls on a greensward
fitted with electric projectors so that mere nightfall shall not
cut short the delightful animosities of that game. I hear old
Nevin tunes coming faintly through the redwood trees. I
hear the gong which warns the swimmers in the pool that

luncheon is ready—luncheon served in a sequoia grove, with Mrs. Norris brandishing a huge wooden spoon over the salad bowl, while two youngsters spear the chickens from the pot, another manages the succotash, another the iced tea. I hear them whispering over their plans for some knotty charades they intend to stage that evening. I see the unpretentious house and the row of guest cabins along the leafy ravine. I remember all the friendly lamplight in the windows on the night I drove away, and I know that nowhere in my wanderings around the world have I come upon any home which seemed to me so crowded with laughter and good works and loving-kindness.

Above all, I warn Miss Ferber that no sketch of Kathleen Norris will be ready to sign unless it has a chapter in it about Bill. Something less than twenty years ago, when Kathleen Norris was a writer whose name was just beginning to be one to conjure with on the news-stands, she came into the port of New York from Rio and went to work at the dismaying task of picking up the scattered pieces of her life. It had been broken by the death of her two little girls, and now her small son was an only child. She herself had been one of six uproarious children, so that a crowd was the very breath of her existence.

Rebecca West once said of Herbert Bayard Swope, when he was editor of the lamented *New York World,* that he could not write a letter unless there were four people in the room, and today I doubt if Mrs. Norris could type out a really good chapter on her rickety portable if she did not know that on the stroke of noon, she would have to go downstairs and see about lunch for a half-dozen of the nieces and nephews with whom her home in California is always swarming. It was such a woman who met the greatest impoverishment of her life by going to Bellevue Hospital and demanding a foundling to take care of.

In those more haphazard days a woman obeying such an

impulse did not have to run the gantlet of the vigilant societies which now manage all such transactions in so busi-
nesslike and scientific a fashion that an adoption is accomplished only to the flutter of card-catalogues and the faint
odor of iodoform. At Bellevue, Mrs. Norris learned of a
young girl who had just been brought to bed with an unsanc-
tioned baby which she could not fend for and dared not ac-
knowledge. It was this baby that Mrs. Norris agreed to take
for her own, and every day she visited the hospital to keep an
eye on the young mother and child. This healing start of a
new interest in life, this process of merely getting acquainted,
had been going on for two weeks when, on one of her visits,
she was met by the head nurse with the news—the dislocat-
ing news—that the baby had died.

It was, one may guess, a benumbed Kathleen Norris who
sat down and stared into the future, only half listening to
the head nurse who, bless her, kept right on talking. I suspect
she was a profoundly wise woman, that nurse. She talked
of how, though mere birth and death were all part of the
day's work in any hospital, the breaking of bad news was
always the hardest part of her job. For instance, she was at
that very moment faced with a task at the prospect of which
even her case-hardened heart flinched. Had Mrs. Norris, as
she waited in the anteroom, chanced to notice a shabby little
boy sitting out there, cooling his heels? No, Mrs. Norris
hadn't. Well, *there* was a case, the nurse said. That boy's
mother was a young Frenchwoman—a worker in a laundry
—whom the ambulance had brought to the hospital a week
before from some humble home to which she and her child
had drifted. The two had only each other in the world, and
from sunup to sundown each day he had come and waited
outside, just on the chance that he might be allowed to
speak to her. Besides, he had no home where she was not.

Well, that frail, valiant mother had died a half-hour before, dropping out of sight like a pebble cast into the ocean,

and now it was part of the nurse's job to go out and tell that youngster that, at the age of eight, he was alone in the world. "I don't suppose," she suggested hesitantly—a wise woman, that nurse must have been—"I don't suppose that you would go out and tell him for me."

I have always wished that I might have been eavesdropping on the scene that followed. You must picture for yourself how Mrs. Norris dried her eyes and went forth to this new assignment. How she began by drifting casually into the anteroom, took a seat there among its waiting population, and finally scraped an acquaintance with the boy who sat by himself. My, but she was hungry. She had half a mind to run across to Childs for a bite to eat, but she did so hate to lunch alone. Would her young friend care to come along? His eyes told her that his mouth was watering at the mere mention of food, but he shook his head manfully. No, his mother might wake up, and then he would be called—the nurse had promised—and if he were not on hand, what would his mother think? But that could be arranged. They would leave word in the ward where they could be found, and then the nurse could telephone, if she should wake who would not wake again.

After this first meal together, during which the two new friends got along famously and he told her all about the farm up in New England which was as far away in space and time as he could remember, Mrs. Norris used the same device for persuading him to come to her hotel and see some books which belonged to her own little boy. It was twilight before she told him what had happened, but by then it was a friend who told him, a friend in whose arms he could cry himself to sleep.

Well, that is the end of the chapter, although it is not, by a long shot, the end of the story. For we have not come to that yet. Nor can I tell you what the name of the little boy was. I can only tell you what it is today. It is Bill Norris.

He is a grown-up now. The last time I had news of him, he was a star reporter on the Pacific Coast, and the very apple of her eye.

FOOTNOTE: In behalf of Mrs. Norris's vast following among the members of the W.C.T.U., if that organization has survived its recent encounter with the Juggernaut, further details should perhaps be offered about the aforesaid cribbage contest in a Hoboken saloon. Mrs. Norris and I were partners. Our opponents were Harold Wallace Ross, formerly of Ogden, Utah (who is Editor of the *New Yorker,* and probably the greatest cribbage player since the late Charles James Fox pegged out), and Madge Kennedy, who must, I think, be so disassociated in the public mind with ruffianly behavior and raffish dissipation as to render the further contents of this footnote a work of supererogation. However, the game was staged on the night when all the writing-folk of Manhattan were swarming across the Hudson for the première of Christopher Morley's *The Black Crook.* The insensate cribbage players could find a table only in the bar of one of the more teeming restaurants. If soaped mirrors and brass rails can make a saloon, I suppose it *was* one, but if any members of the W.C.T.U. were present that evening, they can testify that, when it comes to a question of liquor having soiled any of the players' lips, the game might as well have been played in the basement of the First M. E. Church.

*THE story of the man for whom "Ol' Man River" was written, as told by a neighbor who occasionally catches a glimpse of him towering above the crowd.*

SOME NEIGHBORS: II

## COLOSSAL BRONZE

LATE on the first night of 1933, I started back to London from the country house in Kent where I had been spending the week-end to see the New Year in— started back in a hired Daimler which moved majestically through the fog and was about the size and shape of a small house boat. Clutched in one hand was a spray of priceless orchids from the nursery on the place, and in the other was a forty-inch cutlass of sinister appearance.

My host had heard me innocently admiring them, and to my genuine surprise had pressed them into my hands at parting. As I drove off into the night, I made a note to remember that on my next visit I must be overheard expressing my enthusiasm for several paintings there by Augustus John and the late Mr. Sargent, for a small bronze head by Epstein, for the avenue of immemorial yews which glorifies the drive, for the bride of the younger son of the house, and for a small black spaniel bitch named, if memory serves, Tiny.

But as my car trundled along in the midnight fog my

121

thoughts shifted to the music we had plucked from the air after dinner, and, with that as a start, I found myself from there on reviewing, as one might a parade, the long procession of my acquaintance with one who was a groping and perplexed youth when first I met him, and is today a colossus bestriding the world—the wide, wide world which is his home. You see, we had tuned in that evening on the Hilversum station which broadcasts from the Netherlands, and we were the more amused to stumble on someone singing no quaint old Dutch tune at all, but a melody as unmistakably American as *Huckleberry Finn,* corn pone, or the late Calvin Coolidge.

> "He don't plant 'taters,
> He don't plant cotton,
> An' dem dat plants 'em is soon forgotten . . ."

This, mind you, from Holland, on New Year's Night. It was "Ol' Man River," and we realized too, that it was being sung with a voice of such ripe, rich, moving beauty that it could belong only to him for whose uses that song originally was written.

Wherefore, I fell to thinking of all the times my path had crossed Paul Robeson's in years past, and if Sherlock Holmes had been sharing the car with me and could see in the dark, he might have read the sequence of my recollections just from the way I sighed, chuckled, groaned, snorted, scowled, and hummed my way to London. For Paul Robeson and I are old friends and neighbors—neighbors in a sense possible only to those of us whose tent is usually pitched at one or another of the great crossroads of the world. Such a one is a species of innkeeper, and can count the times when this or that person has dropped out of the caravan for a moment and rested under his roof.

Thus Paul Robeson has come my way a dozen times. Often a year or two will go by without my seeing him or having a word from him, and then, unannounced, his great, dusky bulk will fill my doorway and my heart rejoices, for of the countless people I have known in my wanderings over the world, he is one of the few of whom I would say that they have greatness. I do not mean greatness as a football player or as an actor or as a singer. I am not, I think, confusing his personal quality with his heroic stature. I do not even have in mind what is, I suppose, the indisputable fact, that he is the finest musical instrument wrought by nature in our time. I mean greatness as a person.

In his case I despair of ever putting into convincing words my notion of this quality in him. I can say only that by what he does, thinks and is, by his unassailable dignity, and his serene, incorruptible simplicity, Paul Robeson strikes me as having been made out of the original stuff of the world. In this sense is he coeval with Adam and the redwood trees of California. He is a fresh act, a fresh gesture, a fresh effort of creation. I am proud of belonging to his race. For, of course, we both are members of the one sometimes fulsomely described as human.

"Ol' Man River!" I remembered a day in 1926 when Jerome Kern telephoned me in what seemed a state of considerable excitement. That inexhaustible mind of melody had just read a story which he thought would provide him with the libretto for which he had been waiting all his life. It was called *Show Boat*. Had I read it? I had. And did I know this Edna Ferber? I did, indeed. Well, then, would I give him a note of introduction to her? This was too much.

"If you were to call her up and say you were Jerome Kern and tell her you wanted to write a score for that story of hers," I said bitingly, "I suppose she would slam down the receiver and barricade the door."

But he wanted a note, so (serving about as useful a function as did the present Theodore Roosevelt when he kindly wrote to the American Ambassador in Paris a letter intro-

ducing young Captain Lindbergh, in order that the latter
might not be cold-shouldered by our Embassy) I did as I was
bid. And posted it to him. It so happened that that very night
I went to the theater with Miss Ferber and that in the lobby
between the acts none other than the shrinking Kern drifted
in our direction. I assumed, of course, he had done so to
scrape an acquaintance with his favorite authoress, and
scarcely bothered to introduce them. It was only a chance
word which identified her for him.

"You mean this *is* Edna Ferber?" he cried, and metaphor-
ically fell into her arms. From then on, neither of them remembered that I was there.

But even then the exit speech had not yet been written
for my own modest role. Two weeks later, he was on the
wire again. This time he was in too fine a frenzy of creation
to bother with mere introductions. That morning he had
written a song called "Ol' Man River" and please did I have
Paul Robeson's telephone number? A half-hour later he was
climbing the steps to Paul Robeson's flat in Harlem.

Afterwards I heard all about that first meeting. The song
was sung for the first time from a rough manuscript, with
Kern himself at the piano and Mrs. Robeson as audience.
Then the composer was possessed that Robeson should come
right downtown with him and sing it for young Oscar Ham-
merstein, who had written the words.

Paul did not mind, but turned for funds to Mrs. Robeson.
She is a flashing, resourceful woman, far lighter in color
than her husband, being of mixed Negro and Jewish blood.
Hers is the custody of the privy purse. He wanted two dollars for taxi fare. But Kern was going to drive them down.
She knew he would need only fare for the ride back. One
dollar would be plenty.

"Aw, go on," he said; "be all nigger and give me two."

Yet because the production of *Show Boat* was delayed and
delayed, when finally its first curtain rose, Robeson had

been booked for a concert tour and was not free to join the cast and sing his song. He did not become available until a London cast was assembled to duplicate *Show Boat* in Drury Lane. Thus it happened that New York never heard or saw Paul Robeson in this role until after an interval of two years. After only two years it was revived at the Casino in New York in the spring of 1932.

Against the recklessness of such revival after so short a time, Miss Ferber protested vehemently. It was, she said, about as bad an example of showmanship as she had ever known. No one, she said, would come to see it. And when she was voted down, she could at least refuse to attend the opening. Her family might go, and did, but, for her own part, she announced loftily that nothing would drag her there.

As they left for the theater she called out after them, "I am not one to enjoy seeing something I love killed before my eyes." But let me quote from the letter she wrote me about it afterwards:

So at ten minutes to nine I put on my hat and coat and took a walk enjoying the fine spring night and thinking about Life and one thing and another and imagine my surprise to find myself in front of the Casino Theater. There was what appeared to be a mild riot going on outside and I immediately decided that in-furiated ticket-purchasers were already demanding their money back. Sure enough, as I fought my way inside there was a line in front of the box office, though the play had begun. They were milling around and thrusting their hands forward toward the man in the box office. He was saying, over and over, in a firm monotonous chant, "Nomoreseatsnomoreseatsnomoreseatsnomore-seats." I trampled down women and children and pressed my white little face up against the bars and said, "I want to buy a seat." He said, "I'm sorry, Miss Foibah, nomoreseatsnomoreseats-nomore—"

"I'll stand up."

The Casino doesn't allow standing room because there's no place to stand. The last row is smack up against a wall, and that settles it. I went in, leaned against the door and looked at the audience and the stage at the very moment when Paul Robeson came on to sing "Ol' Man River."

In all my years of going to the theater—and that dates way back to the Ottumwa, Iowa, Opera House, when I judiciously regarded the drama from the cushioned comfort of Mrs. Julia Ferber's lap—I never have seen an ovation like that given any figure of the stage, the concert hall, or the opera. It was completely spontaneous, whole-hearted, and thrilling. The audience was what is known as a fashionable one—"carriage trade." Motor cars, evening clothes, warm May night, and a revival ordinarily would make a combination to cause any lover of the theater to rush sobbing into the night. That audience stood up and howled. They applauded and shouted and stamped. Since then I have seen it exceeded but once, and that was when Robeson, a few minutes later, finished singing "Ol' Man River." The show stopped. He sang it again. The show stopped. They called him back again and again. Other actors came out and made motions and their lips moved, but the bravos of the audience drowned all other sounds.

And here, in the last hours of that same year, he had been singing it from Holland—singing it to all Europe, to the islands thereto adjacent, and to ships at sea. As I rode on through the fog, I fell to thinking of the first time I met him. That was in 1922, when he came around to see me in a small flat I had in the gas-house district of New York.

He was twenty-four then, having been born in Princeton, New Jersey, in 1898, the son of a Negro preacher who, through some skullduggery on the part of two scheming divinity students, was ousted from his pulpit when Paul was a little boy. Instead of leaving town under a cloud, old Mr. Robeson got him a wheelbarrow and a rake and went right to work in Princeton as a free-lance gardener, standing his ground until the truth prevailed. He lived long enough to see his son triumphant at Rutgers—a Phi Beta Kappa man and

not only an All-American football player in 1918, but pretty
generally recognized as one of the greatest players the game
had ever known.

Even while he was studying law at Columbia and setting
up his bride in a Harlem flat, he would slip out of town for
the autumn week-ends to finance his studies and his new
household with a few bouts of professional football. There
had been a rather nasty ruckus on the field in Milwaukee
one afternoon in the preceding fall. Paul's team was playing
against the team from Marion, where Mr. Harding came
from. It was a team of Indians, and one of them was a real
bad boy. He had, Paul was warned, a mean trick of sticking
his fingers into the eyes of the player opposite.

In the middle of one play that afternoon, Paul saw those
fingers headed for his own eyes. He also saw red, and
promptly knocked the brave unconscious. At that, the oppos-
ing eleven fell upon him as one Indian. Out of the corner of
his eye, Paul could see his own one-hundred-percent Anglo-
Saxon team-mates discreetly leaving the scene. It looked as if
he might have to beat up all those Indians single-handed.
Before intervention became effective, he had entered upon
this chore with such a genuine pleasure and such concen-
trated destructiveness that the story of his quality as a fighter
spread over the country before nightfall. Drooping fight-
promoters were galvanized into sudden action. Within a
week, more than a million dollars had been confidentially
pledged to back him as the prospective heavyweight cham-
pion of the world. I think he must have shown considerable
promise for, as Frank Lloyd Wright once scornfully re-
marked, there is nothing so timid as a million dollars.

But Robeson would have none of them. He was uncertain
what he wanted to be, but he was quite sure it wasn't a
prize fighter. No, nor a lawyer, either. He would finish the
law course because he had started it, but a Negro lawyer's
chances are slim, and anyway, he felt he was meant to be

something quite different. An actor, perhaps. He had already tried himself out as an actor in a small-scale revival of *The Emperor Jones*. I was skeptical, because the number of available Negro roles was even smaller then than now.

Well, then, he might do something with his voice. He told me shyly that he had just discovered (which is more than the Rutgers Glee Club ever did) that he had a pretty good voice. He would come around some evening, he said, and roar a few spirituals at me. With which promise, he pulled his vast bulk together and roamed off through the gas-house district.

Perhaps I am only being wise after the event, but I think I felt at the time that I had just crossed the path of someone touched by destiny. He was a young man on his way. He did not know where he was going, but I never in my life saw anyone so quietly sure, by some inner knowledge, that he was going somewhere.

When I ran into him in London ten years later—it was the week before Christmas of the year just past—it was plain that he had not only traveled quite a distance, but now saw the rest of his road stretching clear and inviting before him. In those ten years, he had become famous as a singer of spirituals, had, with increasing skill, played many roles both in New York and London, and had set for himself the goal of becoming a jongleur of such equipment that he could forget the frontiers which crib, cabin, and confine the rest of us.

More than any other artist in the world, save, perhaps, their own lost Chaliapin, the Russians are eager to have Paul Robeson come to them, and he is even now getting ready the songs he wants to sing there and the plays he dearly wants to play. For he has found, in the homemade speech of Pushkin and in the rugged music of Moussorgsky, the one medium that really delights him.

My Russian friends tell me he already speaks their language without a trace of accent, and if that surprises you as

much as it did me, I can explain it only by saying that Paul
Robeson has such extraordinary powers of concentration that
he can sit rapt at a Linguaphone twelve hours a day, leaving
it only long enough to go to the ice box for an occasional
glass of milk, but never leaving it at all to answer the persistent telephone. Offers of vast sums for movie and vaudeville work arrive by mail and remain blandly unanswered.
Only when word comes from Mrs. Robeson that the rent is
due on their flat in the Strand, or from Switzerland that his
small son in school there needs a new pair of skis—that
husky kid who adores his father but is pretty patronizing
about the latter's imperfect German—only then does the old
man emerge and sing or play for a week or two to establish
a little balance in the bank. Then back he goes into the
luxurious seclusion of the work which he now at last enjoys
as much as he once enjoyed football.

As an economist, Robeson reminds me of the darky in a
story I used to tell with some condescension and great success. A householder, whose lawn needed cutting, saw Mose
scuffling along the dusty road and called out, "Hey, Mose!
Want to make a quarter?" Mose paused only long enough to
reply, "No, suh, Ah got one." Which used to seem to us more
bee-like economists an amusingly childish reply. Of late I
have had rather less success with this once dependable anecdote. Perhaps there has begun to dawn on more and more
people an uneasy suspicion that Mose had the right idea.
Anyway, it is Paul Robeson's idea.

In those ten years he has jogged on his way unperturbed
by the most head-turning experiences. On my way back from
Kent, I fell to thinking of the time when he played Othello
in London. I did not see that performance, but Rebecca West
and Aldous Huxley tell me they never saw better Shake-
spearean acting in all their days. I know that Alfred Lunt
and Lynn Fontanne plan some day to play it with him in
New York, with Lunt, of course, as Iago, and Miss Fontanne

as Emilia. Perhaps during that engagement my dream will come true, and I will live to hear an Emilia, by a pardonable slip of the tongue, run through the castle crying: "L'amour has kill'd my mistress!"

Then I remembered how confidently, but how inaccurately, the tabloids had prophesied the Robeson divorce during the preceding summer. And the agitation in London when Lady Mountbatten could scotch a preposterous rumor linking her name with Robeson's only by bringing a libel action against the deluded newspaper which had done some baseless hinting. And I recalled, with malicious pleasure, Robeson's little exchange of discourtesies with Lady Astor, whose visit to his dressing room in Drury Lane brought such a rush of southern blood to her head that she seemed to think she was benevolently visiting one of the cabins on the old family plantation.

Indeed, I was just thinking that I would some day do a story about that encounter and call it "Paul and Virginia" when the aforesaid Daimler turned into the Haymarket and drew up at the curb in front of the Carlton. One New Year's Eve reveler, insufficiently recovered from his celebrations, was seemingly impressed with the vehicle and yelled out, for obscure reasons of his own, "Make way for Lord Kitchener!"

This clarion call naturally drew quite a little crowd, which was considerably surprised when there emerged from the car, not the ghost of Kitchener of Khartoum at all, but merely a well-nourished American in a camel's-hide coat with a spray of orchids in one hand, and a dangerous weapon in the other. Surprised, and, I think, faintly alarmed. At least, the block emptied in what is technically known as a twinkling.

Since then Robeson has made a screen version of *The Emperor Jones* in Haiti and for three weeks he played Eugene O'Neill's *All God's Chillun* in London with an extraordinary new-risen actress named Flora Robson.

I have seldom read such tributes as that revival wrung from

the usually comatose critics of the English press. The *Man-chester Guardian* was delirious, and even the old *London Times* picked up her bombazine skirts and did a fandango in the streets. The phrase "great acting" was tossed about like confetti. These two were compared to John Philip Kemble and Mrs. Siddons. Robeson sent me the clippings with a brief message—my favorite among the epistles of Paul. He merely said: "How'm I doin'?"

FOOTNOTE: The Paul Robeson-Flora Robson engagement in *All God's Chillun* was duly reported to me in a letter from Rebecca West. I quote the paragraph:

"Both were monstrously superb. I couldn't have believed Paul could rise to such heights of poetry as the scene where he comes down the church steps with Robson on his arm. He seems to be just beginning. That really just expresses the quality of his performance. It was as if his imagination and his body did not know what fatigue was. I shall never be happy until I see him play Othello with Robson as Desdemona. They are a real team, for some reason. She ate her heart out for three years as a nursery governess, having been told by the Royal Academy of Dramatic Art that she was no good. That three years has given her some of the indifference and detachment that Paul has got for other reasons—a Beethovenishness. You cannot think how he has come on. The other day I met Charles Laughton, who was suspicious and hurt because he had gone to Stratford-on-Avon for the festival and been put in the Shakespeare Hotel in the Titania Room."

*THE story of two shillings, being an account of a small, respectful, and slightly apprehensive dinner given in honor of Moonbeam and Mrs. Patrick Campbell.*

# THE FIRST MRS. TANQUERAY

It happen'd that a few weeks later
Her aunt went off to the the-a-ter,
To see that entertaining play,
*The Second Mrs. Tan-que-ray.*
"Matilda" by Hilaire Belloc

ON the evening of May 27, 1893, when the fateful first curtain rose at the London première of that pathfinding tragedy, Arthur Pinero, who had written it, slipped out of the theater and vanished unobserved into the sheltering darkness of St. James's Park. For better, for worse, his work was done. Now it was out of his hands, and to watch its performance would be like watching a beloved child running heedless and unprotected along a high, narrow garden wall. One false step to right or left would spell disaster. He could not bear to look.

All playwrights suffer these exquisite pangs, but this was a peculiarly anxious night. For here was such a play as was new to his generation in the English-speaking theater. If you will think back and recall that, of our own three favorites of the Mauve Decade—Ada Rehan, Maude Adams, and Julia Marlowe—none of them ever in her entire career portrayed what it was then customary to describe, with a slight shudder, as "a

132

fallen woman," you will realize how bewildering a script *The Second Mrs. Tanqueray* must have seemed to the first troupe engaged for it. And you can imagine with what misgivings Pinero, in his desperate quest of an actress who would consent to soil herself by playing the damaged Paula Tanqueray, was driven, at the eleventh hour, to engage a slim, Italianate and quite inexperienced young woman who had been playing obscurely in the provinces for several seasons, and was hardly known in London at all. Her handsome young husband had gone off to South Africa to seek his health and fortune, leaving her with two babies to fend for. To earn their daily bread and hers, she had, by the amateur-dramatics route, gone on the stage. Her name was Mrs. Patrick Campbell.

In those days, and for many years thereafter, she was, I think, as disturbingly beautiful a woman as ever stepped through a stage door. But she was also tempestuous, undisciplined, and inexpert. At rehearsals she had been electrifying, but could she keep her head in the inevitable agitation of a first night? On this point, everyone, including the author, was skeptical. It would have been asking too much to expect him to sit helpless with folded hands and wait for the answer. Yet he must not seem a deserter and so, knowing to a split second when the first act would end, he timed himself to arrive at the stage door just as its curtain fell. In the alley he encountered the late George Alexander, who was the first *Mister* Tanqueray. That personable, but to me always profoundly annoying, actor was calming himself with a cigarette. Pinero fell upon him. How was she? How had she been?

Alexander shrugged his shoulders. He said something evasive about nerves and confusion. She had, he was afraid, rather gone to pieces. He implied that the management might have known what to expect when they relied upon this pretty provincial. Pinero brushed him aside, strode through the stage door, and went straight to Mrs. Campbell's dressing room. He took both her hands in his and kissed them. "My dear," he said, "if only you will play the next three acts as magnificently as you have just played the first, I will be a made man." Saying which, he wheeled and went back to his solitary pacings in the leafy lamplight of St. James's Park.

He returned to the theater only for the final curtain. The whole house was standing, cheering. The curtain rose and fell, rose and fell, as the lovely newcomer bowed and bowed. Her first-act nervousness, everyone said, had mysteriously evaporated and she had come on for the second act with eyes blazing, head up, her fainting spirit refreshed, her attack sure, herself unconquerable.

I thought of that first performance as I sat in my window a few weeks ago and watched the early lamps of the river craft winking in the September dusk. It is the hour when our East River in New York looks most like the Thames. I can almost believe then that the yacht-landing of the River House next door is Wapping Old Stairs. Or that I am looking out from Adelphi Terrace, where Shaw used to sit at his desk and write those stormy and tumultuous letters to Stella Campbell. Now, incredibly enough, she, who is woven like a strand of alien and exciting hue in the mouse-colored fabric of the memoirs and letters of her time, was coming to my small house to dinner. The table was set and the salad was in the bowl, for I was expecting Moonbeam and Mrs. Patrick Campbell.

Or only half expecting her, perhaps. Whenever my path crosses that of someone who, in his or her own time, is already a creature of legend, I find myself wondering if I am not dreaming. For example, I remember a sharp sense of unreality when I discovered that the fair, slim, reticent young Englishman who was my assistant on the moribund *New York World* was, behind his incognito, none other than the fifth Earl Amherst. In my college days I had so often lifted my reedy tenor in song about the Lord Jeffery Amherst who was a soldier of the King, and came from a far countree, that

I needed some little readjustment to realize that there might actually be a person of that name. So, too, the mere thought of Mrs. Patrick Campbell coming to dinner filled me with just such incurable surprise as I might feel if the boy at the switchboard downstairs were to call up and say, "Lady Macbeth on the wire, sir," or, "Are you at home to Lucrezia Borgia?"

As her taxi wove its apprehensive way through the raucous streets of 1933, I fell to thinking of the season thirty years before when I had first seen her in Sudermann's *The Joy of Living.* Even then she was the stuff of which legends are made. Mrs. Patrick Campbell and her beauty and that preposterous dog, Pinkie Pankie Poo. Mrs. Patrick Campbell and the tanbark which, to the maddened resentment of every other actress in the land, must needs be spread by the management in Forty-second Street lest our uncouth street noises disturb her performance.

In those days, she went from city to city in a private car. Later, we were to treat her more cavalierly. During her *Pygmalion* tour in 1915, for instance, her contract called for such a car, but the management, at inconsiderable expense, bribed the station master in each city to shift it ceaselessly through the yards and so to hound it with tooting, brawling locomotives that, after a few sleepless weeks, Mrs. Campbell, puzzled at the increase of noise in America, elected to stop at a hotel.

The Shaw period in the legend of Mrs. Pat culminated in this *Pygmalion,* the comedy he wrote for her. But just then, as Mr. Shaw himself once told me the story, the late Beerbohm Tree was the only actor-manager in London willing to go through the proverbially depleting experience of playing with Mrs. Campbell. Unfortunately, she would have none of him. She was still bitter about a memory of some years before when, in order to fulfill a regretted contract with her, he had

staged two one-act plays, himself modestly appearing in the
first, and graciously giving her play the place of honor at the
end of the program. To her hurt bewilderment, some part of
each audience left without waiting for it. Only after she had
torn up the contract and gone her furious way did she learn
that each evening after his own sketch was finished, Tree,
with infinite guile, had made a curtain speech so subtly dismissive that he fairly hypnotized people into thinking the evening was over. They were hoodwinked into going home as
effectively as if the orchestra had played "God Save the King."
Wherefore, Mrs. Campbell began the *Pygmalion* negotiations
with the declaration that she would far rather die than appear
with this ancient enemy. But, at some pinch of need, she
changed her mind and the partnership was triumphant.

From behind closed doors thereafter, the listening world
heard the faint rumble of altercation between Shaw and Mrs.
Campbell. At rehearsals she would be maddened by a barb
from that spare vegetarian and would cry out, "Some day
you'll eat a pork chop, Joey, and then God help all women!"
Or perhaps she would merely smolder. On one such occasion,
a frightened minor actor heard her muttering, "That old man
with the beard, he knows nothing! He knows nothing, that
old man with the beard!" Scandalized, the little actor cried
out, "Surely you don't mean Mr. Shaw!" To which the glow-
ering Mrs. Campbell darkly replied, "So he says!" thus wan-
tonly raising a new issue and leading the little actor to wonder for one wild, lunatic moment who *was* masquerading
behind those famous whiskers.

We onlookers have been vouchsafed some glimpses of the
torrent of love letters which Shaw poured out upon her for
several years. It was in that solitary lull before the war when
history itself seemed to hold its breath. In her autobiography,
published a few years ago, Mrs. Campbell printed a sample
few. It was like her to proffer such a fiery particle as this brief
extract from a slightly impassioned Irishman of fifty-six:

There are such wonderful sorts of relations, and close together-nesses, and babes-in-the-woodinesses, besides being in love, which, as you point out, my diet and feeble nature forbid. I may have moments of being in love, but you must overlook them. And now, having expressed myself with carefully punctuated moderation, I shall go to bed quite calmly, and sign myself, oh, loveliest, doveliest, babiest,

Your gabiest,

G. B. S.

"His wildest letters," she adds demurely, "I do not give." She has since *tried* to give them to an entranced public, but she is thwarted by the law which, in both England and America, protects the writer of such heady correspondence. Mrs. Peck discovered this law when she tried to make a book of the letters written her by the late Woodrow Wilson. If I write you a letter, it belongs to you. That is, the document itself belongs to you and it would be your privilege to sell it as a holograph rarity to some presumably feeble-minded collector. But as a piece of literature, good or bad, it belongs to me. The right to publish it remains with me and passes on to my heirs.

Were Mrs. Campbell free to publish her letters from Bernard Shaw, she could derive therefrom a nice little pot of money—enough to insure comfort for her declining years, if only she would abandon her invariable custom of giving it all to the first needy person she meets. But thus far Shaw has obdurately withheld that permission without which no publisher dares move. His last message on the subject read something like this: "No, Stella, I will not play horse to your Lady Godiva."

That effort to publish the Shaw letters marked a recent winter when Mrs. Campbell, being down on her luck, put her belongings in a handkerchief on the end of a stick and went off to Hollywood to seek her fortune. What enchanted me was her unwavering and ingenious rudeness to everyone there who could possibly have been of assistance to her. She would encounter Harold Lloyd or Ruth Chatterton at a party, and murmur, "Now tell me, what do you do? Are you connected with the cinema?" Her failure to be politic took on the proportions of a magnificent gesture. She was like a sinking ship firing on the rescuers.

I remember a night in Katharine Cornell's dressing room. It was during Miss Cornell's season in *Dishonored Lady,* and she was rather hoping that the chaste austerity of her backstage life (just a few good etchings and a book of poems) would favorably impress a sorrowing great-aunt who was horrified enough at her young relative's being on the stage at all, let alone appearing in the role of a murderous nymphomaniac. Unfortunately, the great-aunt's visit to the dressing room was interrupted by the chance and separate arrivals of three such weird sisters as Theda Bara, Mrs. Leslie Carter, and Mrs. Patrick Campbell. Such a horrid confluence wrecked Miss Cornell's aplomb, so I tried to do the honors. "Ah, you're a famous critic!" cried Mrs. Campbell at the sight of me. "Tell me who *should* have played *Dishonored Lady?*" I tried to mask this glancing blow by a flurry of introductions. Surely the great Mrs. Campbell knew the great Mrs. Carter. "Honored, honored!" Mrs. Campbell boomed, and then, without relinquishing the infuriated hand of Mrs. Carter, she confided to me in a whisper that rattled the theater, "I thought she was dead."

That whisper of hers! It sounds like wind in the chimney of a haunted house. It can fill an entire theater, particularly when she is in the audience. Thus at *The Cherry Orchard* I could not help hearing her try to drown out Nazimova. I thought this was naughty of her, and as the curtain fell on the first intermission, I tried to scowl a reproof in her direction. Unabashed, she held me in the aisle with inquiries about Dorothy Parker, whom she admires enormously, but whom she usually refers to, for some mysterious reason of her own, as Dorothy Warren. Mrs. Campbell told me she had been having great success in her lectures by reciting one of Mrs. Parker's lovelorn poems which ends with the lines:

> "There is no edgèd thing in all this night,
> Save in my breast."

By this time the whole audience was watching us, and I felt a thousand pairs of eyes critically surveying my contours as she cried out with considerable archness, "There's no use denying it. I'm sure *you* are the edgèd thing in her breast!"

Only a stout, middle-aged bachelor who has himself been publicly pinioned and then described before an enthralled audience as an edgèd thing in anybody's breast can really savor the extent of my confusion.

One never quite knows how innocent she is on these occasions. Not long ago she was saluted respectfully at a first night by Howard Sturgis, an exquisite from Providence, Rhode Island, who had known Mrs. Campbell's son intimately and in years past had visited at her house in London for months on end.

"Perhaps you don't remember me, Mrs. Campbell," he said diffidently. "I'm Howard Sturgis."

"I'm so sorry," she answered in the most gracious manner imaginable. "I'm always confusing you with the Howard Sturgis who used to visit my son."

"But I *am* that Howard Sturgis," he protested feebly.

"Ah!" she replied. "How you are going to tease me about my vagueness!"

Wherefore, when, with Moonbeam in her arms, she came to dinner at my house and the talk turned on her autobiography and she spoke regretfully of the bouquets with which, in the course of its pages, she had ingenuously showered herself, I said I held only this against the book—that it left the reader unsuspicious of her very genius for disconcerting speech. It was Mrs. Campbell, for instance, who, on a celebrated occasion, threw her companion into a flurry by describing her recent marriage as "the deep, deep peace of the double-bed after the hurly-burly of the chaise-longue." She started to protest that never, never, never did she say such things, but I pointed out that, even in her own cautious narrative, the cloven hoof was occasionally visible.

"But my friend," she said with a windy sigh, "that cloven hoof—it's on the foot I have in the grave."

Whereat Moonbeam yawned. He is a young white Pekingese of great distinction and insatiable appetite. If he lay prone on the window seat close to her little black velvet bag, it was, I suspect, because she kept therein (in addition to her powder puff, her handkerchief, some loose change, and a sample letter from Shaw) a chicken bone for Moonbeam. This refreshment would not be forthcoming until after he had played his scene with her that night at the theater. It seemed to me a meager meal, and I put some slices of white meat in an envelope for him. "It will be enough for both of us," she said, as she gathered him up and went off to work.

I put her in a cab and thought as it went racketing off up the street how tremendous a woman she was, how negligible were most of us beside her, how many and how terrifying were the citadels she had stormed in her long and tragic day, how bright in the afternoon sunshine was the banner that flew ever in her heart.

An hour later, the taxi driver spotted me and drew up along the curb.

"Say," he said, "I didn't like to bother that lady friend of yours, but see what she paid me with."

On the grimy hand he held out to me, there rested two coins of the realm—but not of this realm. They were shillings. I redeemed them, and they lie before me on my desk.

If the Bank of England does not object to hoarding in a modest way, I think I shall keep them.

FOOTNOTE: The subject of the foregoing sketch was vouchsafed a glimpse of it before these pages went to press, and my first day of 1934 was brightened by the receipt of the following telegram from Los Angeles:

SEASONS GREETINGS DEAR MR. WOOLLCOTT THANK YOU FOR YOUR BEWITCHING INACCURACIES I AM NOT AS NICE AS ALL THAT

STELLA CAMPBELL

*PORTRAIT of a poet attempted by one who, abashed by the difficulties of the undertaking, breaks down and weakly resorts to a hundred familiar quotations.*

# OUR MRS. PARKER

WHEN William Allen White, Jr., son of Emporia's pride, was a verdant freshman ten years ago, he spent the Christmas vacation in New York and was naturally assumed as a public charge by all his father's friends in the newspaper business. He had been at Harvard only a few months, but the pure Kansas of his speech was already seriously affected. He fastidiously avoided anything so simple as a simple declarative.

For example, he would never indulge in the crude directness of saying an actress was an actress. No, she was *by way of being* an actress. You see, they were going in for that expression at Harvard just then. Nor could he bring himself to ask outright if such and such a building was the Hippodrome. No, indeed. Subjunctive to the last, he preferred to ask, "And that, sir, would be the Hippodrome?"

I myself took him to the smartest restaurant of the moment, filled him to the brim with costly groceries, and escorted him to a first night. As we loped up the aisle during the intermission rush for a dash of nicotine, I pointed out celebrities in the manner of a barker on a Chinatown bus. Young Bill seemed especially interested in the seamy lineaments of a fellow Harvard man named Robert Benchley, then, as now, functioning on what might be called the lunatic fringe of dramatic criticism. Seated beside him was a little and extraordinarily pretty woman with dark hair, a gentle, apologetic smile, and great reproachful eyes. "And that, I suppose," said the lad from Emporia, "would be Mrs. Benchley." "So I have always understood," I replied crossly, "but it *is* Mrs. Parker."

In the first part of this reply, I was in error. At the time I had not been one of their neighbors long enough to realize that, in addition to such formidable obstacles as Mrs. Benchley, Mr. Parker, and the laws of the commonwealth, there was also a lack of romantic content in what was then, and ever since has been, a literary partnership seemingly indissoluble. At least it has had a good run. Mrs. Parker's latest and finest volume of poems carries on the flyleaf the simple dedication: "To Mr. Benchley," and even a dozen years ago, these two shared a microscopic office in the crumby old building which still houses the Metropolitan Opera.

There was just about room in it for their two typewriters, their two chairs, and a guest chair. When both were supposed to be at work, merely having the other one there to talk to provided a splendid excuse for not working at all. But when Benchley would be off on some mischief of his own, the guest chair became a problem. If it stood empty, Mrs. Parker would be alone with her thoughts and—good God!—might actually have to put some of them down on paper. And, as her desperate editors and publishers will tell you, there has been, since O. Henry's last carouse, no American writer so deeply averse to doing some actual writing. That empty guest chair afflicted her because the Parker-Benchley office was then so new a hideaway that not many of their friends had yet found a path to it, and even Mrs. Parker, having conscientiously chosen an obscure cubby-hole so that she might not be disturbed in her wrestling with *belles-lettres*, was becomingly reluctant to telephone around and suggest that everyone please hurry over and disturb her at once.

However, this irksome solitude did not last long. It was when the sign painter arrived to letter the names of these new tenants on the glass door that she hit upon a device which immediately assured her a steady stream of visitors, and gave her the agreeable illusion of presiding over as thronged a salon as even Madame Récamier knew. She merely bribed the sign painter to leave their names off the door entirely and print there instead the single word "Gentlemen."

Thus pleasantly distracted through the years, Mrs. Parker's published work does not bulk large. But most of it has been pure gold and the five winnowed volumes on her shelf—three of poetry, two of prose—are so potent a distillation of nectar and wormwood, of ambrosia and deadly nightshade, as might suggest to the rest of us that we all write far too much. Even though I am one who does not profess to be privy to the intentions of posterity, I do suspect that another generation will not share the confusion into which Mrs. Parker's poetry throws so many of her contemporaries, who, seeing that much of it is witty, dismiss it patronizingly as "light" verse, and do not see that some of it is thrilling poetry of a piercing and rueful beauty.

I think it not unlikely that the best of it will be conned a hundred years from now. If so, I can foresee the plight of some undergraduate in those days being maddened by an assignment to write a theme on what manner of woman this dead and gone Dorothy Parker really was. Was she a real woman at all? he will naturally want to know. And even if summoned from our tombs, we will not be sure how we should answer that question.

Indeed, I do not envy him his assignment, and in a sudden spasm of sympathy for him, herewith submit a few miscellaneous notes, though, mark you, he will rake these yellowing files in vain for any report on her most salient aspects. Being averse to painting the lily, I would scarcely attempt a complete likeness of Mrs. Parker when there is in existence, and open to the public, an incomparable portrait of her done by herself. From the nine matchless stanzas of "The Dark Girl's Rhyme"—one of them runs:

> There I was, that came of
> Folk of mud and flame—
> I that had my name of
> Them without a name—

to the mulish lyric which ends thus:

> But I, despite expert advice,
> Keep doing things I think are nice,
> And though to good I never come—
> Inseparable my nose and thumb!

her every lyric line is autobiographical.

From the verses in *Enough Rope, Sunset Gun,* and *Death and Taxes,* the toiling student of the year 2033 will be able to gather, unaided by me, that she was, for instance, one who thought often and enthusiastically of death, and one whose most frequently and most intensely felt emotion was the pang of unrequited love. From the verses alone he might even construct, as the paleontologist constructs a dinosaur, a picture of our Mrs. Parker wringing her hands at sundown beside an open grave and looking pensively into the middle-distance at the receding figure of some golden lad—perhaps some personable longshoreman—disappearing over the hill with a doxy on his arm.

Our Twenty-First Century student may possibly be moved to say of her, deplorably enough, that, like Patience, our Mrs. Parker yearned her living, and he may even be astute enough to guess that the moment the aforesaid golden lad wrecked her favorite pose by showing some sign of interest, it would be the turn of the sorrowing lady herself to disappear in the other direction just as fast as she could travel. To this shrewd guess, I can only add for his information that it would be characteristic of the sorrowing lady to stoop first by that waiting grave, and with her finger trace her own epitaph: "Excuse my dust."

But if I may not here intrude upon the semiprivacy of Mrs. Parker's lyric lamentation, I can at least supply some of the data of her outward life and tell the hypothetical student how she appeared to a neighbor who has often passed the time of day with her across the garden wall and occasionally run into her at parties. Well, then, Dorothy Parker (née Rothschild) was born of a Scotch mother and a Jewish father. Her people were New Yorkers, but when she came into the world in August 1893, it was, to their considerable surprise and annoyance, a trifle ahead of schedule. It happened while they were staying at West End, which lies on the Jersey shore a pebble's throw from Long Branch, and it was the last time in her life when she wasn't late.

Her mother died when she was still a baby. On the general theory that it was a good school for manners, she was sent in time to a convent in New York, from which she was eventually packed off home by an indignant Mother Superior who took umbrage when her seemingly meek charge, in writing an essay on the miracle of the Immaculate Conception, referred to that sacred mystery as spontaneous combustion. When, at her father's death a few years later, she found herself penniless, she tried her hand at occasional verse, and both hands at playing the piano for a dancing school.

Then she got a job writing captions on a fashion magazine. She would write "Brevity is the Soul of Lingerie" and things like that for ten dollars a week. As her room and breakfast cost eight dollars, that left an inconsiderable margin for the other meals, to say nothing of manicures, dentistry, gloves, furs, and traveling expenses. But just before hers could turn into an indignant O. Henry story, with General Kitchener's grieving picture turned to the wall and a porcine seducer waiting in the hall below, that old marplot, her employer, doubled her salary. In 1918, she was married to the late Edwin Parker, a Connecticut boy she had known all her life. She became Mrs. Parker a week before his division sailed for France. There were no children born of this marriage.

Shortly after the armistice, the waiting bride was made dramatic critic of *Vanity Fair,* from which post she was forcibly removed upon the bitter complaints of sundry wounded people of the theater, of whose shrieks, if memory serves, Billie Burke's were the most penetrating. In protest against her suppression, and perhaps in dismay at the prospect of losing her company, her coworkers, Robert E. Sherwood and Robert Benchley, quit *Vanity Fair* at the same time in what is technically known as a body, the former to become editor of *Life,* and the latter its dramatic critic.

Since then Mrs. Parker has gone back to the aisle seats only when Mr. Benchley was out of town and someone was needed to substitute for him. It would be her idea of her duty to catch up the torch as it fell from his hand—and burn someone with it. I shall never forget the expression on the face of the manager who, having recklessly produced a play of Channing Pollock's called *The House Beautiful,* turned hopefully to Benchley's next *feuilleton,* rather counting on a kindly and even quotable tribute from that amiable creature. But it seems Benchley was away that week, and it was little Mrs. Parker who had covered the opening. I would not care to say what she had covered it with. The trick was done in a single sentence. *"The House Beautiful,"* she had said with simple dignity, "is the play lousy."

And more recently she achieved an equal compression in reporting on *The Lake.* Miss Hepburn, it seems, had run the whole gamut from A to B.

But for the most part, Mrs. Parker writes only when she

feels like it or, rather, when she cannot think up a reason not to. Thus once I found her in hospital typing away lugubriously. She had given her address as Bed-pan Alley, and represented herself as writing her way out. There was the hospital bill to pay before she dared get well, and downtown an unpaid hotel bill was malignantly lying in wait for her. Indeed, at the preceding Yuletide, while the rest of us were all hanging up our stockings, she had contented herself with hanging up the hotel.

Tiptoeing now down the hospital corridor, I found her hard at work. Because of posterity and her creditors, I was loath to intrude, but she, being entranced at any interruption, greeted me from her cot of pain, waved me to a chair, offered me a cigarette, and rang a bell. I wondered if this could possibly be for drinks. "No," she said sadly, "it is supposed to fetch the night nurse, so I ring it whenever I want an hour of uninterrupted privacy."

Thus, by the pinch of want, are extracted from her the poems, the stories, and criticisms which have delighted everyone except those about whom they were written. There was, at one time, much talk of a novel to be called, I think, *The Events Leading Up to the Tragedy,* and indeed her publisher, having made a visit of investigation to the villa where she was staying at Antibes, reported happily that she had a great stack of manuscript already finished. He did say she was shy about letting him see it. This was because that stack of alleged manuscript consisted largely of undestroyed carbons of old articles of hers, padded out with letters from her many friends.

Then she once wrote a play with Elmer Rice. It was called *Close Harmony,* and thanks to a number of circumstances over most of which she had no control, it ran only four weeks. On the fourth Wednesday she wired Benchley: "CLOSE HARMONY DID A COOL NINETY DOLLARS AT THE MATINEE STOP ASK THE BOYS IN THE BACK ROOM WHAT THEY WILL HAVE."

The outward social manner of Dorothy Parker is one calculated to confuse the unwary and unnerve even those most addicted to the incomparable boon of her company. You see, she is so odd a blend of Little Nell and Lady Macbeth. It is not so much the familiar phenomenon of a hand of steel in a velvet glove as a lacy sleeve with a bottle of vitriol concealed in its folds. She has the gentlest, most disarming demeanor of anyone I know. Don't you remember sweet Alice, Ben Bolt? Sweet Alice wept with delight, as I recall, when you gave her a smile, and if memory serves, trembled with fear at your frown. Well, compared with Dorothy Parker, Sweet Alice was a roughshod bully, trampling down all opposition. But Mrs. Parker carries—as everyone is uneasily aware—a dirk which knows no brother and mighty few sisters. "I was so terribly glad to see you," she murmurs to a departing guest. "Do let me call you up sometime, won't you, please?" And adds, when this dear chum is out of hearing, "That woman speaks eighteen languages, and can't say No in any of them." Then I remember her comment on one friend who had lamed herself while in London. It was Mrs. Parker who voiced the suspicion that this poor lady had injured herself while sliding down a barrister. And there was that wholesale libel on a Yale prom. If all the girls attending it were laid end to end, Mrs. Parker said, she wouldn't be at all surprised.

Mostly, as I now recall these cases of simple assault, they have been muttered out of the corner of her mouth while, to the onlooker out of hearing, she seemed all smiles and loving-kindness. For as she herself has said (when not quite up to par), a girl's best friend is her mutter. Thus I remember one dreadful week-end we spent at Nellie's country home. Mrs. Parker radiated throughout the visit an impression of humble gratitude at the privilege of having been asked. The other guests were all of the kind who wear soiled batik and bathe infrequently, if ever. I could not help wondering how Nellie managed to round them up, and where they might be found at other times. Mrs. Parker looked at them pensively. "I think," she whispered, "that they crawl back into the wood-work."

Next morning we inspected nervously the somewhat in-adequate facilities for washing. These consisted of a single chipped basin internally decorated with long-accumulated evidences of previous use. It stood on a bench on the back porch with something that had apparently been designed as a toothbrush hanging on a nail above it. "In God's name," I cried, "what do you suppose Nellie does with that?" Mrs. Parker studied it with mingled curiosity and distaste, and said: "I think she rides on it on Halloween."

It will be noted, I am afraid, that Mrs. Parker specializes in what is known as the dirty crack. If it seems so, it may well be because disparagement is easiest to remember, and the fault therefore, if fault there be, lies in those of us who—and who does not?—repeat her sayings. But it is quite true that in her writing—at least in her prose pieces—her most effective vein is the vein of dispraise. Her best word portraits are der-vish dances of sheer hate, equivalent in the satisfaction they give her to the waxen images which people in olden days fashioned of their enemies in order, with exquisite pleasure, to stick pins into them. Indeed, disparagement to Mrs. Parker is so habitual that she has no technique for praise, and when she feels admiration, can find no words for it.

Thus when she fain would burn incense to her gods—Ernest Hemingway and D. H. Lawrence—she cannot make herself heard at all, and becomes as gauche as an adoring shopgirl in the presence of Clark Gable. But just let her get a shot at a good, easy target like A. A. Milne, and the whole town listens. Including, of course, the time when, as Constant Reader in the *New Yorker,* she was so overcome by Mr. Milne's elfin whimsicality that Tonstant Weader fwowed up.

It should be added that that inveterate dislike of her fellow creatures which characterizes so many of Mrs. Parker's utter-ances is confined to the human race. All other animals have her enthusiastic support. It is only fair to her eventual biographer to tip him off that there is also a strong tinge of autobiography in that sketch of hers about a lady growing tearful in a speak-easy because her elevator man would be stuffy if she should pick up a stray horse and try to bring him to her apartment.

While she has never quite managed this, any home of hers always has the aspects and aroma of a menagerie. Invariably there is a dog. There was Amy, an enchanting, woolly, four-legged coquette whose potential charm only Dorothy Parker would have recognized at first meeting. For at that first meeting Amy was covered with dirt and a hulking truckman was kicking her out of his way. This swinish biped was somewhat taken aback to have a small and infuriated poetess rush at him from the sidewalk and kick him smartly in the shins—so taken aback that he could only stare open-mouthed while she caught the frightened dog up in her arms, hailed a taxi, and took her up to Neysa McMein's studio to wash her in the bathtub. There Amy regained her trust in the human race, achieved a fearful air of harlotry by eating all the rose-madder paint, of which a good deal lingered to incarnadine her face, and eventually won her way to a loving home on Long Island.

Then there was a Scottie named Alexander Woollcott Parker who reversed the customary behavior of a namesake by christening *me*—three times, as I recall—in a single automobile ride. More recently there has been Robinson, a soft-hearted and languishing dachshund who was chewed up by a larger dog. The brute's owner said that Robinson had started it. Mrs. Parker turned on him with great bitterness. "I have no doubt," she said, "that he was also carrying a revolver." Robinson's successor is a Blue Bedlington named John. Woodrow Wilson was, I think, the name of the dog at the end of her leash when I first knew her. This poor creature had a distressing malady. Mrs. Parker issued bulletins about his health—confidential bulletins, tinged with skepticism. He *said* he got it from a lamp post.

Of her birds, I remember only an untidy canary whom she named Onan for reasons which will not escape those who know their Scriptures. And then there were the two alligators which she found in her taxi, where someone had been shrewd enough to abandon them. Mrs. Parker brought them home and thoughtfully lodged them in the bathtub. When she returned to her flat that night, she found that her dusky handmaiden had quit, leaving a note on the table which read as follows: "I will not be back. I cannot work in a house where there are alligators. I would have told you this before, but I didn't suppose the question would ever come up."

Well, I had thought here to attempt, if not a portrait, then at least a dirty thumb-nail sketch, but I find I have done little more than run around in circles quoting Mrs. Parker. I know a good many circles where, by doing just that, one can gain quite a reputation as a wit. *One* can? Several can. Indeed, several I know do.

But I have not yet told here my favorite of all the Dorothy Parker stories. It was about the belated baby girl who, as the daughter of a successful playwright, is now an uppity miss at a fancy school. It seemed to those of us on Broadway that she was forever being born. For months the whole town had been kept uneasily aware of her approach. For months the little mother had filled the public eye with a kind of aggressive fragility. Until the last, she would pointedly rise at first nights and conspicuously leave the theater whenever the play became too intense for one in her sedulously delicate condition.

Long after Marc Connelly, in behalf of an exhausted neighborhood, had taken the expectant mother aside and gravely advised her to drop the whole project, we were still waiting for the news from that spotlighted confinement. At last it came, and the telegrams of relief and congratulations poured in from every direction. "Good work, Mary," our Mrs. Parker wired collect. "We all knew you had it in you."

*A BRIEF inquiry into the prob-
lem presented by Dr. Kommer
of Czernowitz, a man without a
country or any visible means of
support.*


SOME NEIGHBORS: V

# THE MYSTERIES OF RUDOLFO


IN 1921, Herr Rudolf Kommer, a stout, Mitteleuropa
journalist without portfolio, received word through Max
Reinhardt's brother that the great impresario wished to
confer with him. As a cosmopolite who had translated many
English plays for the German stage and who had spent three
wartime years modestly serving the cause of old Franz Josef
in the United States, he was somewhat optimistically regarded in Berlin as an authority on the vagaries of the American playgoer. Professor Reinhardt was minded to venture a
season in New York and it was his idea that the best production for him to make here would be *Das Welttheater,* by
Hugo von Hofmannsthal. What did Herr Kommer think
of that idea? With great patience and particularity, Herr
Kommer explained that he thought the idea was entirely
without merit. Whereupon the mighty Reinhardt smiled
vaguely and the conference was over.

Six months later Herr Kommer was summoned again to
the august presence. It seems that this time the Professor

was meditating on the idea of launching an American season
with his production of *Das Welttheater* by Hugo von Hofmannsthal. What did Herr Kommer think of that project?
Suppressing an impulse to shriek, Herr Kommer repeated
his grave conviction that it was a terrible idea. Again the
vague, dismissive smile, and, out on the street once more,
the unheeded expert began to suspect that great impresari
never really *hear* unwelcome advice, and are therefore un-
hampered by the misgivings which stay the hands of lesser
men. It was in the hope of verifying this thesis that he responded with alacrity to a third summons some months later.
But this time Reinhardt was full of a notion to produce *The
Miracle* in New York. What did Herr Kommer think of the
idea? Herr Kommer replied with the German equivalent of
"That's more like it" and was soon agreeing to all the clauses
in a tentative contract by the terms of which he was to pre-
cede the other incomparable Max to America and pave the
financial way for him. All the clauses save one. That one
made the whole contract depend on the collapse of certain
negotiations even then under way. It seems there was already
another agent in the field and Kommer was being retained
merely as a card up the Reinhardt sleeve.

At this discovery, he was preparing to depart in a huff
when curiosity prompted him to ask who this agent might
be. It was, they told him, a powerful American theatrical
magnate named Colonel von Singer. They had been profoundly impressed by him when he visited Vienna in 1920.
Hadn't he bought three motorcars there, and given dinners
for at least sixty guests every evening? Even so, Kommer
swore he had never heard of him. The Reinhardt office
smiled pityingly as who should say that Kommer evidently
didn't get around much. But by that time his huff had arrived and he departed in it.

At intervals thereafter he was taunted by telephone with
news of the dazzling progress the mysterious von Singer was

reporting in his American negotiations. But apparently none of this superb field work bore fruit, for finally it was Kommer, after all, who arrived in New York empowered as sole agent for Professor Reinhardt.

Inevitably he thought of his doleful arrival at the same port almost ten years before. Then he had been a fugitive from a prospective internment in England, where the declaration of war caught him red-handed in the act of serving the *Frankfurter Zeitung* as its London correspondent. Landing in our town, he was first depressed by the huge news bulletins with which the façade of the Herald Building announced the capture of his native city by the Russians and still another inglorious German retreat. He did not know then that it was the late Mr. Bennett's policy to announce German retreats with such magnificent élan that, had they all actually taken place, the first contingent of the A.E.F. would have found the Prussian Guard fighting with their backs to the Great Wall of China.

Young Kommer first cheered himself up by buying a gallery seat for Master Irving Berlin's *Watch Your Step,* and further restored his spirits by spending a month in the Public Library, placidly reading the accumulated files of Berlin newspapers, access to which had been denied him in England since the outbreak of the war. Then he went to work on a local Germanophile weekly, loyally toiling for some modest wage and never dreaming until long afterwards that other, more vociferous advocates of the German cause in our town were making *ein schöner Pfennig* out of their ardor.

Well, ten years had gone by since those stressful days, and this time he would not walk humbly. Instead, he drove to the Ritz, engaged a suite, and sat him down to compose a fateful note on the hotel stationery. It was addressed to Otto Kahn. Professor Reinhardt was planning a season in New York. Would Mr. Kahn care to finance it? Mr. Kahn replied that he would be simply delighted. It was as easy as that. Of course there remained some subsequent details requiring Kommer's supervision. For instance, it was his function to keep a zone of quiet around the engrossed Professor, and this involved constant suppression of minor outbreaks from Morris Gest, the Princess Matchabelli, Jake Shubert, and such. This police work occupied a large part of his days, and it was only after *The Miracle* had been launched in triumph at the Century that he found time to look up and identify his evaporated rival, Colonel von Singer. It turned out to be Leo Singer of Singer's Midgets.

Ever since then Kommer has always piloted the Reinhardt craft in foreign waters. But there has been no Reinhardt season in New York for the past six years. Yet each year, for no visible reason, Kommer arrives in the late fall and deposits his duffle at the Ambassador. Every day in the week except Wednesday—when he has to give Mrs. Vincent Astor her German lesson—you will find him ensconced at the Colony Restaurant, playing host to a group invariably graced by one or more of the loveliest ladies of our time. And, except in the summer, when he must direct the social life of the Salzburg Festival from his personal eyrie in Schloss Leopoldskron, Kommer's table at the Colony is vacant only because he is ruling over a similar table at the Ritz in London or at Peltzer's in Berlin.

And always these, his friends and guests, are united in a common wonder. When his back is turned, they clutch at one another, each employing a stage whisper for the single question: "What does Kommer do for a living?" Since he seems to have unlimited leisure for bridge and backgammon, careless observers have ventured to suggest that he lives on his winnings from the celebrated financiers with whom he has friendly jousts. This theory, however, is untenable by anyone at all familiar with his rating as a bridge-player. And to anyone who has ever watched him helpless in the

toils of Harrison Williams, or any other first-rate backgam-
mon-player, the mystery of his ways and means only deep-
ens. Then, of course, it was long a favorite and widely held
explanation that, even in seasons when Professor Reinhardt
was not venturing abroad, Kommer performed invisible
and highly remunerative services for him. But this theory
collapsed utterly a year ago when Professor Reinhardt himself awoke from one of his trances, buttonholed a New
York editor astray in Salzburg, and, taking him aside, whispered to him as follows: "Perhaps you can clear up one
thing that has always puzzled me. What does Kommer use
for money?"

Of course some of those who, in the carefree times of
yesteryear, asked this same question in idle curiosity are asking it now with an eagerness born of a real desire to employ
his formula for their own purposes. It is hereby predicted
that that formula, when discovered, will be found to be only
part of a larger and more important secret. This is set down
in all seriousness and with profound respect by one who
looks upon Rudolf Kommer as a master of a way of life, and
who would gladly follow him to the ends of the earth, as
Kim followed the Lama, on the mere chance of learning
something of the gracious and tranquillizing philosophy that
must be his.

I would not seem to suggest that Kommer does no work
at all. In addition to teaching Mrs. Astor German, he has recently been engaged, for instance, in preparing for the stages
of Central Europe certain comedies by American authors.
But *Dinner at Eight* was the first American play he has
adapted since *Rain,* and the greatest conceivable return from
such intermediary effort could not account for the lavishness
of his hospitality or the carefree bearing of his ambling gait
across the face of the world.

Maybe he is an alchemist. Or perhaps, although it seems
improbable, he may have succeeded in saving some genuine

pre-war money. There was a period, I know, when he
worked furiously. That period did *not* include the six years
when he was *ein verbummelter Student* at the University of
Vienna, or the two years he then spent in the coffee houses
of Berlin, when his entire published works consisted of one
article which appeared in a woman's magazine and for
which he was paid ten marks. Even Kommer, with his
genius for getting along somehow, could not make this sustain him for two years. Therefore, as a sideline, he worked as
companion to a Swedish invalid whom he would call for
three times a week and escort to the Adlon in order that the
poor fellow might revive his drooping spirits by sipping
weak tea and looking at the cocottes who used to display
their wares at what they called the Adlon "fife-o'glocks."
Even so, young Kommer was at least *planning* to write this
and this and this. Finally, a famous author, to whom he was
confiding these fine intentions, removed his pipe from his
mouth long enough to phrase an utterance which made a
profound impression on our hero. That utterance was: "Essays that aren't written are never printed." These luminous
words danced before him as he moved on to England in the
train of the fragile Scandinavian aforesaid. Essays that aren't
written are never printed. So! Immediately he began posting
from London a weekly feuilleton of three thousand words.
For a time these all came fluttering back to him like homing
pigeons and he was almost at the end of his rope (that Swede
had gone back to Stockholm) when a friend suggested that
he might try sending his London notes to some journal
which did not already employ a London correspondent.
This same friend also intimated that Kommer was heroic
but unwise in doggedly submitting his poetry to magazines
which did not by any chance ever print verse. All of this
may move you to suspect that, if he needed such rudimentary
instruction, the youthful Rudolf could not have been what
one would call real bright. You would be surprised to know

how many local Miltons remain not only inglorious but indefinitely mute for lack of just that modicum of shrewdness. One can at least say of Kommer that he did take a hint when one was offered him, and turned overnight into a prolific success. In addition to publishing a weekly letter in the *Frankfurter Zeitung,* he also translated English plays in batches. He did six of Galsworthy's. He did Arnold Bennett's *The Great Adventure* and Chesterton's *Magic.* But certainly his biggest popular success—*Potash and Perlmutter*— made no provision for these, his middle years. It did heap up a very mountain of marks awaiting his pleasure, but before he got around to collecting them, the value of the mark had fallen to almost nothing at all, so that his greatest triumph yielded him, when the inflation was over, $1.98.

There remain two details of his calling card for me to clear up. That card announces, to the thinly veiled distaste of all butlers, that he is Rudolf K. Kommer of Czernowitz. Why "Czernowitz"? And why "K"? Well, in 1887 he was born of Jewish stock in Czernowitz in the Duchy of Bukowina, and, after the Treaty of St.-Germain was ratified, he woke up with considerable irritation to find himself a Roumanian. He has already taken out his first papers as a would-be American, for he does find it irksome to be dependent upon consulates where the attachés speak a language which he cannot even understand. He himself is so little a Roumanian in background that he had never so much as clapped eyes on the man who was long his new sovereign's minister to our country until Anita Loos introduced them to each other in Stamford, Connecticut. Thus strangely do Roumanians meet. That was Antoine Bibesco, the Roumanian prince who is famous for having married Elizabeth Asquith and for having, by his Balkan guile at poker, provoked Herbert Bayard Swope on one occasion to the immortal outcry, "Boy, the Prince's hat and cuffs!"

But why should Kommer name his native city on his card?

160        *While Rome Burns*

Well, it seems that on the Continent the very name Czernowitz has comic overtones. Like Yonkers or Kalamazoo. It is
also a good setting for Jewish jokes. In the music-hall humor
of Mitteleuropa, it blends the functions of Oshkosh and Ar-
verne. Wherefore when, in 1917, the haughty Catholic Haps-
burgs sent our Rudolf on a gumshoeing expedition through
the neutral countries, the irritated Socialist press made a
point of referring to him always as "Herr Rudolf Kommer
aus Czernowitz." Nothing daunted, he immediately accepted
it as a professional title and has used it ever since.

Czernowitz not only cradled the infant Rudolf but more
recently has achieved another fame. A few years ago it sprang
into the headlines when the League of Nations committee
which was investigating white slavery announced that the
European headquarters of the traffic was good old Czernowitz. With an implied "Ah, there, Rudolf!" scores of those
headlines were promptly clipped out and mailed to Kommer
by dear friends seeking to suggest that the mystery about
him had been cleared up at last.

Then there is the "K." It stands for Kätchen. It seems
there is in London a Viennese café of which the familiar is a
singularly surly cat. Daily, the fat Austrian proprietor would
seek to appease it. "Ah, Kätchen, Kätchen," he would say
(that being his curious Viennese way of saying "Kitty,
Kitty"), "it iss useless for you to park and crowl." And one
afternoon it befell at a rehearsal of *The Miracle,* when Kommer was scolding everyone in the cast, that the Madonna
shook her finger at him and said, "Ah, Kätchen, Kätchen,
it iss useless for you to park and crowl." So he stopped park-
ing and crowling, the rehearsal broke up in disorder, and
he has been Kätchen ever since. Kätchen to Lady Diana, to
Iris Tree, to Tilly Losch, to Grace Moore, to Ina Claire, to
Rosamond Pinchot, to Ruth Draper, to Lillian Gish, to Alice
Obolensky, to Elizabeth Bergner, to Eleanora von Men-
delssohn—indeed, to all the fair ladies whom he, in appal-

ling Tyrolean costume, has ever welcomed on the platform of the Salzburg Bahnhof. Kätchen to all the friends there and here whom he has deftly assisted with their elopements and their divorces, whom he has helped into jobs and solvency or out of jail and hock.

But these are his avocations. What, you ask me, does he do for a living? Well, I wouldn't know about that.

*THE story of Joe Cook and how,
on the shore of Lake Hopatcong,
he remembered the old barn back
in Evansville, Indiana.*

SOME NEIGHBORS: VI

# THE LEGEND OF
# SLEEPLESS HOLLOW

ONCE upon a time—to be more precise, it was in the
hour just after midnight on a Friday in the autumn
of 1906—a New York policeman on patrol noticed
three shabby youngsters scuttling up the Bowery with a
valise which they took turns in toting. He halted them and
bade them show him with what loot they were laden. The
confiscated bag was set down on the sidewalk and inspected forthwith. It contained nothing but Indian clubs.
Not the humble kind which meagerly built clerks twirl ear-
nestly by the dawn's early light. But the larger, hollow clubs
which jugglers use, and cover over with green and crimson
foil so that they may gleam like costly jewels when they
are tossed about behind the footlights.

These, the boys insisted, were the property of the smallest
and shabbiest of their number. He admitted as much and
said he had bought them. This seemed grossly improbable.
He was only fourteen, and under-sized at that, and he looked
like the kind of threadbare newsboy from whom benevolent

old ladies buy the afternoon paper out of sheer tenderness. The policeman had his legitimate doubts and asked for further details. Well, it seems these three—the young clubman and his assistants—had been over to the Alcazar in Brooklyn for Amachoor Night. And look, mister, they had won first prize. "Show him the ten-dollar bill, Curly." Curly, apparently, was the treasurer. He obliged at once with a glimpse of the trio's funds-in-hand. Or rather funds-pinned-on-undershirt. After the show, they had packed up and started home afoot across the Brooklyn Bridge. This painful inquisition had been instituted shortly after they reached the Manhattan side.

The big cop still eyed them skeptically. Then, being a fair man, he bade them follow him while he used his key to commandeer a Bowery barber shop. After he had turned on the lights, he climbed into one of the chairs and said: "Let's see your act." If he thought *that* would be a poser, he little knew that a young juggler asks nothing better than an invitation to perform—even at an unearthly hour, and for an alarming audience of one. In fact, all three boys were delighted. In those days, the rear of a Bowery barber shop was a curtained recess where a customer could, if he was a moneyed dandy and had the time, retire and take a bath. Behind this curtain the troupe withdrew and got ready. Then they sprang out and into the fine Tya-da posture with which, plus an air of pleased surprise, all jugglers have made their entrance since the days when Imperial Rome was something new in politics. Then, while the two aides took up positions slightly to the rear, with their hands behind their backs in the approved manner, the small boy began juggling as if his life depended on it. The clubs flashed on high. One would fall to the floor, or almost, only to be caught by an artful waiting foot and sent back into the air. Then, with all three boys springing into action, the barber shop began to look like a kaleidoscope. The show ended with a breathless bow, and the performers withdrew behind the curtain. But they bounced right out again. They wanted to sound out the audience. Gravely the policeman descended from his tilted judgment seat. He shook hands with all three and bade them get along home. And, he added, whenever they got a start in a regular theayter, he hoped they would remember him and send him a coupla tickets.

I wonder if that broad hint has since been acted upon. For in the intervening years, the star of that command performance has been gradually recognized as a whole theater in himself, one of the few comedians who, like Eddie Cantor, Ed Wynn, and Groucho Marx, can be, and sometimes are, a one-man show. His name is Joe Cook, and he is the salt of the earth. But that is another story.

Had the eventually mollified and considerably impressed policeman pursued his investigations further that night, he might have discovered that, whereas Joe had, as he said, bought those Indian clubs himself, the money for the purpose was obtained by a species of embezzlement. When the Cooks had moved from Evansville, Indiana, to New York, Joe was enrolled in the St. Francis Xavier's School in Sixteenth Street. Every morning Mrs. Cook gave him a dime for carfare and twenty-five cents for lunch. By walking both ways and going without lunch, he had succeeded in saving enough money to buy those lovely clubs. He needed them because, ever since he first practiced slack-wire-walking on the clothesline out in Evansville, he had meant to go into the circus. In New York this plan underwent a slight change one day when, with money accumulated by further abstinence, he played hooky and went for the first time to a theater.

It was the old Keith's Union Square in Fourteenth Street, and those were the days when vaudeville was vaudeville. The show began every morning at eleven, and promptly at eleven Joe was in his seat in the gallery, ready to sit agape at such glories of costume and talent as he had never dreamed of. Such juggling! And such spangles! The Keith programs in that golden yesterday were continuous, but, after all, the term was relative and all things come to an end. Finally, Joe could not help noticing, from the departure of the audience and the winking out of the house-lights, that the show was over. Still walking on air, he reached the street at last and was a little taken aback to find the sky dark. An eclipse, probably. But no, the clock said it was close on to midnight. He had been in the theater for twelve hours. At home he found Mrs. Cook in tears. She was so sure a truck had run over him.

As for resuming the pleasant custom of eating during the noon recess, that now seemed indefinitely postponed. How else than by saving his lunch money could he acquire pink tights and velvet doublets and spangles such as those god-like men had worn at Keith's in Union Square? It was not until later that he learned, among other tricks of the trade, that it was better, in the fierce competition of Amateur Night, not to be too gorgeously attired. Indeed, you might be able to outjuggle the best of them, but if you didn't look as though you needed the money, the sappy audience would never award you the prize.

Hence the shabby garments aforesaid, which Joe wore on Amateur Night on precisely the same principle that the late Theodore Roosevelt, when he went a-campaigning among the plain folk of America, used to leave the braided cutaway, exquisitely striped pantaloons, and high silk hat behind at Sagamore Hill and take along such well-worn, grease-stained, shiny clothing as would make the American people feel he was one of them. If Joe did not carry the imitation further by tossing his hat into the ring, it was because he wore a cap, which he took care to twist appealingly in the manner of a waif in need of a meal.

It was, I suspect, that same wistful twisting of the cap

rather than any dazzling virtuosity in mere juggling which helped him carry off the first prize that night at the Alcazar long ago. Carry it off, by the way, under the embittered noses of such lively young contestants as a gawky Jewish girl whose name was (and still is) Fannie Brice; a minute, feather-footed clog dancer named George White, who has long since put away his dancing-shoes and gone in for management; and Violinsky, whom I last heard of sitting with tilted derby as he dealt faro at Agua Caliente, thankful, he said, that they had two bread lines there, one white and one rye.

I speak of Joe himself winning the prize, for the others of his trio were merely his assistants; Joe's brother Leo, who has been dead these many years, and the aforesaid Curly, whose father was head waiter at the Hoffman House and who wore for all such public appearances one of his old man's stiff-bosomed shirts. I do not know what became of Curly. But there is an aging agent on Broadway who still remembers his own astonishment when these three breezed into his office one summer afternoon. Joe was barefoot. Out in Evansville, all the younger set shed their shoon in early June, and Joe, in New York, remained a small-town boy. And, incidentally, still remains one. The agent's startled eye roamed from the stiff-bosomed shirt (with tomato sauce) to the dusty toes. "And who might you be?" he asked feebly. To which question Joe replied, the wish being father to the thought, "We're actors." But it was less through the good offices of this skeptic than through his own unscrupulous determination that Joe landed his first job on the American Roof.

What impressed the manager enough to book him for a tentative week was a photograph of Joe in the act—the incredible juggling act—of keeping sixteen balls in the air at once. What Joe did not believe it either necessary or wise to mention was that these sixteen balls had been strung together by a wire, which the photographer then kindly painted out.

This was the beginning of a lot of skullduggery; of fly-by-night engagements in amusement parks, tent shows, medicine shows, and small-time vaudeville, in the course of which Joe learned his trade, and from which long novitiate he emerged at last as a prime favorite of the Keith Circuit, a quiet trouper who could walk wires, shoot, juggle, and fiddle, and carry off the whole proceeding with an air of wild, unsmiling nonsense which is, I think, his unique gift among the comedians of his day. Sometimes I hear youngsters ask him how to go on the stage. He wears a puzzled look, not knowing how to phrase politely his inner conviction that if a boy has to be told how to go on the stage, he might better give up at the start and study bookkeeping. Anyone who will let anything on earth stop him from going on the stage might better steer clear of the theater altogether. For his own sake. And the theater's.

That vein of nonsense gave birth to the famous curtain speech in which he would patiently explain just why he could never imitate four Hawaiians, a speech he used to rewrite every night for the private amusement of the orchestra. It was a vein which sustained him through an engagement as a co-star with Peggy Hopkins Joyce, whom he used to describe as "that somewhat different virgin." It imparted a character of their own to such harlequinades as *Rain or Shine* and *Fine and Dandy*.

For instance, I remember in that latter extravaganza a scene in which Joe, as the newly engaged factory-manager, took over the office and inspected the letter files. Hauling open one drawer, he paused as though politely surprised. Then, dipping in, he drew out a large pair of shoes. The embarrassed stenographer claimed them as hers. Next, he took out a potted geranium. Then—of all things—a barber pole. Then (with the slight shrug of one who knows you never *can* tell what you'll find in a filing cabinet) he took out a live skunk.

I like to recall the moment when Joe first told the property man what he would want for that scene: a pair of shoes, too big for anyone; a flowerpot with a blooming geranium in it; and a collapsible barber pole which would fold up like a drinking-cup. "And," he said "I shall want a live skunk—housebroken. There must be some place where you can get one. Better get me *two* live skunks."

"*Two* live skunks!" protested the property man, as if he could bear no more.

"Yes," Joe replied firmly. "One will be the understudy."

And of course it is that touch of grave hilarity which has made the fame of Sleepless Hollow, his home on the shores of Lake Hopatcong, New Jersey. You have probably heard of the demented golf course there, with one tee on top of a water tower and one green on an island surrounded by a mean moat, dug for your annoyance, but with another more kindly green that is funnel-shaped, so that the veriest duffer can go home and boast that he made a hole-in-one.

You may have heard of the house-warming, when Joe was advised that some of his guests were high-toned folk, accustomed to footmen and such. When those guests arrived, they began to encounter footmen bowing and scraping at the crossroads, at least two miles from the house. As they drew nearer, footmen recurred with increasing regularity, all clad in costumes indistinguishable from the one worn on state occasions by our Ambassador to the Court of St. James's. When the car reached the house, these guests were fairly smothered in footmen. Joe had thirty-eight on duty. Anything worth doing at all is worth doing well.

You may also have heard about his famous subterranean bar, its walls crowded with the loot of three continents, including, among other rare souvenirs, a baseball kept under a protective glass case, it being the only known specimen of a

baseball *not* autographed by Babe Ruth. You may be told
how that bar is presided over by a genial eccentric who puts
on six fearful disguises during the course of an evening, and
makes at least that many polysyllabic orations. But what you
can never understand until you have been through the experience is that Joe authorizes, or at least tolerates, such
goings-on, not because he thinks they will make the guests
happy but because he knows darned well they will make the
barkeep happy.

You may even have heard that dinner is not served until
midnight, and then is likely to be barbecued meat cooked
under the stars by two clowns out of work. And that your
seat at dinner, as like as not, will be a trick chair that shudders and heaves and even explodes when you sit down on it.

At least, all these are parts of the legend of Sleepless Hollow, and may lead you to suspect it is not the most restful
spot in the world, may even lead you to raise your eyebrows
and decide that you would rather *not* spend a week-end there.
Well, you would be wrong.

And you can savor what the place is really like only when
you drop in some day and make the humbling discovery
that it was not designed for your entertainment at all. Joe
designed it for his own kids. Designed it in memory of the
barn out in Evansville, where he learned to walk the clothesline clad in elegant tights made of underwear dyed blue.

That was the barn which old Mrs. Cook set aside as the
kingdom of the little Lopez boy when, his people having
died and left him on the doorstep of the world, she took him
in and reared him as her own. For Joe's father was a young
Spanish artist, and Mrs. Cook, who played Aunt Polly to the
boy's Tom Sawyer, was his foster mother. That old barn in
Evansville was torn down years ago, but the good people of
the town have put up a plaque in fond memory of the great
shows Joe gave there when he was a kid.

And in memory of that barn there are a thousand joys at

Sleepless Hollow which Joe put in at one time or another for his four youngsters. In particular, there is a real grand-opera house. Yes, sir, a regular theater. Small but regular. It has nine red plush seats (one of them a box-seat with opera glasses attached), an asbestos curtain, a stage alley, four dressing rooms, and everything. And to guard against any hard feelings in the home of one who knows the heartbreaks of the theater, each dressing room is marked No. One.

The oldest boy and girl—just to make it harder, they are called Joe and Jo, respectively—seem each decided on a career. The girl is a pianist. The boy can do all his father's tricks, and, like his father, cannot so much as hear a new musical instrument without taking it behind the barn and staying there until he knows how to play it too. I figure that Joe Senior in his time has made at least forty such trips behind the barn.

Doris, aged thirteen, is already an Elsie Janis in a small way, but Leo, aged eleven, is still undecided, and pretty worried about it. Not long ago I heard him approach his father with an anxious question. Was it possible, he wondered, that he was going to be a midget? Well, that was something to consider. And how soon, the boy asked, would they know for sure?

The last I saw of them, they were walking side by side down a wooded path, the one a miniature of the other, each with his hands clasped behind him, each with a head bent a little in earnest thought, as they discussed, these two, the grave question of the best course to pursue if it should turn out, after all, that Leo did have in him the makings of a midget.

*THE story of Frank Lloyd Wright, an American giant, and some study of the forces which paralyzed him during those years which might have been his most fruitful ones.*

SOME NEIGHBORS: VII

# THE PRODIGAL FATHER

IN Europe and the Far East, there has been for some time past a disposition to refer to Frank Lloyd Wright as the Father of Modern Architecture, and of late this salutation has been caught up and echoed in this, his native land. In my waggish way, I might observe in passing that this would lend credence to a dark suspicion that modern architecture was born out of wedlock. But it is rather the business of this brief monograph to record the news that Father himself has recently been manifesting a renewal of interest in this child deposited on his doorstep, and has even been giving evidence of a disposition to go back to work and look after it.

Today there is less, it seems to me, of the old disparity between the high honor in which Wright has long been held abroad and the position which he was permitted—or let us say encouraged—to occupy here at home. But consider, please, the irony of that disparity in its heyday a few years ago. Here was a native American being hailed overseas as the outstanding creative genius of our time in architecture—an artist whose drawings were pored over and studied by every student in Europe, a pioneer who had profoundly influenced all recent building in Germany and about whom the French and the Dutch were publishing reverent volumes, a man of achievement who had been all but canonized in Japan, whence every year the Mikado still sends several small, dusky disciples to sit at the feet of this Wisconsin Gamaliel. The travel bureaus that guide European sightseers from Niagara Falls to the Mammoth Cave (just as they push Americans around Europe from Salisbury Cathedral to the Grand Canal) learned before long that they could satisfy some of their clients here only by organizing tours to the home and works of Frank Lloyd Wright. Yet if such enthusiasts, on getting off the boat, turned to the mere man in the street and said, "Where is Frank Lloyd Wright?" the answer was either a stare of blank amazement or, as like as not, a feeling that what the funny foreigner really wanted was to be conducted to the far more celebrated Harold Bell Wright. And when, shortly after the war, the French applied to us to contribute an exhibit to the Exposition of Decorative Arts then being organized in Paris, the regretful reply framed by our Mr. Hoover as Secretary of Commerce was explicable only on the assumption that he had never even heard of Frank Lloyd Wright.

As I have said, there have been recent signs of America catching up with Wright. Princeton and Cornell have been summoning the alarming creature from Wisconsin to lecture to their young, and the Architectural League here in New York not only gave a breath-taking exhibition of his work, but followed it with an exuberant dinner in his honor. As he listened to the speeches, Wright, who has always rather enjoyed regarding himself as a bit of an Ishmaelite, must have experienced some of the disquieting emotions which recently perturbed the bosom of another stormy petrel of our time. I refer to one Bernard Shaw, to whom the British government, which he had so often rendered uneasy, proffered humbly and vainly not long ago a seat in the House of Lords. I am sure that both Shaw and Wright had an uncomfortable feeling that they were being honored as if they were already dead.

But if it is true that, at the time Mr. Hoover made his celebrated reply back in 1925, he had not so much as heard of Frank Lloyd Wright, I think it would not be difficult to explain the lapse. For there was a stretch of more than ten years when Wright did little or no work in this part of the world. The Midway Gardens in Chicago, the Larkin Building in Buffalo, the challenging Unity Temple in Oak Park, his own incomparable Taliesin, and a hundred lovely prairie homes in the Middle West—Mr. Hoover should have known about these earlier Wright buildings, some of them now world-famous. But of recent work he may well have heard nothing, and it is my business here to suggest why.

Four years out of that stretch, to be sure, were magnificently fertile. The work, however, was done not here but in Japan. Most of the remaining time was taken up by sleazy scandals and the ignominious procedure which our ugly divorce laws enforce, taken up by witless and vindictive indictments and all the ugly hoodlumism which the yellow newspapers can invoke when once an outstanding and inevitably spectacular man gives them half a chance. Wright gave them a chance and a half. The reporter pack, in full cry, followed his every naïve move, creating an atmosphere in which no artist could work well, and no architect could work at all. When a Samson Agonistes has made sport for the Philistines, he can, if he be a sculptor, say, or a poet, or a painter, retreat to the wilderness and fulfill his destiny. Your architect, on the contrary, must work in and with a community. He must deal with boards of directors, with vestrymen, with trustees, with bankers. He must deflect great forces of capital and labor, and, as Wright himself has been known to say, there is nothing so timid as a million dollars. The great corporation

executive, who could conceivably know by instinct that
Wright would work such a miracle in glass and stone as the
world had only dreamed of, might nevertheless take fright
at the thought of dealing with him. Didn't he look too much
like an actor? Didn't he go about in knee-breeches? And
what were all those old tabloid tales of "love pacts" and "love
nests"? And weren't there an unusual number of murders
committed in his house one night? Perhaps, after all, it would
be better to deal with an architect who, while no artist at all,
had at least never been talked about in the newspapers.

Of course those calamitous chapters, now happily receding
into a misty past, bulk large in Wright's envelope of clippings
in any newspaper morgue. I would like to dismiss them here
in a contemptuous sentence as none of my business or yours,
but they did so paralyze him that a sequence of his best years
was laid waste and the world was irrevocably cheated of some
beauty it could not spare. In this connection, I would like
merely to add the sententious suggestion that when a DeWolf
Hopper marries for the sixth time, the onlooking world
shakes its empty head as if he were some species of libertine,
although anyone with a grain of sense might guess that, at
least in his relations with women, the bewildered fellow was
incorrigibly ingenuous, an incurable romantic, a man more
innocent than his worldly-wise brothers, a Willie Baxter who
never grew up. But, after all, the sapless and the strangulated
have always misconstrued Don Juan.

In those troubled times, Wright went through some black
and searing hours that would have destroyed anyone less
vital. But at least the Japanese interlude was glorious, and in
those four years there must have come to him a sense of accomplishment in a measure that it is given to few men in any
century to savor even once in all their lives. The Japanese
wished to build an Imperial Hotel in Tokyo as a social
clearing-house for their empire. They sent a commission
around the world to select an architect for their purpose and

this commission chose our friend from Wisconsin. It was his task to rear a beautiful and spacious palace that would modestly take its cue from all the folkways and traditions of Japan, but which, in one important respect, must differ from all the other buildings round about. It must discover and express the secret of withstanding an earthquake.

The weight of the deepest sea in the world is forever straining intolerably the tenuous crust of that anxious island, and from time to time its whole surface shudders disastrously. Wright envisaged not only a stately but a flexible pleasure dome which, instead of trusting to any treachous rock, might float instead on a sea of mud as a battleship floats on the ocean, the weight of its floors sustained not by the walls at all but by centered supports which would balance them as a waiter's fingers balance his tray.

It was a scheme to outwit rather than to defy the temblors, and it so departed from every routine of habitual construction that, rather than entrust it to conventional builders, Wright himself took charge and brooded over the six hundred toiling artisans who fashioned it, piece by piece, as a thing at once of fine simplicity and infinite guile. Throughout those years he was generously backed with money, patience, and shelter from interference by old Baron Okura, a hearty little fellow of some eighty summers, who at the time had just been presented with his sixty-fourth child by his sixteenth wife. If our yellow journals ever reached Japan with their tales of his architect's so-called private life, these tales must have impressed the Baron as the insipid misadventures of a comparative anchorite. At last the great palace was completed—a jointed monolith with a mosaic surface of greenish-colored, leopard-spotted lava and slim, fluted, gold-colored bricks.

Wright received as rich a reward as any man could ask when his ship set sail at last from Yokohama, and sixty of his foremen, who had paid their own carfare from Tokyo to see him off, stood on the pier and yelled: *"Banzai, Wrieto-*

*San, Banzai!"* as the ship went down the bay. Then one night in 1924 he was awakened in Los Angeles by reporters bearing the news that the worst earthquake in history had wiped out Tokyo and Yokohama. The Imperial Hotel, the reporters said, had crumbled with the rest. It was only after ten days of uncertainty and conflicting rumors that Wright received this cablegram:

"IMPERIAL STANDS UNDAMAGED A MONUMENT TO YOUR GENIUS IN JAPAN THOUSANDS OF HOMELESS PROVIDED WITH UNINTERRUPTED SERVICE CONGRATULATIONS—OKURA."

It seems the Imperial had rocked in the upheaval, but, as the temblor passed, had settled quietly back into position with no crack or dislocation to tell the story. Since then, whenever a temblor visits Tokyo, all the town tries to crowd into the terraced courtyards of the Imperial, seeking the protection of a god that can laugh at an earthquake.

I first saw Wright himself on an afternoon in 1925 when, on a lecture tour in the Middle West, I found myself in Madison and learned that Wright's own house at Spring Green was only fifty miles away. I wanted to see with my own eyes the home that such a man would build for himself. Taliesin—that means "Radiant Brow" in Welsh—was already famous. Wright had fashioned it out of the wood and stone he found in this valley where, for three generations, his people had lived, and where his toes remembered the very feel of the soil from the barefoot days of his boyhood. To this valley he had retreated some years before from the prosperous suffocation of Oak Park on the complacent outskirts of Chicago.

I had dimly heard the old wives' tale of blasting disaster which had already been visited on Taliesin. A woman with two children had followed him there from Oak Park and found shelter under his gentle roof. This hospitality had outraged the Negro butler, who darkly predicted in the village that God would punish such goings-on. As is the way with

such tormented moralists, he soon got it into his woolly and
demented head that God expected him to do something about
it personally, soon, indeed, had himself and a vengeful Jehovah committed to a hideous partnership. On a night when
Wright was away from home he struck, tossing lighted
torches into a kerosene-soaked dining-room and stationing
himself outside with an ax to slaughter the guests as they
fled through the blazing exit. In the climax of this holocaust
he killed himself, so that there were seven bodies in the ruins
that awaited Wright when he came home. I imagine that the
wretched fanatic counted on going down in history as the
author of one of the most monstrous crimes in American
annals, but it attracted little attention in next day's newspapers, for he had picked a bad night for it. The front pages
that morning in August 1914 were rather given over to the
news that England had declared war on Germany.

I had read enough of Wright's dicta on architecture—maxims, you might call them, and certainly some of them are
silencers—and seen enough of his work to forecast the quality
of Taliesin. I knew that it would pick up its colors from the
red cedars, white birches, and yellow-sand limestone round
about, that it would gratefully take its lines from the crest of
the hill it was to crown, that indeed it would not be so much
*on* the hill as *of* it. I knew that it would be peculiarly suitable to the landscape whence it sprang, and to the needs and
habits of the man occupying it. I would not be equipped to
discuss it in the technical terms of organic architecture, but I
knew it would be different from all other houses in the world,
without any of the visible and aching strain of a conscious
effort to be different. Of course that is the peculiar gift of
Wright and his like in this world—to build freshly as though
we had all just come out of Eden with no precedents to
tyrannize over us. I knew therefore that in Taliesin I would
find nothing alien, nothing automatic, nothing unreasonable.
Perhaps that's the essence of it—reasonableness. Sweet rea-

sonableness. With the sweetness of warm milk, of new-mown hay, and of water, fresh-cupped from a bubbling spring.

All this I expected, but I had not enough gift of divination to realize in advance how inexpressibly consoling would be its every aspect, how happily would the house grow like a vine on that hill-crest, how unerringly would every window foresee and frame the landscape that was to croon to the man within, above all how pliantly the unpretentious home would meet halfway the participation of the countryside. Why, if a lovely tree was in the way of that house, the house just doffed its cap respectfully and went around it.

I spent two wondering hours at Taliesin. A sunset storm was gathering in the west as I drove away. Next morning in Minneapolis I read that, within an hour after I had left, lightning had struck the house and burned it to the ground. You can see for yourself how malignant circumstances have buffeted this man. This giant. This ingenuous giant.

However, it would take more than a few murders, some bolts from the blue, and the ugly lynching-cry of the mob to repress for any length of time a fellow with so rich a gift for life. A new Taliesin crowns the selfsame hill today and the children of a recent and fortunate marriage are at play in the sun-dappled courtyards. I gather from newspaper references to certain glass towers projected for our own St. Mark's-in-the-Bouwerie and to a vast Arizona caravansary designed for San Marcos-in-the-Desert, that, after long years of costly interruption, he is back at work. I am glad, for I think he is a great man. I know how flagrantly he himself had invited some of the thunderbolts that have struck him. I know what perverse and tactless mockery of all who would serve him dances ever in his eyes. I know how near the surface, always, is the untamed imp in him that bids him upset the very apple cart he is hungrily approaching. But I think, too, that no one in the modern world has brought to architecture so good a mind, so leaping an imagination, or so fresh a sense of beauty. Indeed, if the niggardly publisher of this book were so to ration me that I were suffered to apply the word "genius" to only one living American, I would have to save it up for Frank Lloyd Wright.

FOOTNOTE: When I was in Japan, I enjoyed the hospitality of Aisaku Haiyashi. Mr. Haiyashi, who had been for many years the head of Yamanaka's in New York, and was the man who had carried the ashes of poor Professor Fenollosa from a dreary grave in London to their last resting place beside one of the temples near Kyoto, was the managing-director of the Imperial Hotel while it was building. He had staked his honor on Wright's assurance that the Imperial would outwit an earthquake. When Tokyo was riven by the great temblor in 1924, the first, panicky word reaching Haiyashi's house was to the effect that the hotel had split in two and gone down into a yawning chasm. Later tidings that it had, as a matter of fact, survived the earthquake with no damage whatever reached him just as he had gone into his garden to commit hara-kiri, as the least he could do under the circumstances.

Considerable fury was caused in some quarters in the fall of 1932 by the failure to invite Frank Lloyd Wright to contribute to the architecture of "A Century of Progress." At that time it was still thought that the Fair as a challenge to architecture would be met. I found myself presiding at an indignation meeting in New York. The villain of the piece seemed to be that cheerful realist, Raymond Hood. When he rose to speak, he admitted having come late to the meeting. He had, however, felt reasonably sure that his seat would be saved. I could not help wondering from what.

*THE story of Charles Gordon
MacArthur who was designed for
the enlightenment of the heathen
but who went instead to war,
Hollywood, and a good deal of
trouble.*

SOME NEIGHBORS: VIII

# THE YOUNG MONK OF SIBERIA

> There was an old monk of Siberia,
> Whose life it grew drearier and drearier,
>    Till he broke from his cell
>    With a hell of a yell
> And eloped with the Mother Superior.
>
> OLD CHANTEY

BACK in the first year of this century, the six-year-old
son of the minister in a Scranton congregation found
it among the many alarming but as yet unchallenged
instructions then governing his existence that each Sunday he
should repair to a crowded tent across from his father's home,
there to assist a visiting revivalist, who was resonantly calling
the sinners of Scranton back to the fold.

Upon reaching the platform, the terrified child had to
climb a ladder inexorably awaiting him. It seemed to him
only slightly less lofty than the Tower of Babel, which he
had heard unfavorably spoken of at home. Once arrived at
its vertiginous top, he had to stand there until the preacher
turned, held out his arms, and said "Jump." Then, shutting
his eyes, he had to hurl himself into space. The visiting Gan-
try would catch him (or at least that was the rough idea),

lower him to the platform, and pat him benevolently on his curly head, having the effrontery to wear the while an Inasmuch-as-ye-have-done-it-unto-the-least-of-these expression.

"That, O my brothers and sisters," he would say to the congregation, "is faith."

The immediate results doubtless made for penitence among the Scranton citizenry. But it may not surprise you to learn that (after, of course, a necessary interval for growth and reflection) the small boy turned to and assisted Ben Hecht in the writing of that heroic comedy, *The Front Page,* a play of magnificent stride and one so profane, derisive, and hardboiled that, compared with it, *What Price Glory,* its natural forerunner, seems, in gentle retrospect, like a page out of Louisa Alcott.

Sundry artists, sculptors, novelists, and playwrights have attempted more or less faithfully to give you an impression of Charles MacArthur. Always a confusing mixture of Satanic mischief and childlike bewilderment, he is of such fluctuant appearance that even so faithful an artist as Auerbach-Levy once produced a portrait of him that looked at least as much like Fay Bainter or Sinclair Lewis. It is doubtless a similar variability which leads so many women to refer to him fondly as "that little MacArthur," when he is, in point of fact, a good six feet tall, with the hands and feet of the Neanderthal man, and of such considerable peasant strength that, in moments of exuberance, he has been known to take on three taxicab drivers at once in mortal combat.

But perhaps the portrait painters do not notice the fellow's Herculean build because MacArthur himself doesn't notice it. Those who are born lusty never can associate muscle with prowess, and one who is himself no parvenu in brawn could not possibly experience anything akin to the late Colonel Roosevelt's girlish enthusiasm for mere biceps. Not that MacArthur is fearsome only in physical combat. Recently an able young theatrical manager undertook to taunt him with hav-

ing sold himself down the river to sundry Hollywood mag-
nates. This point was well enough taken but it was conveyed
in an obscene, juvenile, and heavy-handed missive with which
the inexpert letter-writer himself was so naïvely pleased that
he made the tactical error of proudly showing a carbon of it
to several embarrassed friends. These were the more amused
when MacArthur, on receipt of it, merely sent it on to
Hecht with the penciled notation "Shelley's loose again."
Then I remember my own experience in the case of an astounding clipping sent me from a New Orleans newspaper. It
was a one-column photograph of myself under the simple
caption, "Soldier-Author." I tried to think which of my
neighbors would be the more outraged by this and decided
to send it to MacArthur. It came back, with no comment save
the notation "For your files."

It is sometimes easiest to convey an impression of such
difficult portrait subjects by trying to visualize them in the
costume of whatever century seems their natural background.
You may picture MacArthur, if you will, in Lincoln green
and pointed cap. He clearly belongs in the early thirteenth
century, astray, as like as not, from Robin Hood's band, and
vaguely headed for the Holy Land, but (with all his worldly
goods done up in a handkerchief) sitting, for the nonce, outside an English inn and willing to delay his pilgrimage indefinitely in swapping yarns and a mug of ale with any passing
friar.

A sketch of him in words is quite as difficult, and though,
from the momentum of habit, this wildly fragmentary biography may be classified as a Profile, please consider it rather
as some miscellaneous pieces of a jig-saw puzzle which you
must put together for yourself.

Here is one piece. When he was a boy of nine, a zealot in
Chicago led him up to a velvet-draped altar before a crowded
audience in Willard Hall and announced that, for his sins,
the child had been visited with an abscess in the neck, which

would cause his death on such and such a date in the spring unless the prayers of those congregations affected by his father's ministry should succeed in averting the doom. The ensuing bouts of prayer lasted for months, and were conducted by two factions, which quarreled bitterly about the divinely revealed date of the fatal day. However, when (perhaps in its own due course) the abscess burst two days in advance of the schedule, both factions blandly claimed the triumph and for a year exhibited the sheepish boy at innumerable campmeetings as the little sinner who had been cured by the prayers of Chicago.

This episode must have left several scars, of which at least one is visible on his neck today. Now, anyone given to the pastime of fitting such jig-saw pieces together would inevitably try to join this curiously jagged one to another incident which, a dozen years later, enlivened one of the darker days of the Rainbow Division. Private MacArthur of Battery F, 149th Field Artillery, had been unwisely assigned by the Colonel to select a battery song and rehearse the troops in it. Some say they never while they live will forget the expression on the face of the Y.M.C.A. secretary when he first heard the result, the troops slogging down the Lorraine road, gaunt, foul, hairy, verminous, but all lifting their hoarse voices in the refrain: "Jesus wants me for a sunbeam."

It is tempting thus to assemble bits of MacArthuriana and make them into a portrait of a man trying to put a lot of territory between himself and his boyhood. But probably there would be a good many unexplained bits left over.

Charles Gordon MacArthur is the grandson of a Scotch lady named Jane Ironsides who, having picked up a loose member of the MacArthur clan in the old country, brought him to Winnipeg as a means of rescuing him from Aberdeen, which it was her wont ever after to describe as "a mire o' Bedlam." Her son William was well launched as a farmer up Winnipeg way when, out of a clear sky, he felt called upon to preach and, beginning on an astonished Saint Paul street-corner many years ago, he has since conducted countless revival meetings (it was the duty of the MacArthur children to go to as many as five different services of a Sunday), reared a dozen churches, and brought up six children in the fear of God and, at least in their childhood, of himself. Once, when he told me that none of his sons had followed in the path thus pointed out, I had what now seems to me the incredible effrontery to ask him if he felt this cast any reflections on his own skill and devotion as a parent. After some thought, the old preacher blandly replied, "The children of the busy cobbler often go barefoot."

It was our hero, his Benjamin, whom he sent to the school for missionaries at Nyack, where now the Charles MacArthurs have their home. From the Nyack seminary, after two or three years of stern schooling in the pieties, the bursting boy ran away to New York and went to work as a necktie salesman in Lord & Taylor's. But he was so far from being an untethered runaway in those days that when, as I am obliged to report they did, the other necktie salesmen would leer and make lewd remarks to the girls at the ribbon counter, the newcomer went white and was at some pains to arrive at the store next day with a Bible for each offender.

Then came Chicago, and his hilarious adventures as a reporter there, all festooned now with rosemary in *The Front Page,* which the authors in their endearing preface have described as a doting Valentine thrown back across the years to the bouncing days of their servitude.

It was while he was trooping on the Mexican border in 1916 that he served with LeRoy Baldridge, the artist. One night it was Sergeant Baldridge's duty to patrol the camp and see that no mere enlisted men were abroad on the evening of the officers' dance. Hearing the sounds of revelry in one major's tent, he took the precaution to glance in, but drew respectfully back at the sight of the gold leaf on the shoulder of one who sat with a bottle on the table before him, quietly singing hymns to himself. Baldridge went away, wondering what officer was thus oddly celebrating his majority, when, a few moments later at the dance hall, he noticed with a start that every major in the regiment was footing it featly on the floor. Racing back across the camp he gave the lone reveler a closer inspection, only to discover that it was merely Buck Private MacArthur, who, before declaring wassail-all in the dim candle-lit tent that night, had taken the precaution to adorn each of his shoulders with the end of a lemon peel.

Such yarns as that one preceded him from Chicago to New York, where he arrived ten years ago. At that time he had not yet written *Lulu Belle* with Edward Sheldon, nor *Salvation* with Sidney Howard, nor *The Front Page* with Ben Hecht. He had not yet married Helen Hayes. He had, indeed, done nothing hereabouts to account for the aura of a legendary figure which yet somehow invested him with an immediate and, to mere plodding onlookers, an infuriating distinction.

I came to the conclusion that this unaccountable importance could be best explained by one who was familiar with his youthful adventures in Chicago. Wherefore, in preparing this rough sketch for the *Dictionary of American Biography,* I journeyed out to Chicago to ask what young MacArthur had done there in his newspaper days. It was a shabby old reprobate, from the very press-room since dramatized in *The Front Page,* who undertook to enlighten me.

"Well, pardner," he said, "there's hardly much I can tell you about Bugs MacArthur, as we used to call him in his younger days here in Chi. Except he was always playing rummy with doomed men in the County Jail death-cell and taking their last nickels from them to keep himself in likker. And there was the time he returned from the Border War with a price on his head and Colonel Foreman's whole Illinois

Militia looking to arrest and shoot him. In the middle of the
hunt, he broke cover and appeared in an old Ford at the head
of Colonel Foreman's triumphant homecoming parade down
Michigan Avenue, with two women dressed up as Mexican
prisoners in chains beside him, and himself holding out the
largest American flag ever seen in Chicago. And there was
the time when he got the idea of reviving hanged people
with adrenalin. He always spent a lot of time around these
kind of folk. I guess he figured on making a fortune through
writing up their psychology for some newspaper syndicate.

"And I remember the time he knocked out his managing
editor, because the petty tyrant forbid him to keep his bicycle
in the local room. And then he and Deanie O'Banion, the last
of the first-class killers around here, used to ride up and down
the boulevards at dawn in Deanie's automobile, Deanie shooting at the arc lights to keep himself in practice and Bugs
singing 'Nobody knows my name, poor boy, nobody knows
my name.' And his being broke, I remember, and having to
board and lay up at his rich brother Alfred's house and
Alfred making him wear kilts and play the bagpipes for company in the parlor, Alfred at that time running for the presi-
dency of some Scottish lodge.

"Those were the days before Bugs learned how to enter a
ballroom and he was always sliding down banisters and
jumping over barrels with red lanterns on top of them and
stealing stars off policemen and he could recite most of the
Bible by heart and was full of rough jokes, like bringing people he said were smallpox patients into saloons and introducing them to the bartenders, who would run into the street
and leave Bugs in charge of the bottles. And all the while
women cutting each other's throats so as to enjoy his sole
attentions.

"As I said, there isn't much to tell you, pardner, about his
younger days, except that everybody who knew him always
lights up when they hear his name and starts to talking about

Bugs like he was a marvelous circus that had once passed their way when the world was young. He sure was a very moody fellow."

Thus my informant. Now, even a quite unanalytical observer might guess that these legends got into circulation in the first place because MacArthur himself has no superior in his land and day as a raconteur. Indeed, it was this very gift that opened the door of the theater to him. When one thinks how many despairing outsiders find the stage-alley a *cul-de-sac,* it is ironical that that portal should have swung wide at once to one who is really so little interested in the theater, so rare, restless, and unresponsive a playgoer.

I am sure that all the MacArthur plays have resulted from the circumstance that a practiced playwright listened enviously to the flood of his idle reminiscence, and at last, as a means of tapping that wellspring of experience for the theater, invited (nay, dragged) him into collaboration.

Perhaps the more resentful of his listeners are sometimes moved to suspect that some of his adventures were entered upon for no other reason than that they would sound well afterwards in seemingly casual conversation. Thus, when he varied the monotony of the hunt for drug-smugglers which he and Sidney Howard conducted in Florida some years ago at the behest of Mr. Hearst, by visiting the local Maison Tellier one day and taking the madame and all her girls out duck-shooting, it is barely possible he knew that the experiences of that day would tell well afterwards. I suspect he was similarly prompted when, instead of the traditional fur-coat or string of pearls, he once, in Chicago, presented Peggy Hopkins Joyce with a package which proved to contain the helmet of the policeman on the corner. The latter was exceeding wroth when he awoke to find it missing. Now I suspect MacArthur meant this whimsy for his memoirs and was therefore the more annoyed when Miss Joyce used it in her own.

A similar itching skepticism may have tantalized those who watched him in the threadbare days of his first arrival in New York when, in financial desperation, he took the post of press agent for a mausoleum then about to open somewhere in New Jersey and, after weeks of inaction, was goaded into frenetic endeavors by the reproaches of his employer, who would meanly insist on pointing out that not so much as a single paragraph had yet found its way into a New York newspaper. The badgered press agent's next move was to wire to the Mayor of Boston, abruptly demanding that the bones of Henry Wadsworth Longfellow be forwarded to a new and more fitting sepulture which a New Jersey corporation was tastefully preparing for the noble dead. Follow-up telegrams exhorted the resentful mayor to put aside all ignoble considerations of local pride and petty jealousy and at once yield up the cherished remains to a more deserving tomb. This correspondence finally so maddened the Boston authorities that they applied to our police to abate the nuisance for them. MacArthur remained unmolested, however, as he had thoughtfully signed the telegrams "Robert Benchley."

When these two romps join forces, the mere onlooker has an almost suffocating sense that they are preparing material for their own subsequent anecdotes. I remember a pleasant spring morning in their needier days when MacArthur and Benchley, their pooled worldly resources having come to exactly four dollars and fifty cents, had spent it all on a Hotel St. Regis breakfast. Emerging, nourished but penniless, they found the more successful world embodied in none other than Charles Evans Hughes, then Secretary of State and at the moment striding majestically down the Avenue. The spectacle filled them with a mysterious resentment. With one accord they yelled at him in shrill, urchin falsetto, "Yah, yah, Secretary of State. What are you doing here, if you're Secretary of State? Yah, yah, Secretary of State." Thus they ran hooting behind him down Fifth Avenue until, in acute embarrassment, Mr. Hughes called a cab, leaped inside it and had his dignity carried beyond their financial reach.

On such occasions one is tempted to murmur, "Come, come, MacArthur, don't be elfin. Do you have to be quite so picturesque?"

But, in all conscience, most of us are so tedious when regarded as spectacles that even such feeble resistance is looking a gift horse—a priceless gift horse—in the mouth.

*WHEREIN it is related how a handsome perfume salesman, having been set two spades doubled, criticizes his helpmeet's bidding and does not live to play another hand.*

## "IT MAY BE HUMAN GORE": I

# BY THE RUDE BRIDGE

L ET me begin by admitting that through the years I have become a more and more spasmodic newspaper reader. This may be due to a conviction that by faithfully absorbing the imparted wisdom of the two Walters (Lippmann and Winchell) I can learn all I really care to know about what is going on in the world. But, occasionally, through this failure of attention to the news columns, I lose the final chapter of some tale that has really interested me.

These somber reflections were induced one day when a chance remark brought to mind the Bennett killing which enlivened Kansas City some years ago, and with a start I realized that although it had involved four shots heard round the world, I never did know what happened afterwards. Wherefore I moved about among my neighbors, as might an inquiring reporter, only to find that, one and all, they too had lost track of the case. Yet at the time there was probably not a literate household in Europe or the three Americas of which the emotional seismograph had not recorded its tremors.

The Bennett killing, which occurred on the night of September 29, 1929, was usually spoken of, with approximate accuracy, as the Bridge-Table Murder. The victim was a personable and prosperous young salesman whose mission, as representative of the house of Hudnut, was to add to the fragrance of life in the Middle West. He had been married eleven years before to a Miss Myrtle Adkins, originally from Arkansas, who first saw his photograph at the home of a friend, announced at once that she intended to marry him, and then, perhaps with this purpose still in mind, recognized and accosted him a year later when she happened to encounter him on a train. That was during the war when the good points of our perfume salesman's physique were enhanced by an officer's uniform. They were married in Memphis during the considerable agitation of November 11, 1918. The marriage was a happy one. At least, Senator Jim Reed, who represented Mrs. Bennett in the trying but inevitable legal formalities which ensued upon her bereavement, announced in court—between sobs—that they had always been more like sweethearts than man and wife.

On Mr. Bennett's last Sunday on earth, these wedded sweethearts spent the day playing a foursome at golf with their friends, Charles and Mayme Hofman, who had an apartment in the Park Manor on Ward Parkway, which is, I think, a shiny new part of the town that was just forlorn, uncropped meadowland in the days when the great Dr. Logan Clendening, the late Ralph Barton, and your correspondent were all sweet-faced tots together in dear old K.C. After dark and after an ice-box supper at the Bennetts', the men folk professed themselves too weary to dress for the movies, so the four settled down to a more slatternly evening of contract bridge. They played family against family at a tenth of a cent a side. With a pretty laugh, Mayme Hofman on the witness stand referred to such a game as playing for "fun stakes," though whether this was a repulsive little phrase of her own

or one prevalent in the now devitalized society of a once
rugged community, I do not know.

They played for some hours. At first the luck went against
the Hofmans and the married sweethearts were as merry as
grigs. Later the tide turned and the cross-table talk of the Bennetts became tinged with constructive criticism. Finally, just
before midnight, the fatal hand was dealt by Bennett himself
and he opened the bidding with one spade. Hofman hazarded
two diamonds. Mrs. Bennett leaped to four spades. Discreet
silence from Mrs. Hofman. Stunned silence from Bennett.
Hofman doubled. That ended the bidding and the play began.

Mrs. Bennett put down her hand. At her trial it was the
policy of the defense, for strategic reasons, to minimize the
part the bridge game had played in the ensuing drama, but
the jury could not be confused on this point and three of the
jurors went so far as to learn bridge in the long leisure of the
jury room. Nor could the mind of that stern realist, Mayme
Hofman, be befogged. When summoned as a witness by Senator Reed, she knew she was really coming to the defense of
Mrs. Bennett as a bridge player.

"Myrtle put down a good hand," she said stanchly, "it
was a perfectly beautiful hand."

In any event, while she was dummy, Mrs. Bennett retired
to the kitchen to prepare breakfast for her lord and master,
who would be leaving at the crack of dawn for St. Joe. She
came back to find he had been set two and to be greeted with
the almost automatic charge that she had overbid. Thereupon
she ventured to opine that he was, in her phrase, "a bum
bridge player." His reply to that was a slap in the face, followed by several more of the same—whether three or four
more, witnesses were uncertain. Then while he stormed about
proclaiming his intention to leave for St. Joe at once and while
Mr. Hofman prudently devoted the interval to totting up the
score, Mrs. Bennett retired to the davenport to weep on the
sympathetic bosom of Mayme Hofman, saying many things,

through her tears, including one utterance which, in my opinion, should give the Bennett case a permanent place in the files of such fond annalists as William Roughead of Edinburgh and Edmund (Whatever became of the Lester?) Pearson of New York. Mrs. Bennett's sentiments were expressed as follows:

"No one but a cur would strike a woman in the presence of friends."

I have not as yet been able to learn whether the game was ever settled, but when Mr. Hofman had completed his work as accountant, he ventured to reproach the host for unseemly behavior, to which comment Bennett replied by a strong suggestion that it was time for the guests to go home. Mrs. Hofman—one can imagine her bridling a good deal and saying that she considered the source—had got into her wraps and Mr. Hofman was tidying up in the bathroom, when he saw his hostess advancing through the den, revolver in hand.

"My God, Myrtle," he cried. "What are you going to do?" He soon learned.

There were four shots, with a brief interval after the second. The first went through the hastily closed bathroom door. The second was embedded in the lintel. The next two were embedded in Mr. Bennett, the fourth and fatal shot hitting him in the back.

The next day the story went round the world. In its first reverberations, I noticed, with interest, that after her visit to the mortuary chapel Mrs. Bennett objected plaintively to her husband's being buried without a pocket-handkerchief showing in his coat. To interested visitors, she would make cryptic remarks such as "Nobody knows but me and my God why I did it," thus leaving open to pleasant speculation the probable nature of her defense.

It would be difficult to explain to a puzzled Englishman, brought up as he is to think of America as a country of breathless speed, how seventeen months could be allowed to pass

before Mrs. Bennett was called upon to stand trial. By that
time I myself had lost track. Wherefore, when the aforesaid
Clendening called at Wit's End one Sunday, I asked what,
if anything, had ever happened in the Bennett case.

"Oh!" the good doctor replied, "she was acquitted. It seems
it was just an unfortunate accident."

For corroborative detail I have since consulted the files of
the *Kansas City Star,* one of the three or four newspapers left
in this country of which the staff still preserves, like the
guarded secret of some medieval guild, the lost art of reportorial writing. The *Star* accounts of the trial are in the finest
tradition of our craft. I cannot hope in so small a space to
reproduce the flavor of Senator Reed's more than adequate
performance. It seems the dutiful Mrs. Bennett had merely
gone for the revolver because her husband wanted to take it
with him to St. Joe; that in stumbling over a misplaced chair
in the den she fired the first two shots unintentionally and
that her husband (pardonably misreading her kind intentions) had sought to disarm her. In the ensuing Apache dance
of their struggle for the gun, it had gone off and wounded
him fatally.

The defense was materially aided by the exclusion on technical grounds of crucial testimony which would have tended
to indicate that at the time Mrs. Bennett had told a rather different story. It was also helped no little by the defendant herself who, in the course of the trial, is estimated to have shed
more tears than Jane Cowl did in the entire season of *Common Clay.* Even the Senator was occasionally unmanned,
breaking into sobs several times in the presence of the jury.
"I just can't help it," he replied, when the calloused prose-
cutor urged him to bear up.

The Reed construction of the fatal night's events proved
subsequently important to Mrs. Bennett, in whose favor her
husband had once taken out a policy to cover the contingency
of his death through accident. Some months after the acquit-

tal a dazed insurance company paid her thirty thousand dollars.

It was Harpo Marx who, on hearing the doctor's hasty but spirited résumé of the case, suggested that I make use of it for one of my little articles. He even professed to have thought of a title for it. Skeptically I inquired what this might be and he answered "Vulnerable."

FOOTNOTE: Protesting as I do against the short-weight reporting in the *Notable British Trials* series, it would ill become me to hoard for my private pleasure certain postscripts to the Bennett case which have recently drifted my way. It looked for a time as if we all might be vouchsafed the luxury of reading Myrtle's autobiography, but this great work has been indefinitely postponed. I understand she could not come to terms with the local journalist who was to do the actual writing. That ink-stained wretch demanded half the royalties. Mrs. Bennett felt this division would be inequitable, since, as she pointed out, she herself had done all the work.

Then it seems she has not allowed her bridge to grow rusty, even though she occasionally encounters an explicable difficulty in finding a partner. Recently she took on one unacquainted with her history. Having made an impulsive bid, he put his hand down with some diffidence. "Partner," he said, "I'm afraid you'll want to shoot me for this." Mrs. Bennett, says my informant, had the good taste to faint.

*THE chronicle of the disappear-
ance of Eugenie Cedarholm and
of the subsequent inconvenience to
which the State of New York
put the man in whose company
she had last been seen alive.*

"IT MAY BE HUMAN GORE": II

# IN BEHALF OF AN ABSENTEE

IN the hope that my precious leader, Edmund Pearson, will one day see fit to include in his incomparable studies in murder the unique case of Eugenie Cedarholm, a spinster, late of the borough of Brooklyn, I hereby assemble, in a form convenient for his gory files, certain data calculated to illustrate the fascination this case can exercise over delvers into criminal lore. It may well be that Brother Pearson will prefer to stay his impatient pen until the statutory time has run its course, and, in the fall of 1934, the missing woman can be declared dead in the eyes of the law. When I was browsing over the records in the court of the Surrogate of Kings County, her official status was indicated by the documents which referred to her merely as "An Absentee."

This complication also hampered a succession of county prosecutors, each of whom harbored not only an overwhelming belief that Miss Cedarholm had been the victim of murder most foul, but a strong suspicion as to who had put her out of the way and an automatic impulse to subject him to the vengeance of the law. But for several years this impulse was thwarted by the fact that the District Attorney had (and still has) no notion whatever as to where, when, or how this murder—if, indeed, there has been a murder—was accomplished.

In the instance of anyone dropping out of sight as completely as did Dorothy Arnold or Eugenie Cedarholm, the indisputable absence of the *corpus delicti* baffles the police power, which lacks a fulcrum, a point of departure, lacks even a certainty as to the jurisdiction in which a prosecution might be launched. Literally it does not know where to begin.

When, in 1910, that infatuated little dentist, Dr. Hawley Harvey Crippen, set sail from England with his lovesick secretary (faintly disguised as a boy) the inquiry provoked by the vague suspicions of his neighbors led to a detective from Scotland Yard digging under a loose brick in the cellar of the Crippen house in Hilldrop Crescent. He found there a bit of abdominal skin-tissue with a two-year-old appendectomy scar on it, and a pyjama-button of a make and date which fixed, within significant limits, the time when these remains of Mrs. Crippen—as scanty remains as ever led a man to the gallows—must have been there interred.

Similarly vague suspicions entertained by the neighbors of Eugenie Cedarholm led in time to a search as exhaustive not only of the cellar and yard of the house in Schermerhorn Street in Brooklyn which belonged to her, but of all the soil in and around the Freeport cottage where, in the early fall of 1927, she was last seen alive. The police dug up quite a good deal of Freeport. They found nothing.

Yet because of their undiminished belief that one Edward Lawrence Hall had killed her somewhere, somehow, and then disposed of her body with greater success than most murderers, in their heat and hurry, ever have a chance to achieve, said Hall is now serving in Sing Sing what, for a man of his age, is tantamount to a life sentence. Whatever reliance his own considerable shrewdness had led him to place in the protective *corpus delicti* law proved illusory. You see, they got him on a forgery charge. There are more ways than one of skinning a cat.

In 1921 Miss Cedarholm, a woman just come of age, succeeded, on the death of her mother, to the ownership of the brick dwelling at 338 Schermerhorn Street. This she continued to operate as a rooming-house, and to it as a lodger there came, in time, this fellow Hall, a grizzly, interesting, and malignly attractive ne'er-do-well in his late fifties who worked, when necessary, in lunch-wagons. In due course, he became the landlady's swain, and in September of 1927, having just taken a cottage at 37 Prince Street, Freeport, he set up housekeeping there with the young woman installed as his helpmeet. Subsequently, in the period of more than a year while his transactions were going unquestioned, he let her Brooklyn house, collected the rent, and cashed sundry checks purporting to have been signed by her.

This profitable procedure might have gone on unmolested to this day if subway condemnation proceedings in Schermerhorn Street had not created a sum of something like fifty thousand dollars as coming due to Miss Cedarholm. This provoked the Brooklyn Trust Company, as impersonal custodians of that money, into asking loudly whatever had become of her. But no one could be found who had clapped eyes on her after that day in October 1927 when the owner of the Freeport cottage had gone around to collect his rent and found his new tenants flown.

Hall, picked up by the police more than a year later and repeatedly questioned by the District Attorney's office and the Surrogate, said that *he* had seen her often enough, and that she was, he was happy to report, in the best of health and spirits. He even volunteered the information that, during the period of her absence from her old haunts and of her

puzzling indifference to her Brooklyn real estate, she had
been busy bearing him three children in lawful wedlock. It
seems that the marriage itself was almost immediately followed by twins. But where she was at that moment he would
not say. It was his repeated explanation that this silence was
dictated by chivalry. Once he let her whereabouts be known,
it seems, her life would be mysteriously endangered. He intimated that a discarded suitor was bent on doing her in. Even
the eventual imposition of a twenty-year prison sentence did
not unseal his lips on this crucial point.

It was this refusal, by the way, which brought him into
contempt of the Surrogate's Court. As part of the routine of
his appeal, he was allowed a flying visit from Sing Sing to
purge himself of this contempt by stating (apparently without fear of contradiction after so long a lapse of time) that on
the day in 1930 when first his refusal was recorded, the Absentee had, as a matter of fact, been dwelling (at an elab-
orately unverifiable address) in Jacksonville, Florida.

But at the time when it mattered and could be checked, he
had persisted in a hundred such refusals. Would not produce the power of attorney under which he professed to
have been acting. Would not say where he had married Miss
Cedarholm. Or where or when their children had been born.
When asked to name at least one physician who might have
attended any of her several *accouchements,* he replied with
dignity that he himself was a doctor. On that point a wife
of his younger days, discovered by the police in Minnesota,
lent him unexpected corroboration. At least she said that of
the six children she herself had borne to Hall prior to his
deserting her, he had delivered her with his own fair hands.
A many-sided domestic creature, this Mr. Hall.

When, four years after the sudden departure from Freeport, Hall was finally brought to book, it was on an indictment for forgery in the first degree. This accusation was pred-
icated upon the lessor's signature in the Schermerhorn Street

lease, which Hall admittedly negotiated, and on the strength of which he had collected the rent for many months. I trust Mr. Pearson will not overlook the interesting point that in itself this lease was not conclusively damaging to Hall. It was easy enough for a handwriting expert, armed with the undisputed bank signatures of Eugenie Cedarholm and even with the dingy matriculation card she had filled out years before as a schoolgirl, to persuade a jury that the lease had never been signed by her. But to go further and prove that the forgery was Hall's work was another matter. This Hall himself made possible during an unguarded moment when he was under fire in the Surrogate's Court. When Lyman Sessen, in behalf of the Brooklyn Trust Company, was fruitlessly questioning him as to the whereabouts of the Absentee, he did beguile the enigmatic witness into writing Eugenie Cedarholm's name five times on as many slips of paper.

These proved to be slips in more senses than one, and to them Hall owes his present lack of freedom. They clinched the case against him at the forgery trial when Hall persisted in acting as his own counsel. As Assistant District Attorney Kleinman was further able to prove, with the help of the fingerprint clearing-house at Washington, that Hall had previously done time in Stillwater, Minnesota, for stealing some lumber, it was possible for the Brooklyn judge to send him up the river for twenty years, a stiffer sentence than His Honor, with all the bad will in the world, could have given to a first offender.

When Mr. Pearson gets to work on the case, I trust he will note one or two minor details which have enhanced its interest for me. I have occasion elsewhere to mention how greatly such mysteries are enriched by the flavor of the proper names involved. The Crippen case, for instance, has entered into legend incalculably the stronger for the circumstance that his fellow-fugitive was so romantically named. Surely you remember Ethel Le Neve. Well, there are some good

names in the Cedarholm case, too. The sleuth who went out
on Hall's trail was Detective Pritting. It was Pritting who
dug up (figuratively) the wife Hall had left behind him in
the midlands. Then consider the outraged Freeport realtor
who came into court demanding that the estate of the Absentee settle with him for the unpaid rent of the abandoned
cottage, and for the storage ever since of all the furniture left
on his hands. His name—and the late Mr. Dickens would
have employed it with pleasure—was Jerry Verity.

Finally, I ask Mr. Pearson to note especially the part played
in the case by Miss Cedarholm's dog, Duke. As I make the
point, I feel myself unconsciously slipping into the manner
of Sherlock Holmes when he made a now quite celebrated
parting shot at one of the plodding Scotland Yard men at
work with him on some newly discovered crime. Said
Holmes, in his most annoying manner:

"I would call your attention to the curious incident of the
dog in the night-time."

"The dog did nothing in the night-time," replied the bewildered detective.

"That," said Holmes, "was the curious incident."

Well, in that spirit I ask Mr. Pearson to make note of Duke.
At present there is not much available testimony about him,
but when first the District Attorney questioned the young
couple who were (and still are) the last among Miss Cedarholm's friends known to have seen her alive or dead, they
talked a good deal about the faithful Duke. These people
were named Swanberg. They had gone out to Freeport in
October 1927 to have Sunday dinner with Eugenie and her
elderly lover who seemed, they said, to be on the best of
terms. I suppose the District Attorney was groping for any
evidence that Eugenie betrayed some forebodings of doom.
Had she seemed happy? No, Swanberg replied, most unhappy. The District Attorney pricked up his ears. But the
unhappiness was all about Duke. It seems that the Halls, as

Landlord Verity knew them, had only just moved in when Duke disappeared, the dog she had had so long and been so fond of and spent such fortunes on when he was sick. Now he was gone. Just jumped out of the window, Hall told her, and ran away. Hall had helped her search all the woods in that part of the country, and had even gone with her when she went up and down Long Island answering advertisements about dogs picked up. But to no purpose.

"Of course," Swanberg told the District Attorney, "when the dog was gone she felt kind of blue. The day we went out there she tried to play the piano for us. But she had to give up. She couldn't. She was feeling so bad. They were going to take a trip to Florida. Then, Hall predicted, she would forget about the dog and everything would be all right. She was very fond of that dog, and you couldn't touch her when he was around."

*THE trials and tribulations of Nan Patterson, the handsome alumna of the "Florodora" sextette who accompanied Cæsar Young on what proved to be his last ride.*

"IT MAY BE HUMAN GORE": III

# THE MYSTERY OF THE HANSOM CAB

IT was in 1905 on May third, my dears, that, for the second and last time, the case of the People of the State of New York (ever a naïve litigant) against Nan Randolph Patterson was entrusted to the deliberations of an infatuated jury. After being locked up all night, they tottered from the juryroom to report that they, like the susceptible twelve who had meditated on the same case six months before, were unable to decide whether or not this handsome wench was guilty of having murdered Cæsar Young. At that report the exhausted People of the State of New York threw up their hands and, to the cheers of a multitude which choked the streets for blocks, Nan Patterson walked out of the Criminal Courts Building into American legend.

It was in the preceding June that the killing had been done. Cæsar Young, that was a *nom de guerre,* his real name was Frank Thomas Young—was a gay blade of the racetracks, a bookmaker, gambler, and horseman, personable, rich, gen-

204

erous, jovial, English. For some two years he was enchained
by the loveliness of this Nan Patterson, a brunette, pompa-
doured, well-rounded show-girl from the sextette of a *Florodora* road company. He had picked her up on a train bound
for California where, according to testimony which later put
all manner of ideas into Eastern heads, they spent several
days together in what must have been a singularly liberal-
minded Turkish Bath. But by the spring of 1904 he had returned penitent to the bosom of his wife and, for a healing
voyage of reconciliation, the Youngs booked passage on the
*Germanic,* due to sail from her pier at the foot of West Ful-
ton Street at 9:30 on the morning of June 4.

On the night before, they had come in from Sheepshead
Bay after the fifth race and taken lodging for the night with
Mrs. Young's sister in West 140th Street. Indeed that last
evening, Young's life was fairly swarming with in-laws, all
bent, I suspect, on seeing that this, their Cæsar, should not
change his mind at the last moment and run back to that
dreadful Patterson woman. At seven next morning Young
jumped out of bed, dressed, and sallied forth, explaining to
his wife that he needed a shave and a new hat and would
meet her on the pier not later than nine o'clock. He never
kept that appointment and, too late to get her heavy luggage
off the boat, poor Mrs. Young decided to let it go on without
her.

Young never reached the pier because, at ten minutes before nine, just as the hansom he had picked up in Columbus
Circle was rattling along West Broadway near Franklin
Street, he was shot through the chest. The cabman, although
subsequently disinclined to recall having noticed anything
at all that morning, was at the time sufficiently alert to draw
up in front of a drug store. Passersby who hurried forward
found within the cab a dying man. Oddly enough the pistol
which had killed him lay hot in the pocket of his own coat
and he had fallen forward across the knees of the fair creature

who was sharing the cab with him. Nan, for it was she, was extremely emotional and clasping her hands in supplication to the Deity, exclaimed (with admirable presence of mind, the State afterwards contended), "Cæsar, Cæsar, why did you do this?"

In the following November, the American people settled back to enjoy a real good murder trial, with Nan's face pale in the shade of a vast black picture hat, with her aged father, a patriarch superbly caparisoned with white mutton-chop whiskers, sitting beside her and kissing her in benediction at the end of every session. For the State appeared the late William Rand, who looked rather like Richard Harding Davis in those days. He was a brilliant advocate, although in talking to a jury, the tobacco-chewing members of the bar would tell you, he did rather suggest an English squire addressing the tenantry. For the defense the humbler Abraham Levy had been retained—the mighty Abe Levy who looked like a happy blend of cherub and pawnbroker and who, as the most adroit and zestful practitioner of the criminal law in this country, was called for the defense in more than three hundred homicide cases. The foreman of the first jury was the late Elwood Hendrick, eventually Professor Hendrick of Columbia, if you please, but—marvelous in this restless city— still living in 1930 in the East Fortieth Street house which he gave as his address on that day when Nan, after looking him sternly in the eye, nodded to her counsel as a sign that he would do as a juror for her.

The aforesaid American people, fairly pop-eyed with excitement, were at first defrauded. On the tenth day of the proceedings, one of the jurors succumbed to apoplexy and the whole verbose, complicated trial had to be started all over again. This form of mishap occurs so often in our courts that there is considerable backing now for a proposed law to provide a thirteenth juror who should hear all the testimony but be called on for a vote only in such an emergency. Roughly the idea is that every jury ought to carry a spare.

In the testimony it was brought out that Nan, aided by her sister and her sister's husband, had in that last spring worked desperately to regain a hold over her once lavish lover, trying every trick from hysterics to a quite fictitious pregnancy. On the night before the murder they had spent some clandestine time together in what was supposed to be a farewell colloquy. It was begun late in the evening at Flannery's saloon in West 125th Street, with one of Mrs. Young's plethora of watchful brothers-in-law sitting carefully within earshot. Nan had reached the morbid stage of predicting darkly that Cæsar would never, never sail next day. Profanely, he taunted her with not even knowing on what boat his passage was booked. Indeed he tossed a hundred-dollar bill on the beer-stained table and offered to lay it against fifty cents that she could not name the ship.

"Cæsar Young, Cæsar Young," she made answer, while abstractedly pocketing the stakes, "Cæsar Young, there isn't a boat that sails the seas with a hold big enough or dark enough for you to hide in it from me tomorrow morning."

Between two and three on the morning of the fourth, they parted—unamicably. Indeed there was testimony to the effect that at the end he called her by an accurate but nasty name, slapped her in the mouth, and threatened to knock her damned block off. It was the more difficult for the State to surmise how a few hours later they ever came together in that hurrying and fatal hansom. It was 7:20 when he left his wife in West 140th Street. It was not yet nine when he was shot at the other end of the city. Nor was all of that brief time at Nan's disposal. For the new hat was on his head when he was killed. And somewhere, somehow he had also paused for that shave.

There were sundry such *lacunæ* in the State's case. The

pistol had been sold the day before in a pawnshop on Sixth
Avenue but the proof that it had been bought by Nan's sister
and her husband was far from water-tight. Anyway the jury
must have been left wondering why, if these people had all
been battening on Cæsar Young, they should have wished so
golden a goose slain. Another weakness was Young's general
rakishness. But the State's chief weakness, of course, was Nan
herself. She was such a pretty thing.

The strength of the State's case lay in the fact that it seemed
physically impossible for anyone else to have fired the pistol.
The direction of the bullet, the powder marks, the very
variety of the trigger-action all pointed only to her. To the
ill-concealed rapture of the reporters, a skeleton was trundled
into court as a model whereby to convince the jury that Cæsar
Young would have had to be a contortionist to have pulled
the trigger himself, as Nan implied he did. Of course she
was not sure of it. It seems she was looking dreamily out of
the window at the time and was inexpressibly shocked at his
having been driven so desperate by the thought of a parting
from her.

It is needless to say that Mr. Levy, who managed to suggest that he was just a shabby neighbor of the jurors, seeking to rescue a fluttering butterfly from the juggernaut of the
State, made the most of that "Cæsar, Cæsar, why did you do
this?" At such a time, could this cry from the heart have been
studied?

"Is there a possibility," Mr. Levy argued, "that within two
seconds after the shot, she could have been so consummate an
actress as to have been able deliberately to pretend the horror
which showed itself in her face at that moment? Do you believe that this empty—frivolous, if you like—pleasure-loving
girl could conceive the plot that would permit her at one second to kill, and in the next second to cover the act by a
subtle invention? Why, it passes your understanding as it
does mine. My learned and rhetorical and oratorical and bril-

liant friend will tell you that this was assumed. My God, you are all men of the world. You are men of experience. Why, you would have to pretend that this girl possessed ability such as has never been possessed by any artist that ever trod the boards, not even by the emotional Clara Morris, not even by the great Rachel, not even by Ristori, not even by Mrs. Leslie Carter!"

Reader, if you are faintly surprised to find the name of Mrs. Carter in that climactic spot, consider that it may have been a delicate tribute to her manager, Mr. Belasco, who was attending the trial as a gentleman (*pro tem*) of the press. Then, as always, the Wizard's interest in the human heart and his warm compassion for people in distress took him often to murder trials, especially those likely to be attended by a good many reporters.

Mr. Levy's "learned and rhetorical friend" was not impressed. Indeed, he could not resist pointing out that Levy himself, while no Edwin Booth precisely, nor any Salvini either, had just read that very line with considerable emotional conviction.

"It does not require the greatness of histrionic talent," Mr. Rand said dryly, "to pretend that something has happened which has not."

Mr. Levy referred a good deal to Nan's dear old dad sitting there in court and, to play perfectly safe, he also read aloud from Holy Writ the episode of the woman taken in adultery. The jury disagreed.

The State tried again in the following April, moving the case for trial this time before Justice Goff, perhaps in the knowledge that, despite his saintly aspect, that robèd terror to evil-doers could be counted on to suggest to the jury, by the very tone of his voice, that hanging was too good for Nan. In his final argument, Colonel Rand was magnificent. In after years at the civil bar he argued in many cases of far greater importance and it was always one of the minor irritations of his distinguished life that laymen everywhere always tagged him as the man who prosecuted Nan Patterson. This gaudy prestige even followed him overseas when he was a high-ranking member of the Judge Advocate's staff stationed at Chaumont for the prosecution of those of us in the A.E.F. who were charged with cowardice, rape, insubordination, and other infractions of the military code.

"Oh, gentlemen, gentlemen," cried Mr. Rand in his peroration, reaching at last his guess at the scene in the hansom cab. "We are near the end, we are near the end now. Going back to revisit his early home and his old friends, a richer, stronger, heartier man than Cæsar Young that morning you shall not find. But the harvest of the seed he had sown was still to be reaped and the name of the reaper was Nan Patterson. And his companion, what were her thoughts? What were her reflections as she sat there by his side? One call, you may be sure, was insistent in her thoughts. One call she heard again and again. 'You have lost, Nan, you have lost. The end has come, your rival has triumphed, the wife has won. The mistress has lost, lost her handsome, generous lover. No more riots, no more love with him. He is going back, he is going back. Cæsar is going back, Nan. Back, back, to his first love. Back to his true love. Cæsar is going back, Nan. Back, back to the woman who had shared his poverty, who had saved his money, who has adorned his wealth. Back. Cæsar is going back to the wife he had sworn before God to love, honor and cherish.' Oh, if she had doubts, they vanished then; then she saw red; then the murder in her heart flamed into action, and she shot and killed. A little crack, a puff of smoke, a dead man prostrate on a woman's knee, the wages of sin were paid!"

Thus the District Attorney. But again the jury disagreed and after a few days he moved for a quashing of the indictment. It was immediately announced that Nan would be starred in a musical show called *The Lulu Girls*. It opened a fortnight later in Scranton, Pennsylvania, and got as far as Altoona, where, although billed by that time as *A Romance of Panama,* it quietly expired. Shortly thereafter Nan was re-married, after a lively vacation, to an early husband from whom she had been obscurely divorced. She then vanished from the newspapers, although there occasionally finds its way into print a legend that she is living in Seattle a life given over to good deeds and horticulture.

Ten years ago an elderly and indignant washerwoman living in a shanty in White Plains found herself surrounded one morning by a cordon of reporters and photographers all conjured up by a fanciful and self-sprung rumor that she was Nan Patterson. The White Plains *blanchisseuse* was furious, as it seems she was not Nan Patterson at all. Why, she had never been in a hansom cab or a Turkish Bath in all her life. She had never even been in *Florodora.*

*HOW a comely harlot from the State of Maine was slain in a quaint New York bordello and how James Gordon Bennett, the Elder, profited thereby.*

"IT MAY BE HUMAN GORE": IV

# LA BELLE HÉLÈNE AND MR. B.

WHEN, on a midsummer night in 1912, in response to a gesture of annoyance from the late Lieutenant Charles Becker, four happy-go-lucky young mercenaries from the underworld drove up to the Hotel Metropole in Times Square, summoned one Herman Rosenthal from a supper table inside, plugged him full of lead as he came out to meet them, and then drove off into the maze of the city, it so happened that your correspondent, a nighthawk of parts in those days, was within ear-shot. I shall always remember the picture of that soft, fat body wilting on the sidewalk with a beer-stained tablecloth serving as its pall. I shall always remember the fish-belly faces of the sibilant crowd which, sprung in a twinkling from nowhere, formed like a clot around those clamorous wounds. Just behind me an old-timer whispered a comment which I have had more than one occasion to repeat. "From where I stand," he said, "I can see eight murderers."

I have often been prompted since to wonder, in studying the faces around a dinner table, let us say, or at a concert, how many present were marked for seeing eyes with the primal eldest curse. Rather more, I fancy, than the average man suspects. Of course, it is a commonplace of the police dockets in every great modern city that many more murderers walk the streets unmolested than are ever brought to book by man-made law. This calculable number must be swelled each year by the vast list of those murders which are success- fully masked as natural deaths. Indeed, of all the maxims in the copybook, the one set down with the least warmth of con- viction is the feeble warning that murder will out. It is just a futile finger which we law-abiding folk shake at our less trammeled neighbors in much the same spirit that a nurse- maid warns her charges about the goblins which will get them if they don't watch out. In much the same spirit, and with about the same confidence of success.

Which bloody reflections were prompted when Russel Crouse called his eminently readable collection of twelve good stories and true under the title *Murder Won't Out*. It is a curi- ous pageant of the unavenged, a procession headed by poor Elma Sands, who, living or dead, was thrown down the well in Lispenard's meadow the year Washington died. Starr Faithfull brings up the rear. This ghostly review is a reminder that the murderer of Dot King may be someone you saw in a restaurant last night, and that the man who killed Elwell— we can be reasonably sure that it *was* a man who did it—still walks the unsuspecting streets. I wonder if, after all this time, long months can slip by without a thought of that cool slaugh- ter ever coming to his mind. Or does the memory of it still follow him around the city? When he hears a quickening step behind him, does he still sweat with his almost irresistible impulse to break into a run?

In some respects a unique interest attaches to the second item in Mr. Crouse's sorry dossier. This is the case of the lovely Helen Jewett. Her real name was Dorcas Doyen. She was a precocious harlot from Augusta, Maine, whose brief but storm-tossed career was brought to an end early on an April Sunday in 1836 when someone killed her with an ax and set fire to her bed in the brothel which Rosina Townsend used to run at 41 Thomas Street, New York. She had already caused a considerable stir, for her beauty appears to have been extraordinary, and she always made a point of wearing a striking gown of green silk when she attended the tragedies at the Park Theater, or when she took the air on the tree-shaded Broadway of her day. On such promenades she invariably carried a letter in her hand. It is the implication of the contemporary comment that this was the device of an artful minx seeking to suggest that her mission on the sidewalk was innocent, but Helen Jewett appears actually to have been a profuse correspondent. She was addicted, I am afraid, to embossed stationery tinted green or rose or blue or gold and, as one of the newspapers noted at the time, she did rather more business with the post office in the course of a year than many a brokerage house in Wall Street.

When her murder was discovered, suspicion immediately pointed to a lover of hers named Richard P. Robinson, a handsome jeweler's clerk, still in his teens, with whom, for two years past, she had been dallying in an amateur way. It was their idyllic custom to spend the long afternoons in the rustic bower behind Madame Townsend's house, reading the scandalous Lord Byron aloud to each other. This practice alone, one gathers from the moralists of the time, would account for all that followed. Of course young Robinson was hauled at once to the scene of the crime. His first remark on entering the room where the butchered girl lay on the charred bed will always endear him to connoisseurs of understatement. "This," he said, "is a bad business." Robinson, whose amorous night-life was prudently conducted under the sobriquet of Frank Rivers, was tried in July at the Court of

Oyer and Terminer. His defense was an elaborate alibi, somewhat impaired subsequently by the fact that his most helpful witness, an obliging grocer, drowned himself two years later by jumping off a boat in the bay. But that was long after the jury had acquitted Robinson, to the noisy approval of a hundred young blades of the town, who attended the trial clad in just such visored caps and romantical Spanish cloaks as "Pretty Frank" had always worn when squiring the "Girl in Green."

Of course the fair Jewett's taking off threw Little Old New York into something of a panic, for when, at three on that Sabbath morning, the first outcries of discovery brought the Watch on the run, a number of purseproud burghers were caught at Madame Townsend's in various states of informal attire. "The evidence in this trial," said the *New York Herald,* "and the remarkable disclosure of the manners and morals of New York is one of those events that must make philosophy pause, religion stand aghast, morals weep in the dust, and female virtue droop her head in sorrow. A number of young men, clerks in fashionable stores, are dragged up to the witness stand, but where are the married men, where the rich merchants, where the devoted church-members who were caught in their shirts and drawers on that awful night? The publication and perusal of the evidence in this trial will kindle up fires that nothing can quench." After nearly a century, one can hear, above all the hubbub, the tinkle of hush-money passing from hand to hand.

It is as a chapter in the history of New York journalism that the Jewett case retains its chief interest after a hundred years. It was so much catnip to "that ill-looking, squinting man," James Gordon Bennett, the Elder, who had launched his precious *Herald* only a year before, and who seized upon the murder of the pretty lady as a stimulus to circulation in much the same spirit that our *Mirror* was to exploit the mystery in De Russey's Lane many years later, when a parson and a choir singer would be found dead under a crabapple tree. What must have been a maddening hitch in Mr. Bennett's subscription campaign was a press-room accident which perversely occurred on the very day before the murder.

TO OUR READERS AND SUBSCRIBERS—We have to apologize to our patrons for the irregularity of the *Herald* yesterday—and probably today. The steam engine attached to the press from which the *Herald* is thrown off, broke a part of its machinery on Saturday, and we could not possibly get out earlier. The constant call for the *Herald,* yesterday, was beyond everything that ever was seen in New York. Single papers sold at a *shilling* each, in Wall Street. At our office, in the Clinton Building, corner of Beekman and Nassau street, *we never charge more than a cent.* We could have sold thirty thousand copies yesterday, if we could have got them worked.

We trust no more such accidents will take place.

The repair work appears to have been prompt for, while the *Sun,* and the *Courier & Enquirer,* and the *Journal of Commerce* frothed at the mouth, the *Herald,* being in the hands of a ravenous reporter, gained ten thousand in circulation, held the gain, and moved on to place and power. In those simpler (and, in some respects, happier) days, every publisher was his own Winchell, and you must picture the elder Bennett, note-book in hand, bustling off to the blighted bordello to make his own observations. If you can endure research without the consolations of tobacco, and if you do not balk at the prospect of an almost inevitable case of eye-strain, you will find rich entertainment awaiting you at the Public Library in the 1836 files of the *Herald* for those weeks when Helen Jewett's murder was the talk of the town. Let me give you a few samples of Bennett's reportorial style:

VISIT TO THE SCENE—Yesterday afternoon, about 4 o'clock, the sun broke out for a moment in splendor. I started on a visit to the scene at 41 Thomas-street. The excitement among the young men throughout the city was beginning to spread in all directions. The house is a large four-story elegant double one, painted yellow, and on the left hand side as you go to Hudson-street. It is said to be one of the most splendid establishments devoted to infamous intercourse that the city can show. I knocked at the door. A Police officer opened it, stealthily. I told him who I was. "Mr. B., you can enter," said he, with great politeness. The crowds rushed from behind seeking also an entrance.

"No more comes in," said the Police officer.

"Why do you let that man in?" asked one of the crowd.

"He is an editor—he is on public duty."

I entered—I pressed forward to the sitting-room or parlor.

After noting that it was "elegantly furnished with mirrors, splendid paintings, sofas, ottomans, and every variety of costly furniture," Mr. B. followed the police officer upstairs to Helen Jewett's room:

What a sight burst upon me! There stood an elegant double mahogany bed, all covered with burnt pieces of linen, blankets, pillows, black as cinders. I looked around for the object of my curiosity. On the carpet I saw a piece of linen sheet covering something as if carelessly flung over it.

"Here," said the Police officer, "here is the poor creature." He half uncovered the ghastly corpse. I could scarcely look at it for a second or two. Slowly I began to discover the lineaments of the corpse as one would the beauties of a statue of marble. It was the most remarkable sight I ever beheld—I never have, and never expect to see such another. "My God," exclaimed I, "how like a statue! I can scarcely conceive that form to be a corpse." Not a vein was to be seen. The body looked as white, as full, as polished as the purest Parian marble. The perfect figure, the exquisite limbs, the fine face, the full arms, the beautiful bust, all, all surpassed in every respect the Venus de Medici, according to the casts generally given of her.

Mr. B. was at his best in his superb particularity. The F.P.A. of that day would have rejoiced at the care with which he listed every title in the library of this booksy Aspasia, naming not only the copy of Lady Blessington's *Flowers of Loveliness* which was found in the smoldering bed and the copy of *Lalla Rookh* hidden under one of her shoes, but all her favorite authors, all the magazines she subscribed to, and (a point of natural interest to Bennett) even the dates on which her subscriptions had been renewed. He was at his happiest when cutting loose in a description of Rosina's place:

Eight young females of surpassing beauty and three or four ugly and horrible as sin, just by way of contrast, drew crowds of travelers, clerks, brokers, gentlemen, blackguards, fools, philosophers, night after night, to those splendid rooms, hung round with elegant paintings, and tastefully decorated with numerous ottomans, scarlet curtains, and other emblems of refinement and elegance. . . . Behind the pile of elegant yellow buildings was a garden decorated with elegant arbors, picturesque retreats, covered in the summer season with beautiful garlands, evergreens, flowers, and all the beauties of the vegetable world. Under the bright shining moon, climbing up the dark blue heaven, during the soft summer months these arbors would be filled with syrens and champaign, pine apples, and pretty *filles de joie,* talking, chattering, singing, and throwing out all the blandishments their talents could muster.

Hot-Cha!

Bennett got out the *Herald* almost single-handed. Sometimes this called for the agility of a contortionist. In our own time we are familiar with the two-faced effect achieved by journals of which the editorial pages can smugly deplore the morbid appetite for the lore of crime, even while the news columns are whetting and satisfying that appetite to satiety. But Bennett could blandly take up both positions in a single article.

Then in the matter of Robinson's trial he did change sides rather dizzily. Indeed it is difficult not to credit the *Sun's* angry charge that he was first influenced to defend "Pretty

Frank" by an offer of money, and then thrown into a pet by his inability to collect it. "Notwithstanding the puny and purchased efforts of a ricketty, tottering print" was the temperate way in which the *Transcript* put it, a characterization which is now a matter of record only because Bennett himself reprinted it and all its like with a gleeful insolence. Crooked or not, he had a flair for news and a magnificent vitality. That vitality built up a powerful newspaper as a legacy for his son. More than fourscore years after the murder at Madame Townsend's, the younger Bennett was still enjoying the profits created by the first, fine, small-town energy of Mr. B. By that time, of course, the softly bred son had become an empty, tyrannous, and grotesque old man who suffered his father's joy and pride to sicken from absenteeism, and left it at last to shiver on the doorstep of the world, exposed to the cold, damp wind called Frank A. Munsey.

*SOME account of the curious
gentry who kill and tell and some
report on the murder of the woman known as Old Shakespeare.*

"IT MAY BE HUMAN GORE": V

# MURDER FOR PUBLICITY

IN a recent June, New York was all agog about the ac-
tivities of a nameless citizen whose nocturnal practice
it was to go about shooting amorous motorists. Seemingly he then took up some other fad and, since no arrest
was ever made, he is already forgotten, so difficult is it for
even the most earnest of us to *stay* prominent in this distracted and distracting age.

The Queens murderer accompanied his misdeeds by a running commentary on them which took the form of pseudony-
mous communications to the *Evening Journal*. From these
one could not help gathering the impression that what he
really enjoyed in his killings was the stir they caused in the
public prints which obligingly fed his hunger for importance.
These, then, were murders for publicity, and only those who
are unfamiliar with the strongly conservative history of man-
slaughter will think that they import a new or puzzling
phenomenon. Both in their curious blend of sadism with
stern moral reproof, and in their eager bid for public recog-

220

nition, they belong in the same *dossier* with the works of Jack the Ripper and the amazing Doctor Cream.

These two werewolves, who prowled the terrified streets of London in the late eighties and early nineties, had this in common—that they both chose their victims from among the women whom the agitated journalists of the day identified as belonging to "the unfortunate class." Then neither could resist writing suggestive and taunting letters to the authorities. Indeed it was Doctor Cream's epistolary habits which finally put the noose around his neck. His exhibitionism was so strong that he went about pointing the finger of suspicion at himself.

It was Doctor Cream's curious custom to roam night-mantled London clad in an opera cape and silk hat and, thus caparisoned, to present little capsules of strychnine to the women he picked up. Unlike most sadists, he was content to absent himself austerely from the final agonies. But one may surmise that he chuckled in the distance. In the case of one intended victim who, as it happens, threw the capsule away, he also gave her theater tickets, apparently with the prankful notion that she should be tapped for Skull and Bones while at the play. But when, as sometimes happened, one of his successes would be ascribed to natural causes by the slovenly physicians, he seemingly felt frustrated and himself dropped the hints which led to the exhumation, the investigation, and his own eventual undoing. Jack the Ripper, who was never caught and never even identified, and Doctor Cream were adroitly blended by Mrs. Belloc Lowndes in her capital and breathlessly suspensive story called *The Lodger,* which belongs to this day in every firstrate library of criminal lore.

The history of Jack the Ripper has, by the way, an interesting American footnote which does not appear in any of the English chronicles of that terror. In 1891, shortly after the grisly series of Ripper murders came to an end in Whitechapel, a favorite London rumor insisted that the mysterious monster had taken ship for our shores and just then, in an unsavory waterfront dive here in New York, a woman was found with her throat cut from ear to ear and her body subjected to the same savage, expert, and pointed mutilation which had marked the Whitechapel murders. Naturally enough it was assumed that Jack the Ripper had advanced upon New York, and the newspapers here gave way to an ecstasy of apprehension.

For this killing, an Algerian named Ameer Ben Ali, but commonly known as Frenchy, was put on trial. Frenchy was prosecuted by that same Francis Wellman who wrote *The Art of Cross Examination*. And his defense was the first of the three hundred homicide cases which made Abe Levy famous in his day above all other lawyers in the old wives' tales of our criminal courts. During the trial, expert witnesses wrangled for days over the chemical analysis of the substance scraped from under Frenchy's fingernails when he was arrested. The State, in its role as manicure, sought to prove not only that this was human gore, but that it was the blood of someone who had recently dined on corned beef, cabbage, and cheese. A nice point. Frenchy was found guilty of second-degree murder, sent to jail for life, and subsequently pardoned.

The Frenchy case, famous in its day forty years ago but since largely forgotten, should, it seems to me, have a prominent place in American murder annals, if only for the felicitous proper names, ideal for melodrama, which were involved in it. Just as an obscure killing in Virginia in 1910 was swept momentarily into folklore because it took place on the Old Midlothian Turnpike, and in the same year the case of that wretched parson, Doctor Richeson, fascinated the entire country because the pretty choir girl he slew chanced to have the arresting name of Avis Linnell, so I think it might be argued that the world's interest in the Hall-Mills case was immeasurably enhanced by the romantical flavor of the phrase "De Russey's Lane."

The names in the Frenchy case were similarly consoling to the connoisseur. Sober homebodies under countless evening lamps shuddered delightedly over the interior economy of the East River Hotel, where no man was allowed to take a room alone, even if he had a quarter, for fear he would stay all night and thus cheat an outraged management out of a chance to rent it again and again in the same evening. But it was the names which held Mother and Father spellbound. There was, for instance, that interesting customer of the hotel, Miss Mamie Minatour. I wonder what ever became of her. And above all there was the victim herself, a raffish sexagenarian prostitute whose poor old body was claimed by a respectable daughter in Salem, Massachusetts, and taken there for burial. On the waterfront she had been variously known by two sobriquets. For reasons on which it is idle but pleasant to speculate, she was sometimes called Jeff Davis. But the commoner nickname, by which this dilapidated and jocular hag entered into legend, was Old Shakespeare.

*A WARNING to Mr. Chester-*
*ton that he should continue his*
*practice of contemplating the So-*
*viet experiment from the van-*
*tage point of his home in Top*
*Meadow, Beaconsfield, Bucks.*

YOUR CORRESPONDENT: I

# MOSCOW

## AN EXOTIC FIGURE IN MOSCOW

MOSCOW, NOVEMBER 1932.

I AM just back from Leningrad and the manager of the hotel has gone off again with my passport. He will brood over it for a week, entering all its fascinating vital statistics in a series of ledgers and in the process discovering —I should think without great surprise—that, although I have been away from Moscow three whole days, nothing has happened in the interval to alter the previously noted fact that I was born in Phalanx, N. J., of all places, on January 19, 1887. It is depressing to contemplate the amount of clerical labor and white paper which, during the past ten years, has been wasted in solemnly recording for the police archives of various countries a date of such scant historical significance.

There is one aspect of travel in the Soviet Union about which no one thought to warn me. Of course I had heard it would be bitter cold and it is true that already Moscow is festively mantled in snow. There is skating on the ponds which fringe the city and the small, pre-revolutionary sleighs (into which I can get only with the aid of several panting *tovarishchi* and a shoe-horn) are out today, busily threading, with gleeful urchin impudence, the baffled traffic of trucks and trams. When the curtain rises even at the pampered Art Theater, an Arctic blast sweeps out over the proletarian audience from the drafty reaches of the stage. But we don't call this cold in Quebec. At least, it seems no more than chilly to one who has ever waited for the last trolley on a street-corner in Utica, N. Y. I suppose it will get quite nippy in January, but as the citizenry has already resorted to fur coats, extra sweaters, tippets, mittens, and ear-muffs, I do not see what there is left for them to add in the event of a really brisk day.

Then on the eve of sailing I had asked an infatuated Communist if, in other respects besides temperature, I would find traveling in Russia uncomfortable. "Certainly not," he replied scornfully, "unless you are one of those who attach more importance to bugs than to spiritual values." Unfortunately it is the bugs that attach importance to me, but it is only fair to say that, after three weeks in this large and angry country, I have yet to encounter my first Russian insect.

But no one had warned me how disconcerting would be the daily experiences of a fat man in the Soviet Union. In this connection it is necessary for me to intrude upon you the fact that your correspondent verges on the portly. Therefore all readers who have been envisaging him as a young gazelle are in error. For candor in this matter, there is dignified literary precedent. When Mr. Shaw, lying sick in his prime, announced that his coffin might at least be followed through the streets of London by all the animals he had never eaten, Mr. Chesterton ventured to suggest that many humans would want to be represented in that sad cortège and that

he himself would be glad to substitute for one of the elephants.

Now every foreigner is used to being stared at in Moscow.
It is his clothes which betray him and it is no uncommon
thing for him to be stopped in the street and asked politely,
wistfully, even desperately, where he got them. But it is my
unfailing and often embarrassing experience that all Russians, young and old, whom I pass on the street not only
stare but halt in their tracks as though astounded and then
grin from ear to ear. This custom dislocated almost to disrup-
tion one detachment of the parading workers on the anniversary of the revolution. The good citizens nudge one another and hold hoarsely whispered conferences about me. The
less inhibited ones burst into shrieks of laughter. Of course
there be those among my friends who would say that the
man in the street in other countries is similarly affected by
the sight of me and is merely more self-controlled. Local
commentators are inclined to suggest that I owe this mild
but constant commotion to my striking resemblance to the
capitalist as he is always pictured in the Soviet cartoons. But
I myself am disposed to ascribe it more simply to the fact
that in the Soviet Union a man of girth is an exotic rarity.
Falstaff or even Mr. Pickwick, astroll on the Nevsky Pros-
pekt, would cause as much of a stir as a mastodon on Fifth
Avenue. And for the same reason.

I do not think I am being either fanciful or sententious
in associating this phenomenon of Soviet behavior with the
food shortage. The other day I was attending a cantata put
on by the children of the workers in a Moscow boot factory.
Spindle-shanked kids of eight or nine wove gravely about the
stage, all carrying red flags and singing what even they
seemed to regard as somewhat cheerless songs about the importance of tractors and the sheer beauty of machinery. I
fell into conversation with a jolly girl of ten who occupied
the adjoining seat and who was obviously more entertained

by me than by the efforts of her school-fellows up on the platform. She improved the occasion by taking a short English lesson. How, in America, did one say "Papa" and "Mamma"? And "Theater"? And "International"? And did Americans live in caves or in houses? I asked if she would like to go to New York and, after looking at me meditatively, she decided she would. "I think," she said, "that there must be plenty to eat there."

Then the other evening while I waited on a windswept doorstep for a friend to pick me up, one of a trio of young Communists—a lad of fifteen perhaps—reached out and patted my façade as he passed by. I feel sure this was not rudely done at all. The grin he gave me over his shoulder as he went on his way was somehow both envious and amiable. Not fond, exactly, but appreciative. That's the word for it. It was an *appreciative* grin. It seemed to say: "Ah, comrade, what a sequence of juicy steaks, what mugs of good beer, what mounds of lovely, golden butter, what poods of fine white bread must have gone into the making of that!"

Still, I am afraid Mr. Chesterton would better stay at home and think ruefully about the Middle Ages. He could visit the Soviet Union only at the risk of sending the entire population into hysterics.

*A PARABLE setting forth one traveler's reflections on the vestigial remains of inequality which, to the loud delight of all conservatives, one does encounter in the Soviet Union.*

## THE CORPORAL OF ST.-AIGNAN

MOSCOW, NOVEMBER 1932.

I HAVE been here long enough to learn what the major industry of Soviet Russia is. It is printing pictures of Stalin. You cannot walk ten minutes in any direction here without encountering twenty. His formidable image is so omnipresent as to provoke in all naturally mutinous hearts an impulse to go out into the Red Square, yell "Hurrah for good old Trotsky!" and see what happens. I myself am half-disposed to make this instructive experiment tomorrow, and if you do not hear from me again, you may assume that I did try it. Please see that my first edition of *David Copperfield* is given to the Hamilton College Library. But despite the Kremlin's implacable insistence, the person who has come oftenest to my perverse mind since I entered the Soviet Union is not Stalin, nor Lenin, nor even Karl Marx, but a minor historical figure to whom previously I had not given a thought in a dozen careless years. I refer to the Corporal of St.-Aignan. He is one of my favorite characters in unrecorded history, and if I give way now to a notion to tell his

229

small story, it is because it has, in this new retrospect, become fraught for me with luminous economic significance.

I should like if possible to quiet whatever apprehensions may have been aroused by that last phrase. It is true that the most appalling birdbrains are wont after three weeks in Moscow to think of themselves as authoritative economists. But on the boat coming over, an eminent publisher made me promise solemnly, over a magnum of champagne, to remember that the mere crossing of the Soviet frontier would not turn me into a Stuart Chase. And even without such an injunction, one soon learns here to share the local antipathy for sociological globe-trotters who, in the morose words of Brother Chamberlin of the *Christian Science Monitor,* "bustle into Russia, rush through a round of visits to model institutions, and bustle out again, feeling that the Soviet Union holds no more mysteries for them." I want to make it clear that my own brief visit here has cleared up only one of the economic mysteries of our day. Do you sometimes wonder whatever became of all those two-dollar bills which vanished from our circulation a few years ago? Well, I know. They came to Russia. Seen again after so long an interval, these forgotten émigrés look like rather dingy bathmats. Because they are honored in Washington, they are positively adored here, and there is no use trying to explain to a citizen that we consider them unlucky. Not when they can buy him a little extra milk for the baby, or permit him to indulge his aged mother in a debauch of butter.

To any American setting out for these parts, all his neighbors come around and say loftily: "Of course, you will see only what they want you to see." By that they mean that the Soviets, with shocking duplicity, put their best foot foremost and seek to make a good impression on the visitor from overseas. The rascals! Now I object to such warnings not only because they happen to be false but because they are intolerably smug. It is their implication that visitors to our own fair shores, instead of being led proudly to Niagara Falls and the Medical Center and the Hudson River Bridge, are taken at once to see the prison camps of the South and the home life of the West Virginian coal-miners. It would be a truer thing to say that when you go to Soviet Russia, you see only what *you* want to see. At the frontier the customs officials may check up sternly on the amount of good coffee, cockroach powder, and American tobacco you are sneaking into the country, but they never think to examine your prejudices. You bring them all in with you.

Except for a few such men from Mars as Walter Duranty, all visitors might be roughly divided into two classes: those who come here hoping to see the Communist scheme succeed, and those who come here hoping to see it fail. One thing gives the ghouls of the latter class tremendous pleasure. That is the abundant evidence that inequality not only exists here but is actually created by the Kremlin; that in order to stimulate production, the Government has thrown all manner of sops to the old Adam in the sluggish Muscovite heart. Admittedly, there are enormous differences, here as elsewhere, between the lot of the advantaged man and that of his less fortunately equipped comrades. Difference, not only in income, which may be quite immaterial, but in access to food, in freedom to move about, in opportunity, in space for living quarters. Why, there be those in Moscow who sleep six in a room, whereas the great Radek, who might be roughly identified as the Walter Lippmann of the U.S.S.R., has a penthouse all his own atop the largest building in Europe. But when you hear that some Russians live on the fat of the land while others are in want, it is important to keep in mind just how lean the fat of the land is at this difficult stage of what might be called, I suppose, the Mobile Experiment. Oh, yes, there are some teacher's pets. But even the luckiest of them remind me of the aforesaid corporal—one gets to the point at last—and in their presence we soft people who have been leading cushioned lives on the other side of the world know just how Sergeant Clutterbuck must have felt when he met up again with the corporal in the mud of St.-Aignan.

It was in the early weeks of 1918 that my friend Clutterbuck was a transient casual at St.-Aignan. That was the camp which vied with Brest for the distinction of being considered the sink-hole of the A.E.F. It was a shivery huddle of barracks and tents, pitched in an almost trackless sea of mud. The fortunes of war soon picked up my friend by the scruff of his gratified neck, dropped him lightly in Paris, and left him there for as pleasant a year as ever a man spent. He had a Ford truck, a wad of francs for rations, an apartment near the Invalides, and a comely mistress who demanded of him not jewels or fine raiment but only occasional slabs of sweet chocolate from the Y.M.C.A. canteen. I doubt if even General Pershing enjoyed the war more thoroughly or saw the Armistice signed with a profounder regret. During that halcyon year, Sergeant Clutterbuck used to remember St.-Aignan only in his nightmares, from which, I am told, he would awake with a shriek of horror. Certainly he never saw it again until he passed through in May 1919 on his way home. Then, the first person he encountered was a corporal whom he had left behind him in the mud more than a year before and who, in all that time, had never once escaped from the sink-hole. Clutterbuck's jaw dropped at the mere thought of such inequity in the distribution of this world's favors.

"My God," cried Clutterbuck, "have you been stuck here all this time?"

But the corporal, you see, had different standards.

"What do you mean 'stuck here'?" he replied. "Why, I'm sitting on the world. Got a wood floor in my tent and everything."

*A WHILOM reviewer of plays
along Broadway goes to the theaters in Moscow and recognizes,
with some difficulty, such old
friends as Hamlet, Topsy, and
Annie Rooney.*

COMRADE WOOLLCOTT GOES TO THE PLAY

MOSCOW, NOVEMBER 1932.

A HAMLET in which the sweet prince was presented as
a burly rascal scheming to supplant his uncle! A
*Hamlet* in which the fair Ophelia (only fair, if you
ask me) emerged as a pliant hussy whose potentialities for
mischief were brought to an abrupt end when she got drunk
and fell in the brook! This I saw with my own eyes last
night. And knew, when the final curtain fell, that I had just
been reminded of a few forgotten things about Elsinore and
Monte Carlo, about princes and revolutionists, about gam-
blers and doctrinaires. And had even learned a thing or two,
perhaps, about Soviet Russia. But first let me go back a little
way.

On a brisk afternoon last week I skated and skidded my
way along the snowy streets of Moscow with a box-party I
had myself somewhat wildly assembled. I do not recall ever
having seen a more violently variegated cluster of playgoers.
First there was a distinguished Franco-Prussian Jew who had
been born in Corpus Christi, Texas, and who was a cousin
of that most monstrously victimized scapegoat of our time,

233

Captain Dreyfus. Then there was a swarthy, keen, and elegant young Oxford graduate whose father was an eminent Celestial and whose mother was a dusky native of Trinidad, himself therefore a living reminder that, in flagrant defiance of Rudyard Kipling, East and West do get together once in a while. Also, there was his wife, an exquisitely fair, fragile, and attractive Russian girl, who will persist in practicing her Chinese and English on him when he would rather talk Russian to her.

The play that afternoon was a self-inflicted agony about miscegenation by our own Eugene O'Neill, a tragedy known in this country as *All God's Chillun Got Wings* but here called *The Negro* and played in Russian—its Negro roles being performed by able young Muscovites with the aid of considerable burnt cork. In the intervals for scene changes, there would also be American songs to create the proper atmosphere. With a perceptible start I recognized one old favorite of my childhood even when disguised as "Onnie Roaney." But if you have never chanced to hear Russian troubadours lifting their voices in Negro spirituals, the more pensive ballads of Irving Berlin, and "Bon-Bon Buddy, the Chocolate Drop," let me console you with the assurance that you have not suffered an intolerable æsthetic privation.

It is characteristic of the Russian stage that in vitality, resourcefulness, and creative imagination, this Kamerny Theater realization of O'Neill's play made its original New York production look like thirty kopecks. It is perhaps characteristic of me that, with the food shortage and the grotesquely misrepresented Five-Year Plan lying just outside the door and fairly aching for comment, I should have been huddled cozily indoors, inspecting life at second-hand.

At that, I am not sure I did not learn more about the Mobile Experiment from attending a dozen theaters in Moscow and Leningrad than I would have done by journeying to the Dnieperstroy Dam in the manner of the more sociological globe-trotters and staring fixedly at its grandiose proportions. Even one who, in decent if exceptional humility, has no notion that four weeks in Soviet Russia will turn him into an authoritative economist, may discover, when he gets home, that he has brought back some thoughts on the subject, even as you may find some sand in your shoes after you have come home from the seashore.

Well, during the intermission we all dropped in on the director, the brilliant and engaging Alexander Tairov, whose working quarters—office, studio, what you will—have a greater dignity, graciousness, and beauty than I ever found in the settings of our own impresari. He gave us tea and raisin cake and wrung from me the promise to send him the score and libretto of this Pulitzer Prize-winning work called *Of Thee I Sing,* of which the tickling rumors had apparently reached Moscow some time before. He already knew it was a saucy derision of the circus of American politics. If he were to produce it in Moscow, he said, he would, of course, be able to sharpen the satire considerably. He could not have been expected to know that its satire was already sharper than a serpent's tooth. It could never have occurred to him that, being notoriously crushed under the feet of their capitalist masters, the authors of that impudent harlequinade had really said precisely what they wanted to.

You see, there had been nothing in Tairov's experience under the Tsar or under the Soviets to make him think it would be possible anywhere for a political satirist to have a free hand. He could not imagine it any more than the urchin authors of *Of Thee I Sing* could imagine functioning at all in a country where any playwright who took such liberties with the Kremlin as were taken by them with the poor old White House would be shot at sunrise.

The Russian stage, with such superb organizations as the Kamerny, the Vakhtangov, and the Moscow Art Theaters, is, I suppose, the finest and most flexible instrument of its kind in the world, just waiting, like the bow of Ulysses, for a great dramatist to come along and bend it to his uses. But there is, I think, no such dramatist even in sight and, as things have been and still are, there could not be. Without going here into the anxious question whether, as the Russians say, our own boasted freedom means nothing more than the poor privilege of starving to death on a park bench, it is impossible to characterize the theater in Moscow without mentioning as its most salient characteristic the fact that it is not free. In a country where everything belongs to the State, including the radio, the stage, and the printing press, every publication partakes of the nature of a house-organ, and you would no more look to the theater for the unpacking of hearts oppressed than you would expect to find revolutionary sentiments in the court circular issued from St. James's, or to find pacifist propaganda in the *Army and Navy Journal*.

I do not mean to suggest that Stalin personally runs through the manuscript of every tragedy submitted. That is not necessary. So essentially craven is the average person (in Russia as well as America) that most human institutions are self-censoring. All small people, whether they be privates in an army or underlings on a newspaper, strive to guess what the big chief is going to want and act accordingly. More than most human institutions, the theater in all lands and times has tended to be servile, fawning at the foot of the tyrant, whether the tyrant was a dictator like Mussolini or a mob like the Broadway public. Thus, during 1917 and 1918 in the land of the free, Newton Baker, as Secretary of War, did not have to come to Broadway and see that, in the interests of the martial spirit, all the Germans in the play should be treacherous spies and unspeakable bullies. The theater took care of that unbidden. By the same token, the priests, nuns, and landlords in the new Russian plays are usually represented as horrid vulpine wretches, without specific orders to that effect having been issued from on high.

You see, the kind of special pleading we stigmatize as propaganda is, for the most part, self-starting. But the state of mind and political control that foments it cannot, at the same time, nourish that freedom of spirit without which no first-rate play, from *The Trojan Women* to *The Front Page,* was ever written. And although Stalin himself has recently called the heresy-sniffers to heel so that such lovely and gently rueful old plays as *The Cherry Orchard* are being acted once more without any interference from the witch-burners—acted, mind you, before keen, ravenously attentive audiences, but audiences so drawn in this transition period from two régimes that you will find the young people laughing a little patronizingly at scenes which move their elders to tears—although, I say, these hungry theaters have access to the classics, I must remind you that even the classics can be twisted to serve the purposes of the new idea.

Not all of them need much twisting. *Uncle Tom's Cabin,* for instance, does pretty well as it is. The most fanatical Marxist could scarcely ask a more satisfying picture of private property at its foulest. I saw it in Moscow one afternoon at a matinée when all the children from one of the schools were turned loose in the theater. They enjoyed it no end, and were simply delighted (as I was) when Legree was slain in time for the final curtain. Their interest was so intense that they all co-operated in inducing quiet in the auditorium by yelling "Silence!" at the top of their lungs. There were some changes even in *Uncle Tom.* For reasons still unexplained, Little Eva, as a character, was replaced by a warm-hearted and buxom young woman named Dora, who brought to the part the most pleasing underpinnings I have seen in Russia. But George and Eliza, Tom himself, a character named Tawpsee—you remember Tawpsee, who just grow'd—and even the bloodhounds, were much as I had always known them. When Legree said there was no more sense in educating a nigger than in putting a corset on a pig, and the audience laughed in pleased proletarian scorn of such capitalistic goings-on, I did suspect that there had been some recent retouching of the manuscript. But for the most part, the audience did its own twisting. Thus, when George and Eliza ran away to Canada, but good, pious old Tom took all his oppression meekly and bet instead on God, the American audiences in my youth used to weep with sympathetic admiration. But, having heard at school that religion was the opiate of the people, the small Muscovites all laugh contemptuously at his spiritless gullibility.

But you might think of *Hamlet* as less nourishing to such special prejudices. That would certainly be true of *Hamlet* as we may guess that Shakespeare himself imagined it, and true also of *Hamlet* as most of us have seen it acted. But the author of any living play always has two incalculable and ever-changing collaborators, the acting company and the audience, and over his dead body (as you might say), without actually altering a word, they can so rewrite his tragedy that he himself would never recognize it.

Once an old Meany of the press, in his comment on some actor's début as the melancholy one, said that scholars should have kept watch beside the graves of Shakespeare and Bacon the night before to see which one of them turned over. On the night when *Hamlet* was first presented at the Vakhtangov Theater, I think the author must have done more than merely turn over. He must have spun in his grave like a top.

My own reactions to it were less violent. Wedged into the keen, threadbare, turbulent horde from the particular boot-factory which had reserved the theater for that evening, I was both engrossed and profoundly impressed by this Muscovite *Hamlet* with its astounding distances, with its great sweep of masonry, and with its lovely pageantry of costume. I never saw it bettered as a sheer festival for the eye. In reporting on it now, I must try to avoid a too slovenly use of

the word "they." I have been asked what I thought of the
way "they" do *Hamlet* in Russia as if the entire population
of the seven Soviet Republics, with Stalin himself making it
unanimous, had decided on this particular perversion of the
text. Of course it is only one director's notion of how that
text might be slightly distorted to adjust it to the Marxist
ideology, if I may fall for a moment into the horrid lingo
of sociological debate. When Akimov proudly presented his
effort in Moscow, the critics, with a freedom their little American brothers do not invariably enjoy, all fell upon it with a
single descriptive term. I do not happen to know the Russian
word for "lousy" (I have reason to believe they must have
one), but whatever it is, the critics resorted to it.

Akimov, the Belasco of the Vakhtangov, started out with
a simple premise. Since *Hamlet* is a play of court intrigue
with all its leading characters either royal or the hangers-on
of royalty, they must all have been mean swine without a
single creditable motive in the lot. Not only was Claudius
a villain, having slain his brother to get the throne, but even
young Hamlet could have been no great shakes. You see, he
was no member of the proletariat, no son of a worker, but,
by the inevitable corruption of his upbringing, a parasite
like the rest of them and, in the exposure of his father's murderer, probably inspired, if the truth were known, by no
loftier motive than an unvoiced desire to get the throne for
himself. With that somewhat partisan premise as a starter,
Akimov rings a hundred changes on the resentful old classic.
I must content myself with mentioning two of them. I could
tell you how he transforms the ghost into a little spoil-sport
device of Hamlet's for starting the ball rolling against the
king. I could irritate you with an account of the care he takes
to cast Hamlet as a prince who really was "fat and short
of breath" and burdened with "too, too solid flesh." I could
numb you with the pedantry of his reasons for splitting the

"To be or not to be" soliloquy into a dialogue with Horatio and ascribing part of it to Erasmus. But I promise to limit myself to two scenes.

In one of the first colloquies of the guilty couple, it is Akimov's notion to have the queen watch while the king poses for his portrait—poses resplendent and awe-inspiring on a platform in a great golden robe of state, with retainers propping him up and easing with their hands the heavy burden of his crown and ball and scepter. Then at a point in the dialogue when the king grows restive, he wriggles out of his costume and leaves all his panoply standing there, a hollow shell, while he himself is suddenly revealed for the poor little spindle-shanked thing he really is. "You see, you see," the play seems to say, "kings were ever thus. What fools men were to grovel before them!" Art under the Soviets is disposed to be thus sententious.

Then please follow Akimov for a moment in his reasons for having Ophelia drowned while in her cups. The argument runs something like this. When *Hamlet* was written, madness was considered pretty comical. Just as the Duchess of Milan used to keep a few hunchbacks around the house because she thought them amusing spectacles, so she also kept mentally misshapen creatures on her staff because it was the fad of that age to think them funny, too. And when Elizabeth was queen of England, it was the style for the court gallants to drive out to Bedlam of a pleasant Sunday afternoon to have a good laugh at the lunatics. Therefore, says Akimov, to the groundlings and to the fancy folk of the first audience that ever attended *Hamlet,* Ophelia's mad scene must have been played for its comedy values. To preserve those values, a twentieth-century audience would need some equivalent. Perhaps the sight of Ophelia with her wits bemused by a swig of vodka would do the trick. No sooner said than done. Well, that, I believe, is the argument. And there is only one thing the matter with it. It overlooks the fact that the author of *Hamlet* was a timeless being, un-bound by the limitations of his contemporaries. To them the poor, crazed Ophelia may have been a real good joke. But she was no joke to Shakespeare.

Plunged in meditation on the way back to my hotel—in the present shortage there is still abundant food for *thought* in Russia—I suddenly recalled an old crony of my salad days with whom I used to engage in nightly jousts at an insidious game called Poker Patience. In these contests, which were conducted for a modest sum, we ran neck and neck for several weeks, until once in the middle of a restless night, there popped into my opponent's head a scheme for playing the game in such a way that he would infallibly beat me. Thereafter he lost steadily, stubbornly attributing each defeat to capricious mischance, and not discovering the factor he had overlooked in his calculations, not discovering the mathematical hole in his scheme, until, I am happy to say, I was several hundred dollars ahead. You see, he was playing a system in his gambling with the lords of chance, and there is a high, alarming cliff at Monte Carlo which is proverbially the place for the last despairing leap of those who do just that and then find out that their little scheme was not watertight after all.

It was Akimov's direction of Ophelia's mad scene which made me recognize him as a man who was playing a system —and not him alone, but all these Kremlinites who, with the grim relentlessness of Calvinists, still have a great milling multitude in thrall. I suppose we are all holding our breaths until we find out if there be a hole in their system too, holding our breaths with some prayerful anxiety, mind you, because, for weal or woe, the outcome concerns us all. The least we can say is that the hapless Russians are the guinea pigs of a great scientific experiment, and whether we are to profit from it by positive or negative example, whether the remedy discovered by those doctors be a deadly poison or another insulin, is the question to which only children yet unborn will really know the answer.

It takes Moscow to send a playgoer away from the theater thinking just like an editorial in *The New Republic*. I confess a faint relief when, in Leningrad, I found at least one entertainment that was not fraught with any significance whatever. In this respect, you cannot trust even the music halls. At the Music Hall in Moscow, the brilliant extravaganza I witnessed did more than trample on the Christian faith. It executed a war dance on the Christian faith. But there was at least one show I saw without so much as a single implication. That was the circus. Its clowns and its acrobats and its animals speak a language that gives the interpreter a night off. In all its tricks and its manners it recognizes no frontier, and has not yet heard about the twentieth century. I could describe the one in Leningrad without changing a word by just cribbing Huckleberry Finn's own account of the one he attended down the Mississippi long ago.

Afterwards I told the comrade in charge of all such light-minded entertainment in Soviet Russia that there were really three great internationals—the Comintern, the Church of Rome, and the circus. I dropped my idle remark in his office. At my grouping of his humble province in such imposing company, he started to laugh with sheer pleasure and then, apparently because there were several people listening and little pitchers have big ears, he hastily disassociated himself from such levity and recalled his chuckle in mid-air.

FOOTNOTE: It might illustrate the peculiar tang imparted to the most frolicsome entertainments in Moscow were I to describe here the above-mentioned extravaganza at the Music Hall. This is the piece called *The 14th Division Enters Heaven*. It might be roughly compared to a blend of an American burlesque show with *What Price Glory*. After the lights have winked out in the theater and before the curtain rises, the balcony, which embraces the audience in a horseshoe curve, is suddenly invaded by a German priest who starts haranguing. Instantly, at a point opposite, a Russian priest appears and also starts haranguing.

Then, one at a time, first a German, then a Russian, soldier, comes into play. Each crouches, each lifts a gun. Finally there are five Russian soldiers aiming at five German soldiers, each group exhorted by a man of God in the same words to kill the other. With that unanswerable prologue the curtain rises and, after a bawdy and comical deathbed scene, the plot mounts to Heaven and one meets, as low comedy characters, the Magdalene, the Virgin Mary, God the Son, and God the Father. Christ is represented as a blond and willowy androgyne in tight blue-satin trousers and silver spats, with a red rose stuck roguishly in his halo. The ladies of the heavenly host are frankly relieved when word comes from the earth that Rasputin has been slain in Moscow and will soon be up. Then the entire 14th Division, due to some calamitous Russian generalship, is wiped out on the battlefield and arrives in a body. This news is less welcome as they strain the resources of the heavenly bureaucracy and, incited by the revolution in Petrograd below, immediately seize the heavenly government. I think the librettist most enjoyed writing that moment in the dialogue when the Commissar examines the local hierarchy on their right to existence. What, for instance, had God ever done? The old gentleman replies with legitimate pride that he had made the earth. But the next question stumps him. What had he done before that? There is a pause, hideous in its embarrassment. You see, he doesn't know. In the ensuing confusion all the characters go into a dance and the curtain comes down on a roar of conscientious proletarian laughter.

*WHEREIN a circumspect visitor to the Soviet Union, on finding himself safely beyond reach of the ferrule, celebrates that discovery by making a face at teacher.*

## THE RETREAT FROM MOSCOW

WARSAW, DECEMBER 1932.

OF course, not every tourist leaving Moscow can expect to have the prettiest girl in town come down to the station and kiss him good-by. Such a boon rewards only those who have given some thought to the small-change of gallantry, which varies from country to country and from time to time. I suppose that in New York one still woos a fair lady's smiles with candy, orchids, and perhaps an occasional wrist-watch. Then I remember that in Peking the guest who was dearest to the harried hostess was the one who had thought to bring her fifty pounds of cleanly ice. But other countries, other currencies. If I found favor with the lovely Muscovite, it was because I had discovered in my duffle just the packet for her. No doubt the late Mrs. Reginald Wilfer would have said I was paying her an indelicate attention, but she herself had no such qualms. She clasped the tender token to her bosom and cried out with unintentional accuracy: "Ah, I am so exciting!" To those of my countrymen who plan visiting the Soviet Union in the near future, my final advice is to say it with toilet-paper.

244

The night-ride to the frontier was uneventful. I shared a compartment with a black-a-vised French Communist who wore plus-fours and puce-colored underwear. As I was nimble enough to pop into the lower berth before he could say Jean Robinson, he was driven into retreat in the upper one, from which dim-lit eyrie he would stick out his head from time to time to ask me hopefully how many strikes were now in progress in New York. Once when I snorted with laughter over the book I was reading—a feeble detective story by William Le Queux—he wanted to know what the joke was, but I despaired of making clear why I was amused by this paragraph:

The head of a murdered woman was certainly an odd thing for a man to carry about in his luggage. The mystery had now assumed the magnitude of a veritable enigma.

Then at noon the next day, the neat, bustling, inexcusably cheerful station at Stolpce, Poland. The first cup of good coffee in weeks. Flagrantly trivial newspapers to read. And a great buoyancy of one's spirits. All returning travelers mention this curious lifting of the sense of oppression—sometimes unnoticed until it does lift, just as you realize how foul the air of a room has been only when you get a whiff from out-of-doors—this exhilarating relief which even one who has hugely enjoyed his stay in the Soviet Union does experience on quitting its territory. There is a good account of that experience in one of the essays on Russia by the incomparable John Maynard Keynes, the Britisher who wrote *The Economic Consequences of the Peace* and married Lydia Lopokova—in the order named, I believe.

There is nothing mysterious about it. Every man who was ever demobilized remembers this sensation of a recovered freedom. Freedom to sit on a park bench and starve, perhaps. But freedom, brothers, freedom. Or let me illustrate the sensation less portentously. Do you remember how in school it was the way of the more spirited youths to choose, when they had a choice, the back seats in the classroom? They wanted to sit as far as possible from teacher. Well, I fancy that the enveloping sense of restriction in the Soviet Union varies inversely with the distance from the inscrutable Kremlin. When I noticed—or thought I did—that, in comparison with Moscow, the people of Leningrad seemed somehow more carefree, I decided it was only because they were further away from teacher. Still within reach of the ferrule, of course. But further away.

I would not seem to suggest that the visitor from afar is treated even in Moscow with anything except the utmost consideration. But the most pampered foreigners at work there become infected by the surrounding unease. For instance, they usually avoid mentioning Stalin by name. You must guess whom they mean by some such subterfuge as His Nibs. We would be subject to a similar tension in New York if men at lunch together instinctively avoided talking out loud about Mr. Curry. A few days ago I was roaming the rooms of the Museum of Western Art, where they have an astounding collection of Van Goghs and Gauguins. I had come to a halt before an early Monet so fraught with an untranslatable nostalgia as fairly to liquefy the onlooker. A noted American specialist drifted towards me and passed on a rumor that had just arrived by the grapevine route from the Ukraine. Without visibly moving his lips, he whispered: "I hear that some of the kulaks down there have shot a few of the Y.M.C.A. boys." This struck me as an explicable if somewhat drastic action, and I did not learn until later that, in the discreet code used by Americans in Moscow, the term Y.M.C.A. means the secret police of the Gay Pay Oo. I suppose that if my friend the specialist had told me the news without recourse to the code and at the top of his lungs, there would really have been no untoward consequences for either of us. But just to play safe, one takes to walking softly in Moscow. Does that give you a clew to its atmosphere?

All the way here from the frontier, we devoured the newspapers. Russian journals making snoots at Stalin from across the border. Polish journals from Warsaw. Even an old copy of the London *Daily Mail* which had somehow found its way to Stolpce. It was not merely their holiday triviality which made them such refreshment. After weeks of high discourse on economic planning, after weeks of restriction to newspapers in which no item affecting less than a million lives could make the front page, and nothing more personal than a tractor could be mentioned at all, it was downright exciting to come upon gazettes in which the individual, as such, recovered his identity. For instance, we read with interest a dispatch from Rome reporting that Otto Kahn had killed himself by leaping from a high point of the Coliseum. He turned out to be a mere journalist of that name from Frankfort. Then the Buda-Pesth police announced with pleasure that they had cleared up the mystery of the disappearance during the past six months of some twenty-five local girls. They had all been found locked up in the apartment of a textile manufacturer who, the newspaper reported, had been "using them for the satisfaction of his anomalies." A different one for each? we wondered. And we guzzled the juicy testimony in the case of the brilliant young London surgeon whose name had been stricken from the Medical Register on the complaint of a Mr. B. This Mr. B. (so identified in the cautious British press) accused the doctor of having got gay with Mrs. B. Examined by his own counsel, the doctor denied adultery with Mrs. B. and denied with even greater heat that he had ever called her Boo. Darling, perhaps. But not Boo. On this point, Mr. B.'s counsel pounced in cross-examination. "Do you mean to tell this court that you never called her Boo?" "Never," the doctor replied stoutly, and then, faltering, he added: "I did sometimes call her Boo-Boo."

Please do not charge me with having invented this. In

this connection I should like to quote a favorite author of mine if only because I could not so much as mention him in Moscow without every Russian's turning pale. I mean Mr. Trotsky. He will soon be back in Prinkipo, sulking in his tenets. In giving a few telltale excerpts from the nitwit correspondence of the late Tsarina, Trotsky exclaims: "Now don't say I made this up. You *can't* make up things like that."

In a few moments I start for Berlin—Berlin, where the elegiac voice of Moissi is imparting nobility to the great final speech of *Zu wahr um schön zu sein* von Bernard Shaw! Berlin, where a package of Camels—God save the mark—costs $1.50! So no more for the present. *Do svidaniya.*

*BLACK boys, face-cloths, lotus seeds, and other confusions awaiting the American playgoer in the theaters of Peking, Tokyo, and Osaka.*

# GOING TO PIECES IN
## THE ORIENT

AND is the Chinese theater better than ours?" Arthur Hopkins asked me—for something to say, I suppose.

I was just back from Peking and had dropped in at the Plymouth Theater in New York to pass the time of day with this chubby and meditative impresario who probably looks a good deal more like Buddha than did any of the sundry conceptions of that mystic which I had found wrought in wood or bronze in the temples of the Western hills.

"Well," I answered, "the audiences are better."

For, as a confirmed playgoer, I had found myself going by rickshaw to a good many theaters in Peking, and nothing in the acrobatic antics of the actors, the nursery naïveté of the plays, or the whine of the ceaseless music had struck me with so sharp a sense of difference as the fine, hearty collaboration of the audiences. They arrive at four in the afternoon and stay until one in the morning, maintaining throughout that

249

long session a state of glistening and exuberant interest that is in painful contrast to the fretful and lethargic assemblage which depresses the actor when the curtain goes up in America. For reasons which are many, obscure, and complicated, our theater has lost most of its festivity, and the average audience, straggling glumly down the aisles, looks less like a group that has come to a party than like a haphazard collection of irritated passers-by who have been forced to take refuge under this roof to escape the congestion of the sidewalks outside.

In Peking the audiences are large, jolly, and communicative. They so savor the fine points of technique that every expert performance is punctuated and encouraged by a very cannonade of shouts from the pit, everybody thundering out the Chinese equivalent of "Bravo!" with a resulting volume that must warm the actor's heart. Their disapproval or disappointment is equally vociferous. It has been years since I have heard any audience in my own land evince half so much interest in anything as was registered in one roar of Pekingese displeasure, of which the echoes still hum in my ears.

Some Chinese friends of mine had reserved a box for a night when a veteran and celebrated actor of warrior roles was announced to play one of his most successful parts. Perhaps I should explain that a long evening's bill is likely to include four or five plays, and that on this occasion the star was not scheduled to appear in any of them until the historical tragedy at ten o'clock. We arrived from dinner a good half hour before this—just in time, indeed, for a considerable intermission. To an alien of negligible ability as a linguist, the intermission is likely to afford quite as much entertainment as the performance. There is much handing out of tea and one is also given lotus seeds to munch. Then face-cloths fly in every direction.

Probably I should pause here long enough to explain the place of the face-cloth in the life of Peking. It is, they say, the dustiest city in the world. That is true at all times, but especially so when a southwesterly wind is scooping up the light, unresisting surface of the Gobi Desert, carrying it for a while, and then, as if tired of it, dropping it negligently on the Manchu palaces. Wherefore, when you arrive at a restaurant for dinner, or drop in on some Chinese household for a game of poker, you are at once proffered a wicker basket in which reposes for your refreshment a face-cloth, warm, moist, perfumed. In Peking—or in Tokyo, for that matter—you reach for a face-cloth instead of a sweet. It is, I imagine, an ideal method of spreading scrofula, impetigo, and other maladies of the human surface.

Well, in the Chinese theater the attendants, who in America would be busy passing out paper cups full of ice water (or even busier urging you to part, for the nonce, with your tight-clutched hat and overcoat), are preoccupied with the distribution of face-cloths. Once used, these are withdrawn from circulation and, I trust, subjected to some cleansing process. Six or seven such discards will be obligingly handed along to the waiting attendant, whose subsequent procedure in retiring them affords the stranger an entertainment of singular fascination. First, he gathers them into a knout and then lets an inquiring eye rove over the balcony. There this reconnoitering glance may light on a momentarily idle co-worker standing near an exit. Without any visible exchange of signals, the first attendant then sends his wad of face-cloths hurtling through the air and, as they describe their perfect arc, the second attendant, disdaining to reach out for them, merely lifts one nonchalant hand and plucks them from the air with almost contemptuous effortlessness.

Also, the intermission is kept lively by announcements. The part of the front wall of the auditorium surrounding the proscenium arch is used for transparencies, and the lighting up of one of these is a signal that a communication is about to be made to the audience or at least to some member of it.

My friends would translate these for me. Thus I would learn that what looked to me like a glorified laundry-check was a notice to Dr. Fu Tze-yi that one of his patients was being so inconsiderate as to have a fit, or to old Mr. Yuan-Ta-ho that his second concubine—or, as he would say, his No. 2 Old Lady—was waiting for him angrily in the lobby.

But one such communication seemed to be addressed to the entire audience, which received it with the mighty roar hereinbefore mentioned. I turned for light to my host and saw that his usually cheerful countenance was fairly wrenched out of shape with disappointment.

"He isn't going to appear," my friend said, and went on to tell me that the message was an apologetic one, explaining with many florid expressions of regret that the star was not feeling well that evening.

Even so, our party decided to stay long enough to see the scrumptious costumes which are traditional in this play, and longer still if, as seemed at least possible, the understudy proved to be a good actor. When it came time, at long last, for his entrance, there was another roar—this time one compounded of surprise, relief, and pleasure.

"Why, it's him!" cried my host, who, in America, had studied at Colgate University.

And then we understood. The star was merely feeling seedy and, while willing enough to go through the night's work, had wanted his following warned not to expect his best. I thought then how many of our own actors would often welcome having recourse to such a comfortable device, and the incident brought to mind the story about the late Harry Kemble, an old-time English actor with a deep voice, a pronounced lisp, and an addiction to spirits. It was Harry Kemble who, in describing the panic among the English *haute noblesse* during the Oscar Wilde scandal, said that "every thuit-cathe in London wath packed for inthtant flight," and it was he who, on the first night of Tree's *Mac-*

*beth* at the Haymarket in London, after faltering through his first scene with that testy tragedian, next startled and out-raged him by turning from him, walking to the footlights and, in a confidential stage whisper to the audience, remark-ing:

"I will be ever tho much better later in the week."

I would like to suggest that it is not mere familiarity with the Chinese language which the stranger lacks when he goes to the play in Peking, any more than an acquaintance with monkish Latin would help an uninitiated passer-by to under-stand and be stirred by the service of the Mass in the Church of Rome. For in their use of traditional symbols the Chinese players, as in all theaters everywhere—as in our own theater every night, for instance—carry out certain conventions based on what the audience has agreed to pretend.

You, yourself, are a party to many such compacts—as, for example, your obliging willingness to pretend in the theater that you are looking into a room from which (by some un-explained process) the fourth wall has been conveniently re-moved. It is true that in China certain conventional arrange-ments of face-paint are notice to the playgoers that the actor is meant to be comic, but what other purpose do you suppose is served by the burnt cork and huge, pale lips of our own Eddie Cantor? In China certain costumes are traditional for certain characters, just as in the Bowery melodramas of my youth a silk hat meant villainy, and a pink dress was the uniform, not only of innocence, but of innocence coupled with such allure as to be in a state of agreeably constant peril.

The Chinese audience, when an actor enters with long whiskers and dressed in a black robe with a white panel down the front, knows that this questionable shape is meant to be a ghost. To me he would suggest rather the dean of the faculty in some fresh-water college. Or perhaps the grand mogul of some fraternal organization on lodge night. But to the Chinese audience, reared on this symbol, he has the dig-

nity of the dead, and the emotion he stirs is fear. One evening when I was following the perambulations of such a
character the lovely Chinese girl who had honored me by
going with me to the play turned pale and began to tremble
at the sight of him. Indeed, she turned her chair around in
the box so that she might not see the stage. Otherwise she
was afraid this phantom would visit her dreams that night
and she would not be able to sleep the sleep of the just.

Of course anyone who ever saw *The Yellow Jacket* when
that transplanted fragment of Chinese art was played in this
country would keep his eyes open in Peking for that famous
functionary, the property man, who moves about the stage
devastatingly indifferent to whatever horrendous scene may
be in progress, and equally indifferent to the fact that the
audience can see him all the time. It is he who, in full view,
sets up the marriage bed for the big murder scene, or peev-
ishly totes in the ladder when, after some rather good lingering death agonies, the spirit of some character must ascend
to heaven. But as a phenomenon to contemplate, he is quite
lost in the eternal, raffish scuffle of a Chinese performance,
and I was much more interested in his little cousins on the
other side of the Yellow Sea. I shall never forget the black
boys of the Japanese stage, those discreet, reticent, silent, helpful attendants whose meek professional lives are minor mas-
terpieces of self-effacement.

When our liner put in at Yokohama, we were boarded by
a swarm of reporters who all had me ticketed in their note-
books as an erstwhile dramatic critic. So each in turn, with
excruciating politeness and some little national anxiety, asked
me what I thought of the Japanese theater. I was tempted to
reply that, as far as I could judge in my first half hour from
a boat in the harbor, it seemed to be doing nicely. If they
could have waited until the end of my first week in Japan,
I could have gone into more detail.

I should certainly have tried to express something of my

admiration for the art and quality of Onoe Kikugoro, the bright particular star of the Tokyo theater, who is, I believe, generally regarded as the foremost actor in Japan. He is a fine clown, a sensitive and subtle player in tragedy, an adept in either warrior or feminine roles, and a master of pantomime. If you would take Lionel Barrymore, Harpo Marx, and Adolph Bolm and blend them judiciously, you would arrive at a result not unlike Kikugoro. I must insist on Bolm, or some equally muscular ballet dancer, being included as an ingredient, for, as is true of all the considerable actors in Japan, Kikugoro has something of the exquisite physical precision of a Pavlowa or a Chaplin.

After the play one night I went to a supper party at his beautiful house, made like some lovely cabinet of sweet, gleaming new wood. The supper was served on a low table of scarlet lacquer, and we all sat around it on cushions. Across one side of the room he has a low, bare stage for private performances, decorated with a single eight-paneled screen of some golden fabric framed in ebony. During the supper, some of his young pupils staged a dance for us. He watched them with a benign aloofness, but when it was over and we all applauded vociferously, he indulged himself in the luxury of a chuckle and drew his hands out from their place of concealment in the sleeves of his black kimono. Not that he meant to applaud. He just wanted us to see how damp the palms were—bedewed with parental anxiety for these young protégés of his.

I think I shall always remember Kikugoro, aided, to be sure, by a photograph he gave me. I proffered a fountain pen for him to autograph it, but he waved it aside and sent for a brush and with that affixed his elaborate signature, lying prone on his stomach as he did so, rather like a plump child daubing water colors on the nursery floor.

While we were at supper his small son was led in for inspection. Though only six—or seven, as they would have it, for they count age from the moment of conception—he has already trod the boards of the Tokyo theater and will, like his forbears for two hundred years past, be an actor. Our host's father was Kikugoro the fifth. He, himself, is Kikugoro the sixth, and with that many data to go on, my ability as a mathematician was equal to the task of figuring out that this lad would therefore be billed as Kikugoro the seventh. But it seems this does not follow. Kikugoro is a professional name, just as Barrymore is the stage name of the Blythe family, but this boy will be allowed to bear it only after he has made good and only if his exacting father regards him as a worthy successor. The reason that dynasties and great mercantile houses do not peter out in Japan as elsewhere is because, whenever a great man—mikado or magnate—begets, as great men usually do, a second-rate son, he promptly adopts some likely successor out of the next generation, gives him the honored name, and to him hands on the torch.

But I was speaking of the black boys who attend Kikugoro throughout his performance, handing him the stool or the sword he may need or tactfully adjusting the sash which may have become disarranged at some moment of histrionic excess. My point is that after the first minute even the newcomer does not notice them, and I'm sure the Japanese never see them at all. I was even more impressed with the success of this illusion when I went to the famous doll theater in Osaka, which is, they tell me, the oldest marionette theater in the world. There the puppets are finely carved, richly clothed wooden dolls about three feet in height, I should think, and, unlike the Italian marionettes, they are not dangled on wires controlled from above but are frankly carried onto the scene, each by four puppeteers. One of these merely holds the doll, the others manipulating the strings that control the head, arms, and feet. The vocal part is entrusted to a reader who sits cross-legged at a lectern on a platform in the place occupied in our auditorium by the stage box. The reader enacts the whole play, using a dozen different voices, laughing, sobbing, weeping, and shuddering like a somewhat intemperate Ruth Draper. The incredible thing about the whole proceeding is the complete invisibility of those puppeteers. They are clad in black from tip to toe, their hands encased in long black gloves, their faces masked by black visors. At first you may smile at the ostrich naïveté of this procedure, but, on my word, you really do not see them. Your eye is caught and held by the puppets and, unless you happen to be a Stark Young or a Kenneth MacGowan, grimly intent on writing an essay on this phenomenon for the *Theatre Arts Monthly,* you really forget, after the first moment or so, that the black boys are there at all.

*UNTIL arrangements are eventually completed to ship you to Nippon on a transport, you can forget your diet-list and dictionary but please remember your shoe-horn.*

YOUR CORRESPONDENT: III

# HOW TO GO TO JAPAN

**H**AVING done a bit of puttering around the Orient one year, I was approached, upon my return to what is sometimes fulsomely called civilization, by a demented publisher. He was aflame with the idea that I should write a book with the title of *How to Go to Japan*. If I was frosty to this suggestion, it was not only because of a conviction that one thing America certainly does not need just now is another book on any subject. It was also because of a careless assumption that such a discourse would be overproduction for Newcastle. I assumed everyone already knew. But, as I have since gathered from the public prints, there are some who, when bound for Tokyo, are so eccentric as to fly by way of Ottawa, Point Barrow, and other way-stations, where the reluctant residents seem to spend most of the year snowed up and running out of cigarettes and vegetables. When I noted that the Lindberghs wound up their journey by sitting for four or five days in a singularly inhospitable part of the Pacific, I felt that maybe, after all, there might be a place for a book on *How to Go to Japan.*

Perhaps it does need to be said—mildly, of course—that the way to go is by boat. The question becomes acute when the air is full of intimations that a good many of us may have to go by transport and battleship. The rest of my advice on the subject could be condensed to a single sentence. You can get along well enough in Japan without a pocket dictionary, but you must take a pocket shoe-horn.

I forget now why I happened to go to Japan. Maybe I was merely obeying the injunction of whatever sage it was who said, "Go west, middle-aged man." For, due to our supine acceptance of British customs (due, in fact, to such ignoble submission to the fashions set by King George as ought to make Big Bill Thompson turn over in his political grave), we still describe as the Far East a part of the world which Americans can reach most quickly by sailing due west.

The shortest route is from Seattle to Yokohama, and it seems even shorter, for the novice such as Will Rogers or myself does find a childish pleasure in contemplating the phenomenon of the disappearing day. Having sailed on the fourth, and being all set to arrive in Japan on the seventeenth, you are cheered en route by the reminder that it is only a twelve-day voyage after all. Of course one gets nothing for nothing in this rigorous world, and the returning voyager must pay for this gain by going through one eight-day week with rather more Mondays in it than he is used to. It was at breakfast one morning on the westbound voyage that the dining-room steward called my attention to the international date line and the rather high-handed decision to have no Thursday at all that week. For a moment I felt singularly bereft and sat staring pensively out the porthole at the vertebrate string of islands in which North America peters out.

"Ah, well," I murmured, in violation of my own rule

against puns at breakfast—"ah, well, I still have my Aleutians."

"Yes, sir," said the steward.

Then the westbound voyage can have other distractions. For instance, ours was enlivened by a storm in which the first officer had most of his ribs cracked and by one sudden death among the passengers which steerage gossip quite generally referred to as a case of murder by poison. But since the demise was officially ascribed (truthfully enough, at that) to acute indigestion, we sailed into port unencumbered by all the tedious red tape of criminal procedure. The suddenly widowed Hindu woman bore up splendidly under the blow, and if I can still recall the flash of her brave smile, it is probably because of a tasteful bit of dentistry by which she had had a gold spade and a gold diamond inlaid in her front teeth.

I have said you would better take along a pocket shoe-horn because not only at temples and palaces but at such homes as you may visit, at the best of the Japanese restaurants, and even backstage at the theater, you will not be suffered to trail the dust of the city onto the spotless mattings of the interior. You must shed your street shoes at the door. Now the Japanese themselves are so practiced and so shod that they can cast a shoe at the drop of a hint, but it is a laborious business for one of my girth and sedentary life to leave his shoon at every threshold, and an even greater chore to resume them on the way out.

So by all means take a shoe-horn. As for finding your own footgear when you come out, I think that is largely a matter of luck. I remember watching some two hundred little schoolgirls who had tripped across a temple garden under a stage snowfall of drifting cherry blossoms. In a twinkling they vanished into the temple itself, leaving two hundred pairs of practically identical shoes neatly lined up outside of the temple steps. I wondered how each would find her own again, but they came swarming out, into their shoes, and away at so rapid a pace that I could not detect the method. My vague speculation as to how each child would find her own pair again dissolved in a dark suspicion that she did nothing of the kind (unless by coinicidence) but just adopted the first pair which came to foot.

Very well, then, a shoe-horn, its work made easier, if you want to go to such lengths, by your wearing a good stout pair of old town pumps. But you will need no dictionary, for wherever you go in Japan, you will find enough people understanding English to make your faltering attempts at Japanese unnecessary. In any town you certainly would find a far greater proportion of natives understanding your speech than you would in an equivalent town in France for all that England lies just across the tossing Channel. If the French in a thousand years have learned less English than the Japanese in a hundred, it is not, of course, because they are slower-witted, but because they would really rather not know English. I am not going to pretend that every rickshaw boy who picks you up will break into flights of Johnsonian English, but I do know that when I made a speech one day at a girls' school in Tokyo, they understood all my little jokes and when, in comparing their school to the one which Jo March launched in *Little Women,* I groped through my memory for the name of it, my rescuing prompter was a round, dusky little Japanese girl who helped me out by supplying "Plumfield" in a stage whisper. I could almost hear Miss Alcott chuckle in heaven.

So the casual voyager to Japan need not spend much time learning the language in the plodding manner of my neighbor, George S. Kaufman, the playwright. In anticipation of his first trip to France, he conscientiously learned one French word a day for several weeks only to have the trip called off after all. Then he promptly started unlearning his new vocabulary at the same rate, and one night when I dropped in for dinner, he told me, with some little relief, that he had only just that minute succeeded in forgetting what *mouchoir* meant.

No, I think you might better devote such ardor of preparation to a few hours a day spent in practicing the lost art of sitting cross-legged on the floor. The Japanese do not expect foreigners to go through all the breathless setting-up exercises which mark their own exchange of ordinary greetings between two acquaintances at a party, but at a chic luncheon in a Japanese household or at a Japanese restaurant you either sit on the floor or go hungry. You see, the food is down there. At the end of my first of such luncheons, I did not need a digestive tablet so much as a good stiff massage. I had, as a matter of fact, been able to forget my diet entirely. So much food had fallen off my chopsticks en route from cup to lip that I got all the good effects of undereating without subjecting my will power to any strain.

Then I had practically no wine at all. The warm, sweet rice wine is poured by the enchanting Pitti Sing whose duty it is to bring in your luncheon dishes on a tray, replenishing your bowls from time to time and, while kneeling attentively on the other side of your little table, to give shrieks of girlish laughter at your mildest sally. This creates in one the pleasant illusion of being a wit and so, I suppose, is an aid to digestion. I had just finished the first appetizing eyecupful of wine when my waitress took the stopper out of the decanter and, with the prettiest gesture imaginable, asked me if I would have some more. I nodded my head in enthusiastic affirmation, whereat, to my considerable surprise, she looked downcast and put the stopper back without giving me any more wine. Four times during the luncheon this singularly frustrating episode was repeated and I left the room thirsty. Afterward I consulted my adviser in such matters and learned that all my pantomime had merely expressed polite refusal.

"But how," I asked with some heat, "would I have expressed the fact that I did want some more?"

"Why," said my friend, "you would have held out your cup."

He rather had me there. But as a rule one has no such trouble in making oneself understood.

If American speech presents few difficulties to the alert Japanese ear, American movies present none at all to the alert Japanese eye. The Mikado's subjects do not carry their sensitive and passionate patriotism to the point of preferring the talkies produced in their own dear country, although I have, as it happens, heard the foremost actor-manager in Tokyo complain a good deal about the Hollywood products. He finds that, after attending them, the members of his company afflict him by overacting, expressing a mild dislike by such facial disarray as they formerly reserved for murderous hatred and indicating a slight surprise by calisthenic contortions reminiscent of epilepsy.

When an ordinary Hollywood movie is unfurled in Japan, the occasional captions are, of course, translated into the language of the country and, as an added help, a functionary, who is a cross between a Greek chorus and an Ellis Island interpreter, stands in the shadow alongside and intones an explanation of what is going on. But I had the distinct impression that the audience didn't need him and, indeed, never really listened to him. At least I had that impression one night when I was a-stroll on the Ginza in Tokyo with old Jim Howe, a reluctant cosmopolite, upon whom the emergencies of the Associated Press had inflicted a familiarity with the Orient. We dropped in at a plebeian movie house and became two indistinguishable particles in a milling multitude that was enjoying every moment of *Tom Sawyer*. I found there was nothing in that tale of a Mississippi village before the Civil War which was at all alien to the sympathies of this Tokyo audience. Indeed, at each point their reaction was in no way different from our own.

I was, however, a bit startled by one curious lacuna. In the schoolroom scene, I saw Tom roll a spit-ball designed, as I remembered well, for his enemy, the teacher. Yet the next thing I knew, he was being punished. In the picture as shown in Tokyo, the actual launching of the rude projectile and the satisfying arrival at its displeased target were omitted. I learned afterward that this had been censored, for the Japanese are so quick to get a good idea, and so hospitable to interesting foreign customs, that the censors feared the showing of *Tom Sawyer* would be followed by a barrage of spit-balls throughout the schoolrooms of Nippon.

Of course, I suppose some of the ideals of conduct committed to celluloid in Hollywood puzzle the Japanese, but then they puzzle me, too. I know they puzzled a Mongolian chieftain whom some politic Americans, attached to the legation, were trying to entertain in Peking while I was there. He looked rather like the late Queen Victoria with her hair in a braid, but he was attended everywhere by bodyguards of homicidal aspect, and his writ ran through a perilous part of Asia about as large as Texas, so we were all disposed to speak him fair. A dinner given in his honor was not without its mishaps, for when the hors d'œuvres were passed, he plucked something shaped like a skewer from his belt and with it speared for himself, at one deft stroke, four fifths of the salami that had been intended for the entire party.

As for the entertainment after dinner, it was disastrous. They showed an American movie wherein that seemly youth, Señor Ramon Novarro, played a sprig of Castilian chivalry. The Mongolian potentate did not care much for Ramon, and when the hero, having rescued the heroine from nameless perils, bore her off to his room and himself tactfully curled up for the night on the doormat *outside* the portal of the chamber, his Mongolian highness became so frankly bewildered that all attempts to explain had to be abandoned and the party broke up in disorder.

I suppose that the reason the wayfarer's fancy is so tickled by watching *Tom Sawyer* in company with some hundreds of gentlemen of Japan who might just have stepped from the chorus of *The Mikado,* is the essential incongruity of the experience. It is like finding the Connecticut Yankee loose again in King Arthur's Court. But every moment in latter-day Japan is kept lively by just such incongruities. I remember my luncheon of delicious *sukiyaki* at Nara, partaken of upon a bamboo balcony. On the greensward below, the deer for which this ancient little town is famous sauntered suggestively in the eternal hope of scraps from our table. They are delightful, the sacred Nara deer, and on the barest suspicion that you have rice cakes concealed about your person, they will attempt, in twos and threes, to get right into your rickshaw with you. On the shore of a tiny lake I could see a score of children, each equipped with a drawing board and all intent on the contours of a dozen elderly turtles basking on a rock-reef by the water's edge. The immemorial Nara quiet was disturbed only by the sweet hum of their voices, the rattle of an ox-cart on a distant road, and the occasional deep boom of the vast gong at the temple on the hill, which meant that some prudent sinner had paid ten sen for the privilege of thus emphatically calling the Buddha's attention to his prayers. Then came the incongruity. It was a sound borne upon the wind across the lake, a rasping sound, its timbre and its cadence familiar and yet (in this pastoral, medieval scene) a little puzzling. Then I knew. It was a radio, reporting the closing prices on the silk exchange.

I have never been in any country where I was so continuously *aware* of the children. They are so numerous that even the Imperial Government has now, I understand, reached the point of approving birth control in a big way. A distinguished Kyoto critic explained it all to me. There simply isn't room.

"But," I said, "you have Korea."

His face clouded with irritation. "No," he said, "Korea is full of Koreans."

And now Manchuria—to the considerable annoyance of the Japanese—is proving inconveniently full of Manchurians. It is hereby predicted that Formosa will, in time, reveal itself as similarly obdurate.

Which leaves only one topic that I have not touched upon —to wit: our future war with Japan about which, from time to time, I have heard the wiseacres talking ever since I can remember. More often of late, than for some years past. Heaven knows, I heard enough about it over there, not from the Japanese, of course, but in the bar at the Peking Club, or in the veranda café of some Pacific liner, or aboard some small craft fogbound in the Yellow Sea. I heard it talked and talked about among the officers of our own Army and Navy who are stationed in the Far East and have a lot of time on their hands. I heard how many years a really satisfactory war would take, how we would have to begin by frankly yielding up the Philippines and then spend two years gathering forces for recapturing them. And so forth, and so forth. Oh, I heard much of the kind of thinking which made the last war come true.

Most of the talk was ever so cheerful, but war is not my trade and I am afraid I kept foreseeing this one in terms of youngsters now oblivious at school and of homes on midland farms waiting every day for letters that will never come. I only hope that if ever there is such a war and we win it, we shall remember that we won it because we were larger, richer, and more numerous, and therefore not feel too proud about it. For I have seen just enough of Japan and the Japanese to suspect that such a victory might be only another of history's insensitive triumphs of quantity over quality.

*A REPORT included here in grateful memory of a delightful experience called "City Lights," wherein we all saw the first actor of our time at his incomparable best.*

PROGRAM NOTES: I

# CHARLIE—AS EVER WAS

MARCH 1931.

A GREAT statue is being unveiled. It is a group of three heroic figures in marble, hidden now under a canvas covering that is like a gigantic tea-cozy. At the tug of a rope, when the right moment comes, these swaddling clothes will fall away and the sculptor's work will greet the sun and sky. For this right moment a mighty, milling multitude waits in the square. Waits while the band plays and the pennants flutter. Waits while the fat governor falls all over himself shaking hands with the more aggressively prominent and hatchet-faced club-women who come simpering into the speakers' stand. Waits while huge bouquets and floral horseshoes are duly hoisted into view. Waits while the dedicatory speeches (fortunately inaudible) are squawked into the microphone.

At last the breathless moment comes. Everyone rises. The military guard of honor goes into a catalepsy of attention. The band lets out a blare of triumph. The rope is pulled. The canvas shivers and drops to the ground. The statue emerges in its splendor. And in the lap of the central figure, on the knees of Columbia herself, a little tramp lies curled up in the comfort of a nap, a homeless waif now grossly intruded upon in his snug refuge, even as he was sleeping the sleep of the pure in heart.

In all officialdom there is consternation unutterable. But from the milling multitude—of which you and I by now are part—comes a fond roar in recognition of this bantam tramp now tipping his hat disarmingly. This *soigné* ragamuffin, who is so visibly sorry to have disturbed the nice celebration, is no stranger. Not he. We recognize his battered but cherished derby, his jaunty bamboo stick, his absurd black patch of a mustache, his monstrous shoes, and the desperate, defiant elegance of his shabby clothes. It is Charlie, Charlie—as ever was. Charlie—with the odds, as always, against him. Charlie —God bless him!

Revisiting us as a comet might. Returning after four years of loitering on the other side of the moon. Bringing to a sore and anxious world a gift of healing laughter and quickening, cleansing, inexplicable tears. A gift comparable, let us say— there is really no good analogy anywhere—to the sweet melodies that Franz Schubert left behind him when he visited this earth. Or comparable—and this is nearer—to the tale a jolly old pedagogue told to some wide-eyed children on a river's bank one afternoon and then put into a book which he signed Lewis Carroll.

Off and on during the next two years, in sundry towns the world around, you may come upon the new Chaplin picture which, for no good reason, is called *City Lights*. It began in February of this year a spasmodic series of releases, and in the town where I happen to live, during the week after its first showing, no one talked much of anything else. A couple of our banks had closed their doors and a few of our judges were hastily leaving town, but as men met on the street the first word between them would be "Have you seen it?" And the question needed no elaboration.

It is a great brotherhood, the Chaplinites. There has been nothing in the world quite like the sheer fraternity of his following since the novels of Charles Dickens were new. When *David Copperfield* was first appearing a few chapters at a time, each monthly installment bound as a slim green pamphlet, there would be a considerable dropping around to any house in the neighborhood that had received one. "Have you read it?" men asked each other in London, when the earliest editions of *A Christmas Carol* were issuing from the press. And the answer would be, "Yes, God bless him, I have." I remember my grandmother telling me how she used to wait each month for the installment of *David Copperfield,* and how it was at a neighbor's house, one afternoon late in 1850, that someone read her the fateful paragraph, just off the boat from England, which reads:

He led me to the shore. And on that part of it where she and I had looked for shells, two children—on that part of it where some lighter fragments of the old boat, blown down last night, had been scattered by the wind—among the ruins of the home he had wronged—I saw him lying with his head upon his arm, as I had often seen him lie at school.

She caught up her shawl and ran home through the twilight with the news, the heart-breaking news, that Steerforth was dead.

Now, as one neighbor to another, as I might call across the fence from my back yard to yours, I here report on the latest installment of a saga told in another idiom by another Charles. This other Charles learned his humanity also in the same streets of London through which he, too, once wandered ragged and hungry as a child.

It has often been said of Charles Dickens (not quite accurately, by the way) that, though he created scores of immortal characters, there was not a gentleman in the lot. It must be said of Charles Chaplin that he has created only one character, but that one, in his matchless courtesy, in his unfailing gallantry—his preposterous innocent gallantry, in a world of gross Goliaths—that character is, I think, the finest gentleman of our time.

In the latest chapter of this gentleman's adventures he has his full share of the anguish of this world. This time his vagrant steps bring him across the pathway of a blind girl who must sell flowers all day long on a street corner. At first sight he is sick with love and pity and from that moment he must needs be her knight-errant, emptying her flower basket with his lavish purchases and luxuriating in the stolen sweetness of her romantic belief that he is some rich and handsome gallant who will one day carry her off on his milk-white steed.

To pay the overdue rent of her tenement home and to buy the surgery that will restore her sight he steals and goes to prison. It is a pretty forlorn knight-errant who creeps out of jail some months later. The shabby elegance is in tatters. The once incorrigibly cheerful face has lost its fine defiance. Newsboys pelt him with their bean-blowers and he can only drag himself along. Then he sees her—her sight restored, her flower-basket expanded into a resplendent shop, her loveliness become radiant. She is the work of his hands—the oblivious work of his loving hands. And at the sight of the little hobo she cries out: "Did you ever see such a spectacle?" and goes into gales of laughter.

As the picture was originally made, Charlie gave one terrified look at this toppling of the tower his dreams had built, then tipped his eternally propitiatory hat and, with his secret locked forever in his heart, went shuffling off into eternity. But now a pang of pity sends her flying after him with a flower for his preposterous buttonhole and a bit of silver for his hunger. As her hand touches his, by a sense far quicker than her new-found sight, she knows him. And the end of the chapter is just the incredulous wonder in his eyes as he looks at her. You do not need sound effects to make you hear the thump of his heart against his ribs, and the glory that shines round him is not made by any lights that electricians can devise.

The picture, of course, is a history of his struggles to fend for her. For her sake he is decoyed into the prize ring for a couple of nightmare rounds that constitute as mad a ballet as ever witch danced on a blasted heath in the dark of the moon. For her sake he goes to work as a street-cleaner. His fastidious displeasure at the goings-on of a single horse lends point to his nimble avoidance of the next street, down which a pack of mules chance to be jogging. He seeks refuge around the corner, only to be confronted there with a sight that discourages him utterly. A moment later the plausible cause of his discouragement lumbers into view. It is an elephant.

But his great hope is pinned to the singularly intermittent generosity of a rollicking old sport who, when in his cups, has a maudlin passion for Charlie, but on sober reflection next day cannot recall ever having seen the fellow before. Thus is Charlie again and again lifted to the stars only to be cast down next morning. The distaste with which the recovering Mæcenas discovers his erstwhile protégé in bed with him cannot be expressed in such poor things as words. And a moment later Charlie, who in last night's debauch had been promised motor cars, a home for life, the kingdoms of the earth, finds himself out on the doorstep in the morning sunlight with nothing to show for his recent dizzying good fortune except one banana, salvaged from the wreck of his hopes as he was in the act of being thrown out by the butler. Well, at that, a banana is something. You can imagine how smartly he peels it as he steps forth once more to make his fortune, somehow imparting to the homely process of peeling a banana the elegant nonchalance of a duke drawing a monogrammed cigarette from a platinum case.

Some will rejoice most in the moment when the sadism of an Apache dance so outrages our Charlie's sense of chivalry that, with dignity but firmness, he kicks the Apache in the stomach. Others will chuckle reminiscently over the episode of the spaghetti course, when Charlie must eat endlessly because his fork has caught up by mistake an interminable paper streamer. But I suppose *City Lights* will be remembered longest for the mishap of the penny whistle. You see, at a party, he is blowing it in a resolute attempt to partake of the general gayety. When some jocund reveler slaps him on the back he swallows the whistle. Thereafter he is most unhappy. The newcomer does not rest easy within him. He begins to hiccup and, at each surge, the whistle within lets out a little, persistent cheep.

This grows embarrassing. Guests draw away from him. A baritone, who is determined to sing, cannot get started. Always his impressive preliminary pause is disturbed by the whistle invisible. Finally, with the feelings of a leper, Charlie staggers out into the garden to be alone in the moonlight with his unhappiness. Just when he thinks he has conquered it, he hiccups again. A taxicab responds, and when it is silently waved away, the driver departs cursing. Another pause. Another hiccup. Several collies respond. When Charlie comes back to the party, he is followed by all the dogs in the neighborhood.

All of which is pretty comical, and each audience in which I have (with the aid of a shoe-horn) imbedded myself for a glimpse of *City Lights* has rocked with laughter—your correspondent doing a tidy bit of rocking himself. Mr. Chaplin's comedic gift is at high tide. Quite as if he thought of *City Lights* as a gauntlet thrown down to all of Hollywood, he has taken pride in cramming this cake with the richest plums of his invention. Yet when, as has occasionally happened in the past fifteen years, someone says to me (just for something to say, I suppose) that this or that new-risen comedian is "funnier than Chaplin," I am always taken by incurable surprise. But only because I never think of the dauntless Charlie as a figure of fun. Or at least not as primarily a figure of fun. Primarily Charlie is innocent courage, gallantry—the unquenchable in mankind—taking on flesh and walking this earth to give us heart.

And if Chaplin, of whose incomparable art and winged imagination this insouciant tatterdemalion is the creature—as authentic a creation, mind you, as Falstaff or Don Quixote—if in our time he is the ultimate clown, it is because he is an artist whose craftsmanship is at once as sinewy and as exquisite as Heifetz's, and whose secret of the sorcery of motion is the same that transformed Pavlowa into thistledown. I would be prepared to defend the proposition that this darling of the mob is the foremost living artist. There could be no conceivable need to defend the proposition that he is the foremost living actor. It so happens that he drifted into the movies as a medium, and whenever the world's first actor makes a picture that matches the best work he has done—*City Lights* belongs in the gallery of immortals with *The Kid* and *Shoulder Arms* and *The Pilgrim*—why, surely some such immoderate fandango in the streets as this discourse involves is, as they say, indicated.

But just as no one can rely on the grandfather's clock in the hall who does not keep in mind that the creaky old timepiece is always about half an hour fast, so, perhaps, you ought to know something of the predilections of your oracular correspondent. For one thing, I suppose I should break down at this point and admit that if there is one thing I cannot abide in this raucous age it is the transitory monstrosity known as the talkie. This aversion is essentially undebatable, just as I could never explain to the manufacturer who put out a Venus de Milo with a clock in her stomach that he had, to my notion, got hold of a bad idea. His dashing invention won first prize in the Bad Taste Exhibition held in New York twenty years ago, and yet it seems to me, as I look back on it, no uglier a piece of fancy work than this idea of a talking photograph.

I have made this avowal thus far down on the page, not to be furtive about it, but only because it does seem to me irrelevant. Chaplin is Chaplin, and nothing can be proved by him. The fact that the public has clasped to its multitudinous bosom this movie without a single spoken syllable in all its crowded length is no proof that the talkie is doomed or even on the wane and no proof that any other player would be thus accepted at his face value.

So much for *City Lights*. So much for Charlie. Please think of my testimony as one of thankfulness. I sometimes wish I had lived in my grandfather's time instead of today. The pattern of life was less complicated then. This was a cleaner, greener land, and a man who took to the highroad might breathe, instead of gasoline vapors, a forgotten boon called air. But there are times when I would not swap places with my grandfather, and one of those times is when there is a new chapter of the Charlie saga to be seen in town.

I wrote that last sentence in the present tense. But that was bravado. For there is no use pretending that we can count on such chapters as an endlessly recurrent phenomenon. Indeed, there must, I think, fall across each screen on which *City Lights* is shown a shadow not cast by any of the properties or puppets of the Chaplin lot. It is the shadow of a foreboding, an uneasy feeling that in this visitation we are seeing our Charlie for the last time.

Well, that is as may be. At all events, his like has not passed this way before. And we shall not see his like again.

*A BEMUSED report on Miss Lillian Gish's venture in the provinces with the tear-stained relic which an earlier America billed as "The Fate of a Coquette."*

PROGRAM NOTES: II

# CAMILLE AT YALE

OCTOBER 1932.

HERE are some program notes set down by one who is uneasily aware that he has already become an Old Playgoer. At least I feel a growing kinship with the aged banker who once wrote me that, beginning with Samuel Phelps at Clerkenwell, he had seen seventy-eight Macbeths and that, as I could well imagine, Walter Hampden was the worst of the lot. There comes a time when such a one totters off to a fresh revival with the acquisitive eagerness of a maniacal philatelist in pursuit of a fugitive Nicaraguan. In short, he goes only to complete his set. Thus I suspect it was chiefly as an irrational collector of theatrical memorabilia that I hied me to New Haven one day last week to see the tear-stained relic which the young man who wrote it called *The Camellia Lady*. The audience was recruited to a considerable extent from the undergraduate body at Yale. Then Boardman Robinson was there because his son was playing a footman in Act One—a foot-

275

man who, by Act Four, had joined the *jeunesse dorée* and, unless my eyes deceived me, was dancing heartlessly in the gambling hell on the night of Marguerite's great humiliation. Also present—in New Haven, that is, not in the gambling hell—was Thornton Wilder, there because he had never chanced to see the play before. But scattered throughout the theater were enough of us incorrigible old-timers to have justified some such notice in the program as "Wheel-Chairs at Eleven."

It would be a satisfaction, I thought, to see the lovelorn Marguerite played, for once in a way, by a young actress who, in her own person, would suggest the cool, sweet, fragile, phthisic courtesan that the younger Dumas had in mind when he wrote the play. That was Alphonsine Plessis who, doing business under the name of Marie Duplessis, was once, for a little time, the talk of Paris. Dumas, *fils,* had an affair with her which his father was able to break up without having to appeal to her better nature. He broke it up by the more prosaic device of treating his son to the expense of a trip to Spain. By the time the youth returned to Paris, his lady lay buried in Montmartre Cemetery where you can see her grave today. While he was busy covering it with camellias and himself with reproaches, the poor girl's creditors were auctioning off the contents of her flat. Sundry agitated old gentlemen from the Faubourg St.-Germain bid high for such desks and cabinets as might conceivably shelter the letters they had been so careless as to write her. All this was noted with fine English disapproval by Mr. Dickens, who was in Paris at the time, and who, bless his heart, went off, buckety-buckety, to attend the sale.

The grief of the bereft Dumas took the form of a novel, and from that he made the play which was first acted in this country by Jean Davenport under the title of *Camille: or The Fate of a Coquette.* It was then successfully taken over by the lovely Matilda Heron, who translated her own version but still clung to the preposterous Davenport title, which has always bewildered the French. (Miss Heron's grandson, by the way, has made a name for himself in the theater, said name being Gilbert Miller.) From the first, America delighted in *Camille,* and up to thirty years ago most of the actresses, foreign as well as native, played the part at one time or another—even Modjeska, despite William Winter's plea to her that she not degrade her art by portraying a fallen woman, and despite the pitfalls of a Polish accent which necessitated her crying out "Armong, I loaf you!" The Marguerite Gautier of Dumas's imagination was a wasted, waxen girl who died when she was twenty, but she was so often depicted in nineteenth-century America by robust actresses in full bloom that I suppose most people grew to think of her as one who had died of gluttony.

Then I suspect I was drawn to the ticket booth of this latest revival by an incurable wonder about Lillian Gish. A mockingly elusive phenomenon, Miss Gish. Was she a good actress? Was she an actress at all? After seeing the pastel wraith which she substituted for the smoldering Helena of *Uncle Vanya,* I rather thought not. But she was so grotesquely miscast as the disastrous woman in that lovely play that I went to *Camille* with an open mind. It is still open.

I do not envy the task of the reviewers who must try to make an intelligible report on that baffling performance. It will be easy enough to describe its obvious shortcomings, its emotional emptiness, the pinched little voice which reduces all her colloquies to an arid prattle. One has the illusion of watching *Camille* played by a small-town high-school girl. This is part of an abiding immaturity which one finds difficult to describe in such words as will distinguish it from arrested development. It is the immaturity of a pressed flower—sweet, cherishable, withered. It has a gnomelike unrelation to the processes of life and death. It has the pathos of little bronze dancing boots, come upon suddenly in an old trunk. It is the ghost of something that has passed this way —the exquisite print of a fern in an immemorial rock. It is of a quality for which I can find no words. As you see.

Then, when one has said all that, how shall one find other words for certain moments of loveliness which, by sorcery, she does impart to this fond and foolish old play? All around her in the death scene there is a shining light which the puzzled electrician cannot account for. And when she retreats into the garden in Auteuil, there passes over her a shadow as delicate and fleeting as the reflection of a cloud in the mirror of a quiet lake. Or am I babbling? I really do not know how to translate into print the tantalizing mystery of Lillian Gish. I do wish America had never been wired for sound.

Even so, I shall buy me a ticket when next she treads the boards in our town in another play. Even after seeing *Camille*. Even after reading that astounding opus of Albert Bigelow Paine's declining years, *Life and Lillian Gish,* which, insofar as I have had the strength to examine it, seems to me, in a quiet way, the most sickening book of our time.

*THE best play written for the English stage in this century and the finest work yet wrought by an Englishman out of his war experience.*

PROGRAM NOTES: III

# LEST WE FORGET

CERTAIN of the foot-loose folk of the world who stray over the face of the earth telling at hearths and taverns of the strange new things they have just seen on the other side of the mountains, began at the end of the past winter to spread, little by little, the tidings of a play that was holding the theatergoers of London in such a thrall as no one living could remember. It was a piece called *Journey's End,* an English war-play written by one who, lest we forget, tried to set down out of his own memories something of what men said, and did and thought and felt, in the trenches, which eleven wasted years ago ran across France and Belgium and the hearts of men. This play had been written, it seems, by a young insurance adjuster in the hope that the amateurs in his village on the Thames would want to play it as their annual benefit for the rowing club. The rowing club, though sorely tempted at this chance to escape the anguish of paying royalties, declined it firmly. Nor could the

London managers be made to see any advantage to themselves in producing a work so flagrantly, so comically lacking in the standard ingredients of theatrical entertainment.

Why, the only setting was a dim, foul, candle-lit cellar, the only costumes old khaki uniforms, the only dialogue the spare, unedited unheroic colloquies among some British officers in a dugout near St.-Quentin! Their quarrels, their grousing, their homesickness, their panic, their unworded resolution. *Journey's End,* indeed! Journeys end with lovers' meetings, but this impractical creature had written six scenes without a single feminine character in any of them. There were, the managers protested, no love-scenes! That, the shamefaced author had to admit, was true. For I suppose that transcripts of existence fairly aching with the love a man may have for the green land from which he was exiled, and for the house where he was born, the love of life and friends, and the sky at dawn, and courage—such transcripts would scarcely be recognized at first sight by a theatrical manager as love-scenes.

So *Journey's End* was produced at all only because some actors out of work decided to rehearse and play it without salary for a single Sunday night performance. And it was thereafter able to find a theater to go on with only because a passing dilettante saw their performance, liked it, and put up the few hundred pounds necessary to make such tenancy possible. It has since been deemed advisable to lease another stage for the next two years, so that that first London company need not be disturbed during the early part of its engagement.

The second troupe opened in New York during the last week in March. Stray passers-by cannot hope to get seats for it at present, but they will surely find it easier next spring. The third company will arrive in New Brunswick the second week of September to start a slow journey across Canada to the Pacific. The fourth company is due in Chicago the same week.

Indeed I think there will be no time, in your day or mine, when, somewhere in the English-speaking world, there will not be an audience sitting silent at a performance of *Journey's End*. I think that not in our time will the sun ever set on the play that the little insurance adjuster wrote for the Kingston Rowing Club. I think that not in our time, by song or gesture or word or deed, has any Englishman so eloquently spoken the cause of his tribe before the peoples of the world. I think that no braided mission, no silk-hatted plenipotentiary sent out by England since the war began, has so fairly represented her—so fairly told us the best that she has and is.

It is my recommendation that you go out of your way, if necessary, to see one of these companies. Myself, I journeyed from Florida to New York chiefly to sit me down before the play, of which the tidings had spread so fast and so far. It was worth the trip. To be sure, after all those hot and cindery miles, the thing was over and done with almost before I knew it. The youngest lieutenant in the battalion, the pink-cheeked boy, fresh from an English school, had just been shot in the spine and carried down the dugout steps, to die in the arms of his captain, who, four unsuspecting years before, had been his roommate at school, and his hero on the cricket field.

The captain had no time to think of all that, however. Outside, the sound of shelling was rising to fresh fury, and his men were calling him. One saw him reach silently for his helmet and walk to the foot of the dugout steps, saw his lean body wavering a little as from an incommunicable weariness, silhouetted for a moment against the patch of morning sky visible there above the fretwork of barbed wire and the crumbling dirt-edge of the parapet.

That was all. Then the whine of a shell, a hit on the dug-out roof, the crackling of its timber supports, the caving in of the sandbags. On that, and to the rat-a-tat-tat of machine-gun fire, the curtain fell.

The auditorium remained a little while in darkness. Of the usual scramble toward the aisles there was no sign. No one in the crowd around me moved. No one applauded. No one spoke. For a long time I had the illusion that no one even breathed. It seemed to me that, by its truth and its pity and its passion, a work of art had commanded one of those moments of tribute—silence, which the governments ask for on Armistice Day—ask for and cannot get.

Then the curtain rose again, and there, as at any play, was the troupe of players lined up for our applause. I suppose it was as good a way as any of letting us know that the play was over. My own first response was one of ingenuous sur-prise that all of this had been done by a dozen strangers. In creating their illusion they were aided by a cellar smelling of candle-grease, bacon, and whisky. Aided also, I suppose, by a little of something we must call magic. Somehow, cer-tainly, they had made me see the whole Empire in its agony; the front line from Flanders to the Alps; the miles of churned-up soil, bare of life as the face of the moon; the geysers of earth where the shells were hitting; the lumber-ing crawl of the transports, the ambulances laden with pain, the stain of blood on bandages. All this, and then beyond, not more than a hundred yards beyond, the enemy—thousands of guns, hidden, cleaned, oiled, and ready; millions of bul-lets lying in pouches; countless Germans crouched, waiting for the order, breathless in the moment of intolerable quiet that comes before an attack. Then, as the curtain fell for the last time, the lights in the house came up, and out we all went, blinking and blundering, into the shrill, preposterous streets of New York. . . .

I only hoped no one would stop me to ask if *Journey's End*

were well-written. It would have been like asking someone in the milling, dusty crowd at Gettysburg whether Lincoln had been in good voice, like asking whether Paul's message to the Corinthians should or should not be included in a letter-writer's manual. If you must know, *Journey's End* had enough theatrical guile in it to make a dozen thrillers. It had been fashioned with uncanny judgment, put together with the same felicity of selection that keeps a poem like Gray's "Elegy" alive from generation to generation. That alone would account for the clutch it takes and keeps on each playgoer's attention. But that alone would not account for the far-away look in the eyes of the silent and dispersing audience, such a look as one had not seen since that day when the cables reported that an unknown youngster named Lindbergh had come down out of the skies and landed in a field near Paris.

*Journey's End* is as British as Piccadilly, but it has something to say to all the world. And I think I know why the world takes it as parched earth takes the rain. Quietly, almost abstractedly, in the manner of a man who says one thing while he is thinking of something else, this play is a reminder to a starved generation that now and again certain members of the human race can and do behave so gallantly that one is not ashamed, after all, to belong to it.

Already legends are forming around *Journey's End*. You will hear that R. C. Sherriff put his play together not out of things he had imagined or, as most dramatists do, out of things he had seen tested in a hundred other thumb-marked plays, but out of the odds and ends of the courage and cowardice, sorrow and laughter, meanness and magnificence he found recorded in a yellowing packet of letters which he himself had written home from those same trenches a dozen years before.

Seemingly those letters contained no reference to the trenches ever being visited by ravishing French peasant girls with high heels, sheer stockings, and a disposition to say "Ooh, la la" at appropriate intervals. So, like the intermezzo of our own superb *What Price Glory,* his play is made out of the dramatic stuff of the front itself. Made, for instance, out of the horror of this young nerve-rasped captain who must order his adoring schoolmate of yesteryear on a raid that is almost certain death. Made, for instance, out of the wonder of that scene when an old granny of an officer, who must go with him on this raid, keeps the youngster's mind off the ordeal they both must face by talking furiously to him, while the remaining eight minutes tick off into eternity, of shoes and ships and sealing wax and of the Roman road that ran through the village where he lived in England. Made out of the pregnant moment when the boy, in the midst of all this high-pitched chatter, sees suddenly that the older man has taken off his ring to leave behind in the dugout, and knows as suddenly, from that mute tale-bearer, what manner of mission will take the two of them across the parapet a minute later. Knows and goes white and sick. And does not flinch.

The sheer authenticity of *Journey's End* must have had its origin in the author's deep respect for the memory of the things he had seen. That authenticity is guarded now by the men who stage and play it. The man whom Gilbert Miller engaged to direct the American performance was a British captain, captured during just such a raid as the play chronicles. As a matter of fact he learned his present craft by putting on the amateur performances which the British prisoners gave in a German camp.

This Colin Keith-Johnston, who so admirably plays the captain, wears the same uniform he wore when he was shot down near the ruins of Albert during the spring of 1918. Indeed, all of the New York company saw service, save the one who plays the youngest lieutenant. I am sure he, too, would have been adequately military and alarming were it not for the fact that the Germans elected to cross the Belgian frontier when he was only six.

Probably I need not add that, just as Mr. Sherriff was able to fill his play to the brim with the emotion of those half-forgotten days, so, by the interval of a decade that had run since those days marched into history, he was also able to impart to it something of history's perspective. Therefore, there is no moment in all its scenes so filled with a cathedral hush as that one in which Osborne, the older captain, and Raleigh, the youngster newly arrived from England, talk to each other about the Germans.

"The Germans are really quite decent, aren't they?" Raleigh asks. "I mean, outside the newspapers?"

The older man nods an affirmative, pauses a minute, and then says:

"I remember up at Wipers we had a man shot when he was out on patrol. Just at dawn. We couldn't get him in that night. He lay out there groaning all day. Next night three of our men crawled out to get him in. It was so near the German trenches that they could have shot our fellows one by one. But, when our men began dragging the wounded man back over the rough ground, a big German officer stood up in their trenches and called out: 'Carry him!'—and our fellows stood up and carried the man back, and the German officer fired some lights for them to see by."

Young Raleigh's eyes are big as saucers.

"The next day," says the older man, "we blew each other's trenches to blazes."

"It all seems rather—*silly,* doesn't it?"

Osborne nods his head.

Recalling to us all, I think, that there was no episode in all the hubbub and excitement of *The Big Parade* so moving and so momentous as that one when the terrified young doughboy gives a cigarette to the German kid dying in the shell-hole beside him.

From the fraternity of that scene, however, you cannot safely advance to the conclusion that those who call themselves pacifists will find much aid and comfort in *Journey's End*. I think they will find it less an indictment of war than a finger of accusation pointed steadily at the shambles of slack and selfish and silly living which we have the effrontery to call peace. After all one can ask of no fine play— even of one so nobly conceived and so modestly presented as *Journey's End*—that it do more than enlarge the heart and quicken the imagination of those who see it. Yet—who knows?—here and there in the world men may come away from this play newly critical of the dubious structure of civilization for the saving of which all this blood was shed, and —who knows?—newly and highly resolved that these men shall not have died in vain.

FOOTNOTE: Mr. Sherriff's beautiful novel, *The Fortnight in September,* is abundant evidence that there was nothing accidental about the magic of *Journey's End*. It was a year or so after the first New York performance of his play that I first met its author. He came to lunch with me at Sovrani's, in London. We had a prolonged and rather pretty struggle for the check, with me capturing it triumphantly at last only to discover that I had prudently come away from the hotel without any money. I have since run into the play in various parts of the world, from Clinton, N.Y., where it is frequently revived by the undergraduates at Hamilton College, to Tokyo, where it became so involved in the Japanese Little Theater movement that Sherriff's royalties in yen amounted to about a shilling a month. I once saw it presented by the New York company at a command performance at West Point, and at the ensuing reception heard the barrel-shaped old Commandant reprove Colin Keith-Johnston, for having, as Stanhope, been "too gentle with the poltroon." In Singapore, for one performance, the Stanhope was Noel Coward, who ran into a touring company in the Far East and joined it long enough to rehearse and play *Journey's End.* There was time for only two rehearsals, but the performance itself was fairly smooth, except for a distraught moment in which, for unfathomable reasons, Mr. Coward kept referring to the First Platoon as "the First Platoolium"; and except, too, for a critical moment in the final scene when, in his grief and sorrow, Stanhope bent so far over the dying Raleigh that his steel helmet fell off, hit the defenseless juvenile in the head and knocked him unconscious. This, while unpleasant for him, was not noticed by the audience. No other detail of this Singapore performance need be noted by annalists of the stage, except, perhaps, for the circumstance that the troupe toured the Far East repulsively billed as "The Quaints."

*A GRUMBLING and belated review of the remorseless and venerated trilogy by the same sacred cow who wrote "Strange Interlude."*

PROGRAM NOTES: IV

# MOURNING BECOMES ELECTRA

FEBRUARY 1932.

TO a woman I know, lunching one day last fall at the Colony Club, there floated from a nearby table a fragment of conversation that was as tantalizing as a bit of lamplit melodrama glimpsed through a tenement window by a passing elevated train. It was evidently a chat across an omelette by a man and woman each of whom had recently been to see that glum three-decker by Eugene O'Neill called *Mourning Becomes Electra*. The man could not pretend that he had enjoyed it, and indeed he was muttering mutinously because all the town was ringing, like some overworked welkin, with its praises. The woman, as she completed the ritual of the finger-bowl and drew on her gloves, interrupted with a single question put to him in a voice that was fairly Arctic in its superiority. "Just tell me this, my dear," she said, "has there ever been any incest in your family?" The reply was a mere mumble, but from the context

288

the eavesdropper could gather that the man was disavowing all knowledge of any such domestic *contretemps* under his ancestral roof. "Ah!" cried the woman, with a triumphant pounce on his bashful admission, "then you simply cannot begin to appreciate *Mourning Becomes Electra.*"

In the rather blinding light of which incident, I am driven to conclude, from the considerable patronage which the play has since enjoyed, either that our knowledge of intramural sport in America needs revision, or that the interesting unknown at the Colony Club had been in error in thinking that the new O'Neill play was addressed to any audience so special.

In the ensuing weeks, sundry preoccupations kept me from investigating the matter myself, but strongly contrasted and, on the whole, inconclusive reports from other playgoers would drift my way from time to time. I am minded to chronicle here the adventure of one man. He is a dramatist of considerable repute who wandered into New York last fall after a prolonged absence in far places. In a reckless moment he proposed an evening at the play to a woman whom he cherishes because she has fair hair, a serene brow, and a consoling habit of silence. Trustingly he left the choice of the play to her, and was considerably taken aback when she nominated *Mourning Becomes Electra.* It dismayed him because of his own deeply entrenched conviction that this O'Neill was a good deal of a troglodyte—honest, blunt, clumsy, humorless, and without enough perceptive knowledge of the human heart to handle the themes which his well-nursed ambitions were leading him to attack. Boldly the author of the first vivid sea-pieces had come ashore and begun the peopling of his stage with characters he himself did not know much about, hardily undertaking, in the succession from *The Great God Brown* onwards, the writing of plays which called (and called in vain) for the touch of one who was both poet and prophet. In the lamentable

*Dynamo* and in *Strange Interlude* (that *Abie's Irish Rose* of the pseudo-intelligentsia) he had finally taken on a kind of bombazine pretentiousness. Small wonder it was with laggard steps that my friend escorted the fair lady to the Alvin.

I suspect that the first two stretches of the play—let us say up to the killing of Mrs. Mannon's lover—must have held him enthralled. O'Neill is a master of the theater as an instrument, and better than most he can make it say what is on his mind. I myself have not much interest in, nor respect for, the contents of that mind as they have been revealed thus far. But when he is not straying off into the dismal swamps which lie on either side of the road he knows so well, the fellow has a magnificent stride. To my notion all of the early part of *Mourning Becomes Electra* has the sinewy and homely narrative strength of—let me reach for a comparison which does him neither too little nor too much honor—a novel by Charles Reade. I would not be surprised if my friend wondered a little that this good, plodding, journeyman job could have been hailed as a work of burning beauty, a mountain peak looking back across the centuries to *Macbeth* and *Œdipus Rex*. But I do not see how the play, at least in its earlier scenes, could have bored him, and I doubt if it did.

When, however, he came to the sheer wallow of the trilogy's third part, I know he felt that all his misgivings had been justified. To him the long, floundering scenes between the brother and sister had the groggy quality of a wrestling match in its final stages. They gave him the itch. His collar shrunk. He felt that the world must be going mad. It simply could not be true that anyone, anywhere, any time could think this blubber good. He turned to his guest to exchange a companionate glance of sympathy, and at what he saw his heart stood still. For there she was, staring at the stage, her lips parted, her whole being absorbed. He looked at her incredulous. Could it be—it must be—that he was wrong? This O'Neill did know, after all, what he was doing. And just then she, noticing that his eyes were on her, leaned closer to whisper a question in his ear. His delighted ear. His radiant ear.

"Do you happen to know," she asked, "whether they have kitchenettes in the Beverly-Wilshire?"

In confessing that my own thoughts wandered further than the Beverly-Wilshire during certain stretches of *Mourning Becomes Electra,* I must add that I saw the play when it was being listlessly performed for the hundred and fifteenth time before an audience so bronchial that the infuriated players doubtless felt the only real sin the Mannons ever committed was in building that pillared mansion of theirs on the edge of a frog-pond. Along the deep ruts of the play some of the actors moved like bemused clothing store dummies. The giving of such a tragedy with the same troupe six times a week for twenty weeks, is part of the suicidal insanity of the theater in our land and time. The Guild must often wonder why, when it aspires to be an art theater, it should ask or even permit a company to enter into so benumbing a peonage, but after all such folly is only one aspect of the witless jig we have all been dancing on the red-hot stove lid of American life.

*A CRISIS in the life of Mr. Duffy and Mr. Sweeney which is now remembered as indisputably the greatest moment in the history of the American theater.*

# THIS THING CALLED THEY

W HEN, in the course of human events, it may become necessary to elect a successor to Walter Hampden as president of the Players, I hope it will occur to someone to nominate Jimmy Duffy. He could be described as a vaudeville actor without portfolio. The Players might do worse, and probably will. For Mr. Duffy is dear to all the people of the theater. It was thanks to him that, once upon a time, They got Their comeuppance.

I sometimes think there could be no better five-year plan for America than a resolution to cut the word "they" out of the national vocabulary, if only as a means of keeping it in mind that it is we—you and I, that is—who retained the Volstead Act in force, and put children to work in factories, and finance the underworld, and leave our public business in the hands of lightweight men like James J. Walker. But swearing off on the use of this injurious pronoun would work a certain inconvenience in the theater, where, unless otherwise defined, the word has a special meaning. In the theater, They are the audience. To the actor making an exit, his fellow-player in the wings does not whisper "How are you?" Not at all. He whispers "How are They?" "How are They?" Harpo Marx once asked the late Mr. Vokes, as those famous old tramp comedians, Ward and Vokes, came off after a turn in Cleveland. "Ah!" said Mr. Vokes sadly, "these people don't get the humor of the bum."

There is a disposition in the theater to suspect at times that They act in cahoots, mysteriously passing the word around on certain evenings to stay away in a body. Then it has been noted that when They are in an ugly mood at one playhouse, a similar hostility prevails all over town. Certainly it is true that the actor on the stage as the curtain rises knows, before ever the first cough rends the air, whether They are with him or against him. In this respect audiences differ as night from day, as a furnace from an ice-box. Sometimes They are charming. Sometimes They are almost more than one can bear. And what the outsider may not realize is that if this variation is a matter of decision on Their part, it is a decision made before the curtain rises.

It was at a matinée at the Orpheum Theater in Memphis some years ago that for once in a way They got what was coming to them. On that historic afternoon the long-unspoken grievance of a thousand and one actors, living and dead, found voice. The spokesman, the mild but effective spokesman, was the aforesaid Mr. Duffy. In consequence of his modest effort that day, his standing in vaudeville has never been quite the same since, but actors should hold him always in grateful memory. If, not long afterwards, the team of Mr. Duffy and Mr. Sweeney disappeared from the two-a-day programs, it was probably because the powers that were had already suffered a good deal from their insouciance. The two first met in the cast of a camp show organized by Frank Tinney, sometime Captain in the United States Army. Thereafter they joined forces, and you may have seen them.

They were usually billed either as "Russian Entertainers Extraordinary"—extraordinary was putting it mildly!—or as "Two Minds Without a Single Thought." Their act was marked by a certain labor-saving nonchalance and by a kind of mild dementia that puzzled the average playgoer, but was nicely calculated to reduce some such sympathetic soul as our Mr. Benchley, let us say, to tears of helpless laughter. Clad in fur coats, it was their practice to drift vaguely onto the stage, collapse slowly by some kind of wilting process until they were lying end to end in the footlight-trough, and there hold a colloquy which would last until their act was finished.

It was often an anxious problem in management to get them both to the theater on time. Once, in Canada, when their position on the bill was preceded by a mind-reading act and Mr. Duffy was reported missing as their time approached, Mr. Sweeney had the presence of mind to slip into the audience and scribble enough questions to keep the mind-reader working overtime, and finally, when this device had spent itself, to send an usher up with a slip of paper which put the crucial question: "Where is Mr. Duffy?" Mr. Duffy was, as it turned out, dozing at that moment in a limousine parked near the stage-door. It had tempted him on his way to work.

Another time, in Chicago, Mr. Sweeney had to warn the stage-manager that Mr. Duffy was even then lingering in a Turkish bath and would therefore inevitably be late. He was wrathfully told to get the culprit on the telephone at once. The stage-manager himself roared into the mouthpiece: "What is eating you, Mr. Duffy? You ought to be here and made up this minute. Why, you're on now."

"Are we?" Mr. Duffy replied, and then after a pause he asked anxiously, "How are we going?"

But the misdemeanor which permanently alienated the affections of the late Mr. Albee came that afternoon in

Memphis. It seems that the two minds without a single thought were not attuned to the audience that day, which was more than merely unresponsive. Its silence had a kind of malignance. The good people of Memphis appeared actually to resent the antics of these zanies. It was as if They all had come to the theater to think over Their private worries and did not wish to be disturbed. After ten minutes of this congealing experience, Mr. Duffy rose, brushed the dust from his knees, and stepped forward with an ingratiating informality. Shyly he said he just wished to thank Memphis for one of the most heart-warming receptions within his memory as a poor strolling player.

"And now," he added, his manner changing subtly to the cheerful bustle of a master of ceremonies, "if you will all just remain seated, my partner, Mr. Sweeney, will pass down the aisle with a baseball bat and beat the be-Jesus out of you."

*"STEPPING WESTWARD,"* *the autobiography of the grand old lady of Gardiner, Maine, who enriched the world with the little book called "Captain January."*

BOOK MARKERS: I

# THE GOOD LIFE

THERE once reappeared in the village of East Dennis on Cape Cod, a sea captain whose ship, which sailed from that part of the New England coast many years before, had long since been given up as lost with all hands. Now here at last was the skipper again—old, gray, silent. Yes, the ship had gone down, and he alone still lived to tell the story. Only he would not tell it. Indeed, in the years which remained to him, he made just one allusion to the disaster, but the single sample was enough to suggest that the whole story might have been worth hearing. That was when a young neighbor, coming into his son's office, greeted the old captain, who looked up from under shaggy eyebrows but did not answer.

"Why, Father"—this, afterwards, in filial remonstrance—"didn't you know that man? That was Wilbur Paddock."

"Know that man?" was the grim reply. "I ate that man's uncle."

Those of us who are, perhaps, excessively articulate are at

times thus wholesomely reminded that, just because some of our neighbors are taciturn, it does not follow that they have nothing to tell.

"Mother," said the daughter of a grand old woman down Gardiner, Maine, way, "you must know many Gardiner stories that I have never heard. I wish you would tell me some of them."

Mother—erect, stately, her hair a silver crown for the rose-tinted oval of her face—smiled and her sea-blue eyes seemed to look beyond the gleaming ribbon of the Kennebec, back over eighty Gardiner years.

"Well," she said thoughtfully, "there was So-and-So: he had an Affinity and they lived in a tree in front of the house. Will that do?"

Which admittedly tantalizing colloquy, and the East Dennis anecdote, too, I have blandly appropriated from the memoirs of another grand old woman of Gardiner, who has been so busy all these years—what with traveling a good deal and bearing seven children and writing more than sixty books—that only after she and her husband had celebrated their sixtieth wedding anniversary did she find time to set some odds and ends of her story down on paper. Her name is Laura E. Richards. She has led the good life. And, to my notion, written one. It is called *Stepping Westward* and I despair of finding any formula by which I can hint to you one-half the pleasure and the rue I experienced in reading it.

Mrs. Richards was born Laura Howe, named for that Laura Bridgman, a blind deaf-mute, who, while the world held its breath, was led by the strong, kind hand of Dr. Howe along the same difficult path out of the wilderness which, in a later generation, Helen Keller was to tread. Mrs. Richards's mother was that Julia Ward Howe whose imperishable monument—a noble shaft—is "The Battle Hymn of the Republic," and whom one glimpses briefly in *Stepping Westward*. Somehow, I see her clearest in the country-house not far from Narragansett Bay, locked away in the stifling, pine-smelling attic, the myriad wasps buzzing around her oblivious head the while she penned a tragedy for dear Mr. Booth, or worked away at her Greek. Mrs. Howe never took up Greek until she was fifty, but as the Wards—thanks be!—were a long-lived lot, she got forty years of fun out of it.

I seem to be holding up patches for your inspection. But, after all, *Stepping Westward* is just that—a crazy-quilt put together by a brisk, twinkling, wise old woman. I think of her as sitting in a bay-window, the sills bumptious with geraniums. She paws over hoarded scraps of velvet and silk, some bright, some somber, some fresh, some worn. Her needle travels swiftly. Now you hear a tolerant chuckle at something the grandchildren are up to in the garden below, and now, while the needle pauses, you see a far-away look, as if she were listening to laughter at candy-pulls long ago. And hearing, over and above the ghost of old sleigh-bell music borne faintly down the wind, the sound of long-silent voices lifted on the frosty air in "Seeing Nellie Home."

Pleasure and rue. Pleasure at the thousand and one charming memories which popped into her head as she was writing her story. The memory, for instance, of the Beacon Street Apollo, who was so aware of his beauty that, when he sent his card up to the fair lady on whom he was calling, he scribbled under his name: "Prepare to meet thy God." Or such a memory as Uncle Richard, who was blind, but a good backgammon player for all that and mighty severe in his judgments. You hear him say with calm finality: "The trouble with Mr. Thackeray, my dear, was that he was not a gentleman." It seems that on his first visit to this country, the author of *Vanity Fair* had violated Uncle Richard's code of propriety by waving his legs out of a cab window, while driving down Beacon Street, to express his delight at the large audience assembled for his first lecture.

Pleasure and rue. Rue for the spacious days in which this

gracious life of hers was led, and a feeling—a panicky feeling—that we shall not know their like in this land again.

I was led to *Stepping Westward* by a review of it in the annoying but essential *Times*. I cannot pretend that the critique was inspiring. Indeed, it was a pedestrian effort soon exhausted by the triumph of describing Mrs. Richards as "the finest type of American womanhood." Rather it *goaded* me into examining her book by an astounding omission. Under the headline, "The Daughter of Julia Ward Howe" (as if Mrs. Richards were no one in her own right), it rattled on for some seven hundred words without a single allusion to *Captain January*. I could not believe my eyes. It seemed the equivalent of a monograph on Joel Chandler Harris which omitted all reference to Uncle Remus. Had this reviewer never heard of *Captain January?* Could it be that there was growing up in this country a generation which did not know that lovely story? Boy, my knapsack and passport!

I found out that Mrs. Richards, herself, did something to mislead the *Times* reviewer. Though in her time she dashed off *shelves* of books—cheerful rubbish, many of them, I fancy—now they do not loom large in her own mind, and really the old woman in the bay-window could afford space for only one chapter about her adventures since she "commenced author." Listen to her:

I mean to be a model of reticence about my published works. ("Gad, she'd better!" said Carlyle, when Margaret Fuller announced that she "accepted the universe!")

As her first-born lay prone on her knees, Mrs. Richards used the baby's admirable back as a writing-desk and turned out jingles which were posted, with becoming trepidation, to *St. Nicholas,* the verses all adorned by illustrations which were supplied by Johnny Mitchell, a would-be architect who worked in the same office with young Mr. Richards. So they made their first public appearance together—Laura Richards and John Ames Mitchell, who was later to edit *Life* in its great days, and was to write—thanks be!—the story called *Amos Judd*. But maybe the *Times* reviewer never heard of that one either.

Of *Captain January,* I learned with interest from the publishers that it has sold more than three hundred thousand copies in the forty years of its life, learned with delight that it still thrives and is today a part of the living library of America. So *that's* all right. I learned, too, from *Stepping Westward* that the disconsolate manuscript of *Captain January* came out of her desk drawer at last, some years after it had been rejected by every publisher in America and England whose address she happened to know. I also learned (with a shudder) that in 1927 there was actually a Baby Peggy Edition of *Captain January.*

Dear Mrs. Richards, here at least is a review of your enchanting *Stepping Westward* by one who does know *Captain January.* Knew it by heart when he was ten, and has since reread it every time he chanced to spend a week-end in some country-house the better for its presence. Reread it only the other day just to make sure, and not without some honorable moisture on these old lashes. It is one of the great stories of the world, and I suspect that generations yet unborn will honor you for it. In the most unexpected places all over this country today—in the hearts of many a bogus curmudgeon like myself, for instance—there is a lot of love for you which you know nothing whatever about.

FOOTNOTE: The tremendous Laura E. Richards shelf, hereinbefore airily dismissed with a wave of the hand, included, of course, a lyric passion of my childhood called *A Legend of Okeefinokee,* and certain books for girls about a recurrent heroine named Hildegarde. Though my own youth was spent in ignorance of Hildegarde, I find others of my neighbors were more fortunate. Anne Parrish confesses that she still reads the Hildegarde books every year, and I find this tender recollection in a letter from Kathleen Norris, to whom I had presented a copy of *Stepping Westward* to sustain her on a train trip from New York to California. Mrs. Norris made this report:

"The Laura E. Richards book is enchanting, and I've read every word of it; just as Teresa and I battened on Hildegarde and Rose so many years ago. In the days when Baby Ruth was pantingly expected in the White House (*we* knew that ladies knew *long* before the baby came!) our ambition was to have a room like Hildegarde's with 'Forget-me-not' and 'Non ti scordar di me!' and all the other languages on the same phrase lettered about the walls by 'a fond father.' Hildegarde's room was even so. How is that for remembering? That was almost forty years ago.

"What a woman, and what a full and glorious life! Turning *her* hard times into Merryweather—it's a pity some of our distinguished contemporaries don't know about it. And what a line she gives me, who never was allowed to read Reade, as anti-Catholic: 'Take the bay darling out of me sight, and leave me the cream-colored love!' This phrase will be discovered in my heart when I die."

*A MARGINAL notation for those readers who might be misled by the official mystifications about the death of the unknown woman who lies in a celebrated grave.*

BOOK MARKERS: II

# THE WIFE OF HENRY ADAMS

THE most beautiful thing ever fashioned by the hand of man on this continent marks the nameless grave of a woman who is not mentioned in her husband's autobiography. It is the ineffably tranquil bronze—the hypnotically tranquil bronze—which you will find in an evergreen thicket of cypress, holly, and pine on a slope in Rock Creek Cemetery, Washington. I have often encountered a popular disposition to call it "Grief," but if there be one thing indisputably certain about the utter composure of that passionless figure, it is that it is beyond grief, as it is beyond pain and all the hurt the world can do. In the more than forty years of its standing there, it has become a recognized node in the increasing vibration of American life. Scurrying little pilgrims—Soames Forsyte, Louis Calhern, your correspondent, the whilom editor of *Babies: Just Babies,* and all the ragtag and bobtail of latter-day America—go to it, stay a while, and come away again. The oblivious figure challenges each and every one. Motionless, it reaches out and

303

draws a holy circle around its bit of fragrant earth, saying with such an imperious force as no mere prelate ever commanded, "Here, here is sanctuary." This is the statue of mystical contemplation which Henry Adams commissioned his old friend, Augustus St. Gaudens, to make when Marian Hooper Adams died. Now it marks his grave, too—his, and the grave of the unknown woman.

It was characteristic of one who always moved about upon this earth with something of the shrinking gait of a professional violet crossing a ballroom floor that he should have omitted from *The Education of Henry Adams* all reference to the more than twenty years of his marriage, thus unfortunately implying, at the very least, that he had learned nothing from his wife. But that honored, if somewhat trying, book was written and published under such circumstances as hedged it 'round with privilege. I cannot think that the same privilege extends to the new and attenuated monograph about him written and recently published by James Truslow Adams for reasons which, after an attentive and puzzled reading, are still obscure to me. This time there *are* a few pages devoted to Mrs. Adams, painting the marriage as an uncommonly happy one and investing her with considerable charm. But when he comes to her death, the new biographer lapses abruptly into an owlish, ostentatious silence and tiptoes past that locked door. Beyond speaking of the night in December 1885, when the thread of Henry Adams's life was snapped "by the death of his wife under peculiarly tragic circumstances," the present chronicler contents himself with saying, in a funereal manner worthy of the late Mr. Wopsle, "We shall not here lift the veil which Adams himself always held over his grief." This eruption of reticence, whether dictated by the aforesaid chronicler's own instincts, or enforced upon him by the families affected, will, I am sure, be described by certain temperaments as an exercise in good taste. I do not myself so regard it. I say it's spinach.

To be sure, this is the viewpoint of one whose blood is watered and darkened with printer's ink, but surely even those in whose confused thinking reticence is somehow bound up with the eternal verities must admit that there is a statute of limitations on privacy. The only dispute, then, could turn on the question as to when that statute runs its course. Some who might reluctantly admit that the once private life of Nero now lay wholly within the public domain may still have been considerably taken aback when, only a century after Lord Byron's death, one of his descendants honored by publication and supported by documents the old rumor that the poet had had a child by his own sister.

Then others who might share my own brisk feeling that it was high time such incestuous sheets were aired would still not be as maddened as I am by the over-exercise of discretion which sees to it that even today, more than sixty years after Charles Dickens was buried in Westminster Abbey, the young woman who was the first person mentioned in his will is not yet mentioned in his biography.

But without attempting here to seek any agreement as to just when a biographer may properly go through the ceremony which the present one describes as "lifting the veil," I may still question the wisdom of James Truslow Adams in pointing to the veil at all. For it seems to me that such hugger-mugger is an affront not only to the reader but to the memory it professes to serve. At least let me point out the sheer nonsense of any suggestion that her privacy *is* respected by such a finger-on-lip gesture. For, of course, his sedulous averting of the gaze as though there had been some deep damnation about her taking off, his broad hint that there was such a mystery about the death of Mrs. Adams as might not be gone into even fifty years later, does unleash the wildest surmises. And such surmises howl in the night, as the master of the Kremlin discovered when he somewhat enigmatically interred his own good lady.

Those responsible in the present case must not complain if they soon encounter a rumor that Marian Adams was hanged by the neighbors as a practitioner of lycanthropy. This untoward result would seem all the more ironic to those knowing that behind this particular veil is only the quiet fact that on an evening in December 1885, the poor lady merely exercised her inalienable privilege of taking her own life. I would like, on some other page and day, to discuss the smug arrogance of those busybodies who always speak as if self-slaughter were, *ipso facto*, a shameful thing. But here I wish to make only the one point—that when, like the burglars Harold told about in *The Golden Age*, James Truslow Adams vanishes into the shrubbery with horrid implications, he is committing himself, consciously or unconsciously, to the dubious policy of introducing into biography the closet of Bluebeard.

*THE corresponding secretary's
report to the members of that club
who have a special weakness for
Florence Atwater and a clowning
blackamoor named Gamin.*

BOOK MARKERS: III

# THE GENTLE JULIANS

IT was in the autumn of 1918 in the enlisted men's
Y.M.C.A. at Bar-le-Duc, that I joined the Gentle Julians.
It was a chill and cheerless day, I remember, relieved
only by the news that a fresh consignment of Camels had
arrived at the canteen, where they could be had for three
francs forty centimes a carton, and that, in the air raid the
night before, the bomb that fell through the roof of the
bordello had—you can imagine the general hilarity!—killed
an M.P.

Two large, ruddy, kind-faced, flat-heeled American women
had been up since daybreak, ladling cocoa into an endless
line of doughboys. I finally got me a messcup full of this
pleasant beverage, and, having found a torn fragment of a
magazine wherewith to tidy up my corner of the table, I was
sipping it elegantly and, as ever, looking for something to
read with my meal. The only literature within reach was
the aforesaid scrap of paper. So I read that. It contained one
undamaged paragraph, wherein someone disposed effectually

of those rabid food-conservationists back home who were writing to the papers urging that dogs be killed as parasites. With a Velasquez available, these stern economists would burn it rather than go chilly, not having noticed how wasteful the Creator is proved to be when He made themselves.

"They take the strictly intestinal view of life," the paragraph went on to say. "It is not intelligent; parasite bacilli will get them in the end."

I am able even now to quote it exactly, because I came upon it again on the Rhine, in a stray copy of what proved to be *Collier's,* wherein I found intact Booth Tarkington's chronicle of Gamin, the French poodle that stormed the citadel of that aged and peculiar man, the father of Julia Atwater; the poodle that, seemingly turned out by some frenzied topiarian, had a bang like a black chrysanthemum, eyes like winking garnets, and a clown's heart so golden that he sometimes reminded Mr. Tarkington of the Jongleur of Notre-Dame. This chapter from the history of Gamin, at once so touching and so magnificently comic, seemed to me then, as it seems to me now, one of the great dog stories of the world, fit company on the shelf for the noble tale of *Rab and His Friends,* for Mr. Ollivant's *Bob, Son of Battle* and for *The Bar Sinister* by Richard Harding Davis of blessed memory.

It was not until three or four years later that I renewed my acquaintance with Gamin, when I found that his adventure at the Atwaters' was but part of a new, or at least newly assembled, book called *Gentle Julia,* which, after many readings and many artful efforts to seduce me into infidelity, remains the book I most cherish out of all that Mr. Tarkington has written. I suppose it is not so distinguished a work as the unforgettable *Alice Adams,* which is a brilliant novel, even if it did win the Pulitzer Prize. I know it is not, by a long shot, the Tarkington book which has been most widely sold, as anyone would know who had come upon the re-

print of the Penrod stories in every book-stall in Europe.
But in the hearts of the Gentle Julians it has a place all its
own.

For there is that about this chronicle of the Atwaters which
creates a fraternity among those who delight in it. It would
take a longer examination than there is room for here to in-
quire what quality it is in certain books which creates such
a fraternity—such a society, for instance, as the Janeites, of
which Mr. Kipling is the recording secretary. Myself, I belong to several, as monstrously varied in character as if a
man were to list the Knickerbocker and the Hudson Dusters
among his New York clubs. I am, for instance, an old
*Wuthering Heights* boy. Recently, in London, Sir James
Barrie was talking about the late Thomas Hardy. He had
found only one shortcoming in Hardy. It seems the fellow
had never read *Wuthering Heights*. At which sentiment my
sense of brotherhood with Barrie transcended any mere
Hands-across-the-Sea emotion. I felt as if he had given me
the grip.

Such wildly disparate works as *Wuthering Heights, Moby
Dick, Bunker Bean,* and perhaps (though it is too early to
say), *Death Comes for the Archbishop,* have the power to
create such fraternities. I have attended a good many informal meetings of the Gentle Julians. I saw Kathleen Norris
at one. She is a life member. Recently she bought a copy
for a friend at a second-hand book store at the cost of a quarter—easy come, easy go—but, just as she was about to present
it, glanced once more into its familiar pages and decided
she needed it herself to sustain her through an impending
journey. That night there were several complaints to the
porter about the mystery of Lower 10, from behind the curtains of which recess there kept issuing at intervals peals of
maniacal Irish laughter.

Another Gentle Julian in good standing is Edna Ferber.
Just as my grandfather's conversation was never quite intel-

ligible to anyone who did not know Dickens, so only the addicts of *Gentle Julia* are not too shocked when Miss Ferber describes any group of her neighbors as vile things upon whom she would not wipe the oldest pair of shoes in the world, nor too puzzled when she declares that the King of Spain is her very ideal and that she would marry him tomorrow.

These Tarkington tales are fond. Even in their most devastating passages they are clearly the work of one who absurdly retains a liking for the human race. The human race, surprised and gratified, reciprocates, and therefore listened hungrily all one winter for any news of the operations on its friend's eyes. Not that the blindness had stayed his hand. A dictated novel called *Young Mrs. Greeley,* for instance, was in his best vein. But it was good to know when the good news came at last—it was heartwarming to know—that he would see the flowers in his garden at Kennebunkport that next summer and the blue of the sea beyond.

*THE report of an afternoon call
on an old and wounded pirate in
his final lair upon the Azure Coast.*

BOOK MARKERS: IV

# THE LAST OF FRANK HARRIS

WHEN I read in the cabled obituaries that the can-
tankerous Frank Harris had spent his last months
writing a biography of his erstwhile hireling, Bernard Shaw, I found myself thinking of the last time I ever
saw that stormy petrel. It was in the summer of 1928. I had
known him first when he was spending the war years here in
resentful exile from the London of his lost heyday, lectur-
ing angrily on Shakespeare to sparse audiences at the St.
Regis and, after failing to persuade any publisher to sponsor
his life of Wilde, putting it out himself with money advanced
by Otto Kahn. His carefully plastered hair and his bushy
mustache were of a blackness suspect in a man already sixty.
There was a distinct air of skullduggery about him, and he
looked like nothing in this world so much as a riverboat
card-shark of a bygone day.

Then a dozen years later I went to call upon him in his
frowzy flat on the Cimiez Hill in Nice, where he was com-

ing to the end of his days, and had come, I think, to the end
of his rope. He was surrounded by bits of Roman statuary
unearthed in ruins thereabouts and these disputed what
space there was with unsold stacks of his own more contra-
band works, from which any caller might purchase as many
volumes as he could carry away. I had a feeling that, if he
had lived on a New England highway, he would have kept
a small roadside stand to tempt the passing motorist with
homemade pornography—smoking hot. He was a frail and
frightened old man then with the scorn gone out of his voice
and pathetically glad to see any caller to whom he could
talk of the great days when, in the nineties, he had edited
the *Saturday Review* in London, and launched Shaw as a
dramatic critic at six pounds a week. What was left of his
hair was still firmly black, and with his high, shiny collar, his
striped, starched shirt-front, and his tan shoes with uppers
of white velour, he looked more like a Mississippi gambler
than ever. But his youthfulness had something synthetic and
implausible about it. One had the uneasy notion that he was
being held together by adhesive tape and might come apart
at any minute.

Shaw was much on his mind just then, for every issue of
the Nice *Éclaireur* was agitated by the circumstance that the
great Socialist was spending his vacation on the Riviera that
summer. Each arriving train disgorged a French journalist
hurrying, *porte-plume réservoir* in hand, in quest of an inter-
view, and the hostess of every villa on the azure coast tossed
under her rented *moustiquaire* in night-long speculation as
to how she could get Bernard Shaw to come to dinner. Harris
knew that his whilom colleague had already been stopping
for three weeks at a little hotel at Antibes less than an hour's
motor-ride away along the white road to Marseilles, but he
had not yet come to pay his respects to his old chief.

It was easy to see that this hurt Harris grievously and that
he ascribed the neglect to the influence of the disapproving

Mrs. Shaw who, as a form of literary criticism, had been known to burn one of Harris's later works in the Shavian fireplace at Adelphi Terrace. Wherefore there was a gleam of malice in his reminiscence of the days when Shaw was courting "the Irish millionairess with green eyes." Shaw's already published letters of that period are full of indecision on the subject of the ample Miss Townshend, and I remember Harris's twinkling account of the actual proposal. In those days Shaw was a passionate cyclist, and as he was also uncommonly brittle, one or another of his valuable bones was usually in splints. One such catastrophe of the highway deposited him in front of Miss Townshend's home with a broken leg.

"Well," Harris said, "there he lay being nursed within an inch of his life and simply terrified by a conviction that if he lingered another day in that softening atmosphere, he would ask the woman to marry him. So before he had learned how to manage his crutches, he attempted flight. But he slipped on the top step and crashed to the bottom, not only breaking his fool leg again, but cracking the other as well. The next thing he knew, his fair protectress was engulfing him in her solicitude. He had just strength enough left to lift his head and murmur, 'Will you marry me?' 'Yes,' she said. Then he fainted. And that," said Harris, "was that."

I was glad to hear later that Shaw did manage to get over to the Cimiez Hill before he went back to England, and that he and Harris spent an afternoon in exuberant disputation. It must have been then that he agreed to supply some data for the aforesaid biography, and I know that he, himself, went over the proofs. I find myself wondering in what parts of pity, amusement, irritation, and affection his thoughts were compounded when he went away from that meeting in Nice —two men saying good-by to each other for the last time. I am sure he must have noticed this at least—that the scalawag Harris had carried one thing into exile with him which neither his own wild folly and arrogance nor the world's malignance could take from him. It was a talisman which could have clothed even prison walls with such glowing tapestries as never loom produced, and filled the meanest garret with such music as not even Otto the Magnificent can command for his feasts. I mean his knowledge of the world's great poetry and his undying love for it. To this he was faithful. Its presence made a priest of him.

I remember that while we sat at tea that afternoon in Nice, he started to illustrate a point by quoting from *Antony and Cleopatra*. But the argument was forgotten, for the sheer music of the line seduced him. With eyes half closed, he went on with the scene, speaking each verse with a voice that had an ancient magic in it. In no time, he had forgotten that I was there, and I felt I ought to take my hat and slip out of the temple unnoticed. If I did not do so, it may have been because I knew that, when he came back to earth, he would be excessively vexed to find that I had got away without a parcel of books.

*A REVIEW of Mr. Shaw's
"Black Girl in Her Search for
God" and some speculation about
the effect of a certain "sweet savor" upon an Irish philosopher.*

BOOK MARKERS: V

# THE NOSTRILS OF G.B.S.

FEBRUARY 1933.

SOME five or six years after the war, Mr. H. G. Wells amused himself and the readers of the *New York Times* with an article in which he played a few rounds of that faintly Olympian indoor sport called the Lifebelt Game. On a single pier he placed two men of light and leading. One was Professor Pavlov of Leningrad, the imperturbable investigator who, Tsar or no Tsar, through flood, famine, war, revolution, and the angry dictatorship of the proletariat, has gone calmly on with those patient studies of the brain-mechanism which are reported to the world in the phrase-coining and moment-ous book called *Conditioned Reflexes.* The other occupant of the aforesaid pier was Bernard Shaw, who has recently de-scribed himself as the unofficial Bishop of Everywhere, and who does seem, of late, to have undertaken an episcopal in-spection of his diocese.

It was the point of the game that they should both fall into the sea, and that Mr. Wells should come bounding to the rescue—but with only one lifebelt. Which was the more valuable man? To which of them, in the interests of humanity, should he throw the single preserver? While we onlookers pictured Pavlov and Shaw splashing with pardonable anxiety in the brine, Wells paused to consider this question and, at the end, politely affecting to be still undecided, he handed the lifebelt to the reader and went about his business. But this indecision was a mere pretense. In his audible musings, Wells implied pretty clearly that he would have flung the belt to Ivan Petrovich and, not without regret, of course, have let Mr. Shaw go to the bottom. After a dignified interval, quite as if he had been crossly treading water all this time, the voice of Shaw issues somewhat tartly from the deep. It is to him, it seems, that the lifebelt should be thrown. At least it should be if the only other candidate for salvage is to be that old Pavlov.

This hint to the holder of the lifebelt is as broad as it is long, and you will find it in the small *conte philosophique* called *The Adventures of the Black Girl in Her Search for God,* which, made into a singularly beautiful book by the lovely designs of John Farleigh, was rushed to the English presses in time to get into every Christmas stocking in the United Kingdom. Why it should not yet have reached the bookstalls in America is one of the minor mysteries of the trade. Quite as many words of immeasurably less moment are cabled daily to this country, for all the world as if there were some hurry.

Taking a missionary Bible as her guidebook, the questing Black Girl visits all the authorities from the God of Noah to Mohammed and Voltaire. Even the God of Micah so alarms her by his roar of displeasure that she runs like a lamplighter, thereby amusing a myopic sage who is watching from a nearby log. "In running away," he kindly explains, "you were acting on a conditioned reflex. Having lived among lions you have from your childhood associated the sound of a roar with deadly danger. This remarkable discovery cost me twenty-five years of devoted research, during which I cut out the brains of innumerable dogs, and observed their spittle by making holes in their cheeks for them to salivate through instead of through their tongues. The whole scientific world is prostrate at my feet in admiration of this colossal achievement and gratitude for the light it has shed on the great problems of human conduct." And that is but the beginning of a colloquy which turns the great Pavlov into a figure of fun. Of all the deities inspected by the Black Girl, none is treated more contemptuously than this god of science.

When the story is finished, Mr. Shaw moves among the audience, distributing blueprints to explain his meaning. The English critics were irked by this medicine-man procedure, but that is only because they persist in thinking of Shaw as an artist when all his ancestral voices bid him strive to be not an artist at all but a teacher. And, though going on seventy-seven, he is, I think, the greatest of his time. When class is dismissed this time, I come away with a new notion about dear teacher. It suddenly occurs to me that his angers and emphases are more understandable to any reader who realizes that there is one scent which offends the Shavian nostrils beyond all others, one smell which, quite literally, maddens him. That is the odor of burning flesh. He has, for instance, been able to contemplate the Soviet liquidation of the kulaks with singular equanimity so long as these recalcitrant farmers are merely exiled in droves or shot like grouse. But I seriously believe that if the Communists were to burn one of them at the stake, the Kremlin would lose Bernard Shaw overnight.

Consider the Black Girl's encounter with the God of Noah. She finds him a well-built, handsome, aristocratic man, wearing a beard as white as isinglass, a ruthlessly severe expression, and an absurdly decorous nightshirt. He thunders in part as follows:

Kneel down and worship me this very instant, you presumptuous creature, or dread my wrath. On your knees, girl; and when you next come before me, bring me your favorite child and slay it here before me as a sacrifice; for I love the smell of newly spilled blood.

Of course she considers him a vain old bogy man of such bullying egotism as would be tolerated in an earthly father only if he were rich, aged, and of indisputable testamentary capacity. But this exigent Jehovah also demands that her relatives bring plenty of rams, goats, and sheep to roast before him lest he prove his greatness and majesty by smiting them with the most horrible plagues. And it is clear from the context that what Mr. Shaw most profoundly dislikes about the God of Noah is just this singular appetite for the "sweet savor" of sizzling carcasses. Indeed, you are driven to conclude, it seems to me, that not only Shaw's repudiation of that clumsily imagined god, but also his special anger at the martyrdom of Saint Joan and his horrified aversion to pork chops, are all, somehow, reflections of the same mysterious deep distaste for burning flesh.

*A SINGLE stone shied at two*
*such strange birds as "Philoso-*
*phy 4" and the same author's*
*abject monograph on the late The-*
*odore Roosevelt.*

BOOK MARKERS: VI

# WISTERIA

NOVEMBER 1930.

I HAD meant to reserve this space today for a nice, judg-
matical review of Owen Wister's *Roosevelt: The Story of
a Friendship*. But there is that about the flavor of this innocent exhibition of hero-worship and snobbery which in-
duces a malaise in me and unfits me for dispassionate comment on this portrait of one Harvard man by another. Mr.
Wister is the deep-dyed product of feudal Philadelphia. And
seemingly, when the blue blood of Germantown is blended
with the Harvard crimson, the result gives one a really oppressive sense of having been born in the deep purple. Any
public manifestation of that sense provokes in members of the
rabble an urchin impulse to shy a few such stones as this one.

You see—unjustly, I am afraid, perhaps even perversely—I
keep thinking of this fond tome as a sequel to "Philosophy 4,"
a Harvard short story which Mr. Wister published nigh on to
thirty years ago. "Have just been reading 'Philosophy 4,' "
Roosevelt wrote him in 1916. *"You* may think it a skit. *I* re-

319

gard it as containing a deep and subtle moral." Now that story had seemed to me about as subtle as a kick in the face. Indeed, it seemed to me when I first read it (and it still seems to me) one of the most smugly offensive bits of callow, unconscious Bourbonism I ever encountered.

"Philosophy 4," as you may recall, is the story of an ant and two grasshoppers, in which the grasshoppers triumph gloriously. They are two rosy, handsome, elegant Sophomores, scions of the Colonial aristocracy. Having improvidently cut all the philosophy lectures, they realize on the eve of examinations that they must hire a greasy grind to tutor them from his faithfully taken notes. And then, to Mr. Wister's undisguised delight, they pass with higher marks than he does. Oscar, the grind, is the butt of the story, a pale, cautious, bespectacled son of Jewish immigrants, who is painfully working his way through college, struggling for every penny and developing in the process such shifty, calculating eyes that Mr. Wister really cannot abide him. You feel the fellow would never have made the first ten of the Dickey.

On the other hand, Bertie's and Billy's parents owned town and country houses in New York and were named Schuyler and things like that. Money filled the pockets of Bertie and Billy. "Therefore," says the stupefying Wister, "were their heads empty of money and full of less cramping thoughts." Bless the man, that sentence is sound Shavian doctrine. But a little later the story says: "Oscar felt meritorious when he considered Bertie and Billy; for, *like the socialists,* merit with him meant not being able to live as well as your neighbor." Indeed, there is a Let-them-eat-cake tone to the entire context which suggests that, after all, it will be some little time before we can hope to hail the author as Comrade Wister. To be sure, a little later in the narrative there seems to stir, even under the fine linen of the author's bosom, a faint sense of the story's mean and contemptuous insolence. He hastily makes the usual and familiar disavowal. It seems that some of his best friends at Harvard were poor students. For one willing publicly to make so handsome an admission, Comrade Wister is scarcely adequate as a salutation. Let us call him Greatheart and be done with it.

Now even so leisurely a commentator as your correspondent, who usually discovers a book about a year after it has gone out of print, would scarcely be thrown into a pet over this 1903 yarn of Owen Wister's today if its tone were not continued right on into this monograph on Roosevelt. After all, "Philosophy 4" is a story about three Harvard Sophomores by a fourth—the fourth having remained a Harvard Sophomore for twenty years after graduation. It is interesting, therefore, chiefly as a phenomenon of arrested development. There may be some, to be sure, who might feel that Mr. Wister never does gain perspective with the recession of an event into the past, that his chapters on the war in this book, for instance, might have been written in 1918 for all the clarification of focus and readjustment of values acquired in the interim. It is then his fault, perhaps, if one gets a troubled impression that Roosevelt himself, during the war, knew no more what it was all about than the least of us did—that, indeed, the thwarted Colonel's attitude throughout was indistinguishable from that of the spinster who was having the time of her no longer young life dispensing sweet chocolate and arch smiles at Yaphank.

But it would be quite unwarranted for me to pretend that it is either the scantiness or the obtuseness of Mr. Wister's opus on Roosevelt which chiefly afflicts me. I am not even much disturbed by the hushed tones of the narrative, although toward his hero Mr. Wister did seemingly preserve, to the last, the manner of an awe-struck schoolgirl in the presence of her matinée idol. No, what irritates me almost to the point of intemperate statement, and even incivility, are the book's little patches of the aforesaid deep purple. They begin at the beginning when young Theodore Roosevelt, Harvard

'80, is boxing in the gymnasium at Cambridge before a gallery full of Saltonstalls and pretty girls with nice furs. But the master patch of all—a tiny one, but how purple, how purple! —is that line at the end when the autumn of 1918 came to Sagamore Hill. The elder Roosevelts were watching the war from that manorial shelter. Poor Quentin lay dead in a French meadow. And the others? Mr. Wister accounts for them in the perfect Tory sentence of our time, a phrase that is an amalgamation of Harvard and Philadelphia combining the worst features of both. "Theodore, Kermit, and Archie," he says, "were with their soldiers."

Their soldiers, forsooth! Well, well, one can only hope that these liegemen, when they were demobilized, found snug berths at Sagamore Hill, that they always tipped their caps respectfully as Mr. Wister drove through the lodge gates, and that one and all they married worthy, apple-cheeked lasses who could be counted on, if only for Mr. Wister's sake, to bob curtsies in the lane when Theodore, Kermit, and Archie came riding by in their fine carriages.

*A RESPECTFUL review of the*
*able and valuable book written*
*by Frederick Palmer about the*
*work done by Mr. Baker of*
*Cleveland as Secretary of War.*

BOOK MARKERS: VII

# THE TRIUMPH OF
# NEWTIE COOTIE

JANUARY 1932.

IS yours a mind which, like my own, can be unduly
plagued by the circumstance that one picture on the wall
hangs slightly askew? Does such a dislocation make you
fret and fidget until at last, while matters of immediate personal moment wait, you drag over a chair, climb up on it,
and straighten the darned thing with your own hands? If so,
you know the quality of the sense of relief that gradually took
possession of me as I read this new book which Frederick
Palmer has written about a chapter in the life of an erstwhile
mayor of Cleveland. I mean the Cleveland lawyer whom
chance and Woodrow Wilson called to the post of Secretary
of War just in time to direct the affairs of that office during
the period of considerable activity which was its lot in Mr.
Wilson's second administration.

I say "new" book advisedly, for although you may have
read the selections from it which were first published serially

in the *Legion Monthly,* something like two-thirds of the entire work did not become available until Mr. Palmer's two fat volumes appeared on the book-stalls in November. From their pages you may learn, if you wish to, with what incomparable ability Newton Baker performed the task which Wilson set before him in America's emergency, and you may realize (for the first time, perhaps) how well this quiet man has deserved of the republic.

And I say "for the first time" just as advisedly. Because, although we all know that through two subsequent administrations the opposition spent a king's ransom vainly dredging the War Department records in the hope of finding some small trace of malfeasance, even so interested and intelligent a student of the war as Mr. Palmer himself did not know, until he gained access to the documents, how uncommonly well Mr. Baker had deserved of the republic. Indeed, there is an extra chuckle in the book for those enough in the know to realize that Palmer was, if anything, an anti-Baker man who was swept off his feet by the sheer force of the facts unearthed in his own researches, and was by those facts turned into a profound admirer. As it worked out, the chief strain of the task the publishers assigned him proved to be the strain of suppressing his growing impulse to toss his hat into the air and cheer in the properly suspect manner of a campaign committee.

If this was true of an observer so advantageously placed as Palmer was throughout the war, how much more must it be true of laymen too easily impressed in 1917 and 1918 by the hostile critics who, as if by common consent, hit upon the silent, busy Secretary of War as the scapegoat upon whom they might vent their sundry wartime disgruntlements? Chief among these critics were the late Colonel Roosevelt, an Achilles sulking in his tent, and George Harvey (an editor), who, having had his feelings hurt by the sometimes glacial

Wilson, found a singular relief in calling Mr. Baker Newty Cootie, and announcing, from time to time, that the War Department had ceased to function.

Now, at Mr. Palmer's heels, you can go back over that confusing time, checking up the diatribes with the facts, and thereby learning how often Mr. Baker was thinking and working a mile and a year ahead of his noisiest critics, how often he was blamed for the sins of Congress, and how often a Harvey polemic denounced Newty Cootie for failing to do something which, as a matter of record, Newty Cootie had already quietly attended to. Yet it has been apparent, from time to time (as when even the *Britannica* came out with an infected account of Baker), that enough of the old animosity lingered vaguely in the public mind to make such a corrective as the Palmer book desirable in the minds of all who can be irritated by a picture left askew on the wall.

If the straightening process was still needed at so late a date, it is partly due to certain habits of Mr. Baker's own singularly serene and gracious mind. While in the Cabinet he was, by all the instincts of his nature, indisposed to answer back. Indeed, he never did so except when it seemed valuable for the morale of the faithful band toiling night and day under him that he should expel any anxious public illusion that they were sluggishly failing the Army in its hour of trial. But as the civilian head of a force in which buck-passing was the favorite sport, it was his usual custom to take all the bucks handed to him and slip them into his pocket without looking up from his work. Into that capacious pocket, for instance, went the small matter—yes, the relatively small matter—of Leonard Wood. Now we all know that if that thwarted chieftain was kept at home while the fight was on, it was because Pershing simply would not have him around the premises. But at that time, it seemed best for the service that Pershing should be spared the reputation of having made so unpopular a gesture. Wherefore, when people snarled at Mr. Baker for "persecuting" General Wood, Baker said nothing and went on with his work.

This habit became so ingrained that, even when the Armistice was signed, and the war of the memoirs began, Mr. Baker could not be induced to speak up in his own behalf. He, at least, has written no book. There are times when this exasperates me, for, compared with most historical documents, a mere office memorandum of Baker's has such shining lucidity that reading it is a refreshment in the sense that breathing mountain air is a refreshment. Then I have a lively curiosity to know what a man at once as informed and as wise as Newton Baker really thinks of Foch's work, and of Pershing's. And whether, since it was his assignment to see that our part in the World War was well done, he thinks now that this country or the world is any better off *because* it was well done. Or any better off because we went into the war at all. Or any worse off. But Baker remained silent, and, though I sometimes regret that silence, I think I understand its spirit, and to that spirit my hat is off. Knowing, as he knew, that the great multitude who had had the bloody and painful part of the job to do would pass nameless and undistinguished into history, and seeing, as he must have seen, how many of the minor chieftains were busy window-dressing their own silly little reputations, he could not find it in his heart to care much what anyone, then or later, should say about himself. Suppose they misjudged him. What of it?

In the front of the second volume, Mr. Palmer quotes a paragraph from a letter Baker wrote some time after the war to a neighbor who was trying to get him indignant about the subsequently abated inaccuracies in the *Britannica*. Here it is:

"I am not so concerned as I should be, I fear, about the verdict of history. For the same reason it seems to me unworthy to worry about myself, when so many thousands participated in the World War unselfishly and heroically who will find no place at all in the records which we make up and call history."

That paragraph is, to my notion, a bit of evergreen which will lie fresh and sweet on the tomb of the Unknown Soldier in Arlington long after all the formal wreaths laid there by all the silk-hatted statesmen of our time have withered to dust.

I do think I should add that this disposition to let his work speak for itself, this absence of concern about the verdict of history, amounts with Mr. Baker almost to a lack of what used to be called a decent respect for the opinion of mankind. Or, if not quite to that, at least it reveals him as lacking that streak of shoddy, that lingering childishness, that touch of the prima donna—call it what you will, but it is the alloy that makes gold into currency—which in so many great men has made them relish the approving roar of their contemporaries and so love the hot breath of the crowd on their necks that they were perhaps all the better equipped for leadership in a democracy. Certainly it is a lack which makes Mr. Baker the despair of all the men who have been vainly trying to persuade him to let his name be put up at the next Democratic convention.

When you are going to catch a train, it is just as well for you to know how slow your watch is. When you are reading a book review, it is sometimes helpful for you to know something of the reviewer's bent and bias. In that sense, I think I should report that this review is written by one who would, if he got a chance, cast his vote for Newton Baker for President of these United States with greater satisfaction than the Constitutional provision for universal suffrage ever before afforded him. Wherefore, in reading Mr. Palmer's deliberately restrained narrative, I first found myself almost lame from wishing he would come right out and say, in so many words, that here was the ablest Cabinet member to serve this country since Alexander Hamilton. But when I reached the final page, I was glad he had not set up a possible resistance by any such roll of drums. With far more effectiveness than my impatient zeal would have let me achieve, Mr. Palmer let the facts say it for him.

They say it for him in a book which has extraordinary cumulative force, a book written from so rare an eminence that it gives the whole sweep of our war effort from the lumber camps of Oregon to the dripping shambles of the Argonne, a book further marked, to my notion, by its good temper and its sagacious moderation. As I put it down I am tempted to say of Frederick Palmer, as Booth Tarkington said of that literate marine, Captain John W. Thomason, Jr., "Here is a gentleman who knows how to hold his hand."

FOOTNOTE: The foregoing review, first published in the *American Legion Monthly,* was later circulated privately in pamphlet form as part of the sporadic and unsuccessful effort to persuade Mr. Baker to campaign for the Democratic nomination in 1932. He acknowledged and discouraged the effort in a letter to me which began "My dear Captain" and reached me on Christmas Eve. I replied with a night-letter to Cleveland which ran something like this:

ONE WHO AT THE TIME OF THE ARMISTICE HAD DOGGEDLY RISEN BY SHEER MERIT TO THE RANK OF SERGEANT HEREBY WITH UNAFFECTED DELIGHT ACCEPTS HIS DIZZYING PROMOTION TO A CAPTAINCY AND WISHES YOU WITH ALL HIS HEART A MERRY CHRISTMAS.

This, in turn, elicited a letter still obdurately addressed to "Captain Woollcott." I quote a paragraph from that letter.

"Your gracious telegram has just been received. During the war when I was receiving some officers in France, I greeted a colonel as 'General.' He looked at me with stark amazement and asked, 'Do you mean it?' He later became a General. My voice has, of course, lost some of its potency in the matter of promotions, but my mind is just as vigorous on that subject as ever, and both because I am too proud to have any of my orders disregarded and also because I recognize merit when I see it, you are henceforth 'Captain' Woollcott."

T12 G